Modern European History
1871–2000

Modern European History 1871–2000 brings together a unique selection of documents covering the period. The collection is organised by topic, and a clear historical context and chronological chart provide background for each section. This second edition brings the book up to date and includes such key themes in European history as:

*   Bismarck and Imperial Germany
*   France 1871–1944
*   the Russian Revolution
*   the origins and aftermath of the First and Second World Wars
*   Fascist Italy and Nazi Germany
*   the Spanish Civil War
*   the Cold War
*   European integration 1945–1999.

Containing documents such as extracts from diaries, speeches, treaties, poetry, radio broadcasts, photographs, cartoons, political posters and propaganda, this is an essential resource for students of modern British and European history.

David Welch is Professor of Modern History and Director of the Centre for the Study of Propaganda at the University of Kent at Canterbury. He is editor of the Routledge *Sources in History* series. His previous publications include *The Third Reich: Politics and Propaganda* (Routledge, 1993) and *Hitler* (UCL Press, 1998).

Modern European History 1871–2000

A DOCUMENTARY READER

Second edition

David Welch

London and New York

First published 1994 by Heinemann Educational

Second edition first published 1999
by Routledge
11 New Fetter Lane, London EC4P 4EE

Simultaneously published in the USA and Canada
by Routledge
29 West 35th Street, New York, NY 10001

Routledge is an imprint of the Taylor & Francis Group

© 1999 David Welch

Typeset in Baskerville and Gill Sans by Routledge
Printed and bound in Great Britain by Biddles Ltd,
Guildford and King's Lynn

British Library Cataloguing in Publication Data
A catalogue record for this book is available from the British Library

Library of Congress Cataloging in Publication Data
Welch, David.
Modern European history 1871–2000: a documentary reader / David
Welch. – 2nd ed.
Includes bibliographical references and index.
1. Europe – History – 1871–1918.   2. Europe – History – 20th century.
I. Title
D395.W38   1999
940.2–dc21   99–14506

ISBN 0–415–21581–1 (hbk)
ISBN 0–415–21582–X (pbk)

To

JAMES JOLL

who was such an inspiration for so many historians

Contents

Maps

Documents

IMPERIAL GERMANY, 1871–1918

FRANCE, 1871–1944

RUSSIA IN REVOLUTION, 1890–1918

THE ORIGINS OF THE FIRST WORLD WAR AND ITS AFTERMATH

FASCIST ITALY

NAZI GERMANY

RUSSIA UNDER STALIN

THE APPROACH TO THE SECOND WORLD WAR

THE ORIGINS OF THE COLD WAR

EUROPEAN INTEGRATION

Author's acknowledgements

I would like to acknowledge colleagues at the University of Kent at Canterbury who have read and made valuable comments on parts of the manuscript. In particular I would like to thank William Fortescue, Richard Sakwa, Clive Church and Ian Manners for their painstaking efforts to improve the text and to James Ellison for his contribution to the use of sources. Obviously, I alone am responsible for the inadequacies that remain.

A wide-ranging book such as this must rely heavily on researches undertaken by others. I would like to cite in particular the wealth of statistical information to be found in C. Cook and J. Stevenson, *The Longman Handbook of Modern European History: 1763–1985* (Longman, 1989), which I found an indispensable source of reference.

Every effort has been made to contact copyright holders. Any omissions or errors will be rectified in subsequent printings if notice is given to the publisher.

David Welch
Canterbury
January 1999

Abbreviations

A.H.R.	*American Historical Review*
C.E.H.	*Central European History*
C.H.J.	*Cambridge Historical Journal* (later, *Historical Journal*)
Econ.H.R.	*Economic History Review*
E.H.Q.	*European History Quarterly*
E.H.R.	*English Historical Review*
E.S.R.	*European Studies Review* (later, *European History Quarterly*)
G.H.	*German History*
H.	*History*
H.J.	*Historical Journal*
H.T.	*History Today*
H.W.J.	*History Workshop Journal*
I.R.H.S.	*International Review of Social History*
J.C.H.	*Journal of Contemporary History*
J.H.I.	*Journal of the History of Ideas*
J.M.H.	*Journal of Modern History*
P.P.	*Past and Present*
R.P.	*Review of Politics*
S.R.	*Slavic Review*

Introduction and guidance on using documents and sources

The aim of this book has been to produce an accessible one-volume documentary reader that covers a number of the most important topics in European history, 1871–2000. No book of this scope can be entirely comprehensive, but the topics I have chosen provide, I believe, a 'flavour' of the key events. I have attempted to bring these periods alive by drawing on a rich variety of sources and documents that illustrate some of the main individuals, events and issues. The range of sources is deliberately wide and includes speeches, treaties, newspaper reports, diaries, poetry, statistics and oral accounts, together with the visual evidence, such as photographs, posters and cartoons, that provides a source just as important to historians as the more traditional written sources. The use of documentary evidence is intended to reflect the skills historians have to master when challenged by problems of evidence, interpretation and presentation.

How to approach documents

The use of a document exercise, usually based on 'gobbets', is an established element in most history courses. 'Gobbets' invariably consist of brief extracts from documentary sources, and students are asked to respond by answering specific and general questions. Some of the documents included in this volume are relatively short and in the 'gobbets' mould. However, most of the sources chosen are much longer and require greater concentration and stamina. Wherever possible, I have attempted to retain the integrity of a document and have not simply presented a brief extract, which can be misleading. Documentary evidence (as opposed to a few lines selected from a document) thus forces the student to confront a series of questions that professional historians also have to grapple with. Such questions can be summarised as follows:

*   *What type of source is the document?*

    Is it a written source, or an oral or visual source?
    What, in your estimation, is its importance?
    Did it, for example, have an affect on events or the decision making process?

- *Who wrote or created the document?*

  A person, a group or a government?
  If it was a person, what was their position?
  What basic attitudes might have affected the nature of the information and the language used?

- *When was the document written?*

  The date, even the time might be significant.
  You may need to understand when the document was written in order to understand its context.
  Are there any special problems in understanding the document as contemporaries would have understood it?

- *Why was the document written?*

  For what purpose(s) did the document come into existence and for whom was it intended?

- *What was written?*

  This is the obvious question – but never be afraid to state the obvious! Remember it may prove more revealing to ask the question 'What is *not* written?' – that is, read between the lines. In order to do this you will need to ask what other references (to persons, events, other documents, etc.) need to be explained before the document can be fully understood.

Students should bear in mind these fundamental points and think about their response to documents. Above all, ask yourself the question, what, as a historian, can I *interpret* from this piece of evidence? You will need to identify the document clearly; set it in its historical context; comment on specific points; and sum up the document's historical significance.

I have tried to bear these points in mind when analysing documents. I hope you will too. My choice of documents has been governed by their contemporary significance (that is, their immediate impact on events) and also by the extent to which they provide an insight into an event either as a contemporary observation or as a later analysis by historians. But do remember that the documents have been *selected*. They reflect individual choice and opinion; they are not intended to be definitive. Other historians would, no doubt, have included different sources, and they would certainly have provided different interpretations. Thus an important element in the historian's arsenal is not simply the accumulation of data – but the application of skills that allow such material to be *interpreted*.

The documents included in this volume should not, therefore, be viewed as an end in themselves. Strive rather to adopt a critical approach to the documents and challenge some of the observations that I have made. However, there is no short cut to a critical interpretation of sources. Extensive reading and study are required – not simply of history textbooks, but a range of different sources (novels, poetry, archival film, oral accounts, etc.) that provide insight into the period and give you the knowledge and confidence to make up your own mind. To this end, each chapter contains a selected bibliography consisting of documents and sources, secondary works and articles. Many of these sources can now be found on the Internet. Moreover, to enable you to navigate the stormy seas of history, each topic is placed, wherever possible, in its chronological context, and to remind you of the events, chronological charts are provided.

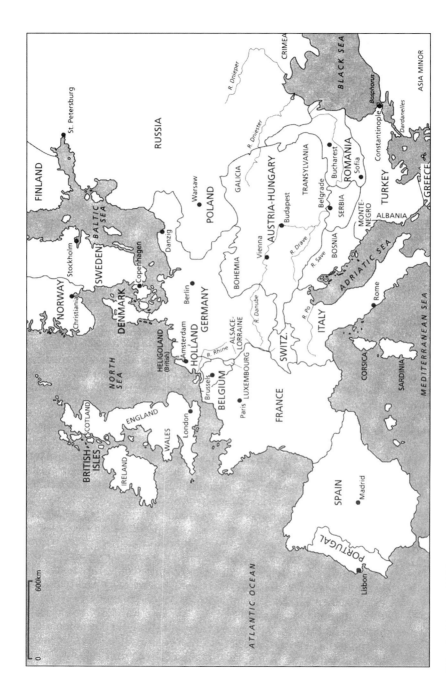

Map 1 Europe, 1871

1

Imperial Germany, 1871–1918

The term 'Germany' had no real political significance at the beginning of the nineteenth century. The numerous states that made it up were loosely bound by their membership of the old Holy Roman Empire. The German Empire, or Second Reich, was created in 1871, and was founded on an unequal alliance between the national and liberal movements and the conservative Prussian state-leadership. The German Empire included Prussia, the kingdoms of Bavaria, Saxony and Württemberg, eighteen lesser states, three free cities and Alsace-Lorraine. It has been stated that the Prussian Chancellor, Otto von Bismarck, united Germany as the result of a series of successful military wars. However, closer examination reveals that the conditions for unification had been achieved *before* Bismarck came to power.

During the nineteenth century there were three major steps towards unification: the creation of the German Confederation (1815); the formation of the German Customs Union (*Zollverein*) (1834); and the period of the decline of Austrian influence (1852–64). Brought about by naked militarism, the creation of the German Empire appeared to have fulfilled Bismarck's prediction of 1862 that Prussia would unite Germany by 'blood and iron'. In fact, the Empire had been established only after numerous compromises had been made and was immediately open to the criticism of being incomplete. Certainly when measured against the great aims of the 1848–9 Revolution – to create unity through freedom to build the state on new political, economic and social foundations – the founding of the Empire signified a defeat for middle-class liberalism. By and large, however, the majority of people warmly greeted the achievement of national unity. The story of imperial Germany after the euphoria of 1871 was the failure to adapt its institutions to the newly developing economic and social conditions.

Left-wing liberal critics dismissed the Empire as an incomplete constitutional state. The liberals claimed that it should be governed on a wider parliamentary basis. A largely powerless parliament (Reichstag) was complimented by an upper house, the Federal Council (Bundesrat), which was made up of delegations from the separate states (not, therefore, representative of the German people as a whole). While the Reichstag possessed rights of veto, legislation was initiated in the Bundesrat, which could dissolve the Reichstag and declare war. The

Bundesrat was effectively controlled by Prussia, which could block any measures deemed harmful to its own interests.

Germany under Bismarck

In reality the system was ruled by one man, who was responsible only to the Emperor. The complicated constitutional system depended solely on the personality of Bismarck, who dominated the government and administration by holding the key positions of Chancellor and Prussian Prime Minister. No firm parliamentary principle was established, such as a government responsible to a sovereign parliament – rather the situation was one of 'government of the parties', a system that was dubbed 'Chancellor dictatorship'. Whereas a democratic, constitutional nation state under the principle of sovereignty of the people had been the aim in 1848, the Empire of 1871 was a nationalist authoritarian monarchy.

The Empire was also incomplete with regard to the social and political demands of the middle-class emancipation movement. Claims that the new state should adapt itself to the evolving industrial society were not met, nor was the demand that the nation should have an active role to play in the political process. The Empire did not aim to make changes, but aimed rather to preserve the old Prussian social order that had been reinforced by the dominant position of the Junkers. The opposition parties – the left-wing liberal Progress Party, the Social Democrats and the Catholic Centre Party – were denounced as enemies of the Reich. The first decade of the Reich was filled with high social and party political tensions.

1.1 'Between Berlin and Rome', a cartoon of 1875 (see p. 3)

Document 1.1, a satirical cartoon of 1875, implies 'a real mix up', and is critical of Bismarck's *Kulturkampf* (cultural struggle) – his attempts to undermine the influence of the Catholic Church in German domestic politics. The cartoon was published in the liberal Ullstein press, which retained an ambivalent attitude towards Bismarck's policies, but continued to satirise him. There is a need first of all to identify the two protagonists and to understand why they should be engaged in a game of chess. Why did Bismarck wish to weaken the Catholic Centre Party and restrict the power and influence of Catholics and the Papacy in German politics? Note also the strange characters on the chessboard. Who do they represent and does there appear to be a winner? It has been suggested that the scope of the *Kulturkampf* was inadequately defined; it took on the nature of a campaign against the Church rather than against the Catholic Party. The cartoon apparently sees the conflict as one between Bismarck and the Papacy, for there is little evidence of the Catholic Centre Party in the cartoon. How far does visual evidence such as a cartoon enhance our understanding of the complexity of historical issues? A cartoon after all, if it is to be effective, needs to make an immediate impression and invariably relies on simplifying issues and events.

Source: Ullstein's *Weltgeschichte*, Berlin, 1907–9, Bildarchiv Preussischer Kulturbesitz, Berlin

Does this undermine its importance as an historical source, or should historians take such evidence seriously?

Bismarck's *Kulturkampf* turned out to be one of the major failures of his career. The Pope declared anti-Catholic laws null and void and forbade Roman Catholics to obey them. Indeed, the influence of the Catholic Centre Party increased rather than diminished during this period, as did its representation in the Reichstag. Bismarck quickly turned his attention to the Social Democratic Party (SPD) and socialist ideas, which were now seen together as the chief internal threat to his domestic policies.

The Anti-Socialist Law of 1878, Document 1.2, was eventually passed with a comfortable parliamentary majority after an election was fought on the issue. How do you explain this and what events had occurred in 1878 to prompt this Draconian legislation? The document stated that the 'aims of social democracy' constituted a 'danger to the public'. All meetings and publications associated with socialist ideas were banned under this vague pronouncement. Trade unions were also declared illegal. Nevertheless, the law did not prohibit the candidature and election of socialists to the Reichstag. Since it is an 'official' Government document, one needs to go beyond the clinical language used here and 'read between the lines' for clues to government thinking. Although such documents do not make for exciting reading, they nevertheless constitute an important source for historians, in that they provide evidence of 'official' thinking on a particular topic. In this instance, do you find it revealing that there is a lack of detailed information substantiating this legislation?

1.2 The Anti-Socialist Law, 21 October 1878

Content: Law against the aims of Social Democracy of danger to the public.

(NO. 1271) LAW AGAINST THE AIMS OF SOCIAL DEMOCRACY OF DANGER TO THE PUBLIC. 21 OCTOBER 1878.

We, William, German Emperor and King of Prussia by the grace of God decree in the name of the Reich, with the consent of the Bundesrat and Reichstag, the following:

1. Associations which further social democratic, socialist or communist aims and thus threaten to overthrow the existing state and social-structure, are banned.

The same applies to associations in which social democratic, socialist or communist aims are directed at the overthrow of the existing state or social structure in a manner which threatens peace and harmony amongst the population. The same law on associations applies to alliances of any kind …

9. Meetings in which social-democratic, socialist, or communist tendencies, directed to the destruction of the existing order in State or society, make their appearance are to be dissolved. Such meetings as appear to justify the assumption that they are destined to further such tendencies are to be forbidden. Public festivities and processions are placed under the same restriction …

11. All printed matter, in which social-democrat, socialist, or communist tendencies appear … is to be forbidden. In the case of periodical literature, the prohibition can be extended to any further issue, as soon as a single number has been forbidden under this law …

16. The collection of contributions for the furthering of social-democratic, socialistic, or communistic endeavours … as also the public instigation to the furnishing of such contributions, are to be forbidden by the police. … The money seized [by the police] from forbidden collections, or the equivalent of the same, is to fall to the poor-relief fund of the neighbourhood …

28. For districts and localities in which, because of the above-mentioned agitation, public safety is endangered, the following provisions can be put into effect, for the space of a year at most, by the central police of the State in question, subject to the permission of the Bundesrat.

(1) That public meetings may only take place with the previous permission of the police; this prohibition does not extend to meetings for an election to the Reichstag or the diet.

(2) That the distribution of printed matter may not take place in public roads, streets, squares, or other public localities.

(3) That residence in such districts or localities can be forbidden to all persons from whom danger to the public safety or order is to be feared ...

Source: *Reichsgesetzblatt*, no. 34, 21 October 1878

Perhaps Document 1.3, a lithograph entitled 'Bismarck deals with the Liberals and the Socialists', provides a more powerful insight into how contemporaries interpreted such repressive measures. Look at the manner in which socialist and liberal elements are portrayed (social-liberal colorado beetles) and the brutal methods being employed to exterminate them. It also begs the question: if the 'House that Bismarck built' was so repressive, how could political propaganda critical of Bismarck be allowed?

1.3 'Bismarck deals with the Liberals and Socialists', a cartoon of 1878

Source: Bildarchiv Preussicher Kulturbesitz, Berlin; and H. Kurz, *The Second Reich* (London, 1970)

Bismarck's campaign against social democracy assumed the proportions of a crusade. As a result of anti-socialist legislation, all socialist and communist associations were disbanded, their publications outlawed and socialist 'agitators' deported. Bismarck's *realpolitik* might be referred to as the 'stick and the carrot'. On the one hand there was the repression of socialist agencies, and on the other he attempted to win over the working class and isolate them from the SPD by a policy of watered-down state socialism, in which the government sponsored certain legislation covering sickness, accident insurance and old-age and disability insurance. Document 1.4 is an extract from Kaiser Wilhelm I's speech at the opening of the Reichstag on 15 February 1881 which alludes to the prospect of new state sponsored legislation for the workers.

1.4 Kaiser's speech at the opening of the Reichstag, 15 February 1881

... At the opening of the Reichstag in February 1879 His Majesty the Emperor with reference to the [anti-socialist] law of 21 October 1878 expressed the hope that the Reichstag would not refuse its continuing co-operation in remedying social ills by means of legislation. Such remedy shall be sought not only in the repression of socialistic excesses, but also in the promotion of the welfare of the workers. In this respect the care of such workers as are incapable of earning their livelihood is the first step. In their interest His Majesty the Emperor had a bill on the insurance of workers against the result of accidents presented to the Bundesrat – a bill which is intended to meet a need felt equally by workers and employers. His Majesty the Emperor hopes that the bill will receive the assent of the Governments of the States, and that it will be welcomed by the Reichstag as a complement of the legislation on protection against social-democratic activity. The now existing provisions which should have protected the worker from becoming helpless through the loss of his earning capacity by accident or old age have proved inadequate, and their inadequacy has contributed no little to turning the members of this class to participation in social-democratic activity in order to seek help ...

Source: G.A. Kertesz (ed.), *Documents in the Political History of the European Continent 1815–1939* **(Oxford, 1968), p. 267**

The Kaiser's speech referred to 'socialist excesses' and expressed the hope that the Reichstag would continue to support the government. But what was the real intention of this speech? Can we assume, for example, that the speech was written by the Kaiser or by Bismarck himself? The intention appeared to be that the promotion of the welfare of the workers was dependent on continuing vigilance against socialist activities. Bismarck encountered strong opposition from liberal groups within the Reichstag who objected to what they believed was state interference in the relationship between employer and employee, especially as employers as well as employees were expected to make financial contributions to these welfare schemes. Given the support of the Kaiser, it is not surprising that, despite some minor defeats, Bismarck's social welfare programme, which was in advance of similar legislation in other European states, was successfully carried through the Reichstag. However, his attempt to alienate the labour force from social democracy failed. By 1913, the SPD was the largest single party in the Reichstag.

Kaiser Wilhelm II and German nationalism

After the accession of Wilhelm II in 1888 it soon became apparent that Bismarck and the new Emperor both claimed responsibility for domestic and foreign policy. Bismarck considered his policy of keeping socialism and nationalism in check, in addition to his plans for maintaining peace, to be threatened. After Bismarck's dismissal in 1890 the Reich was faced with a governmental crisis. Wilhelm II wanted to be 'his own Chancellor'. However, the attempt to set up a 'personal system of government', an autocracy in which ministers would do his bidding, failed. The young Emperor lacked the knowledge and ability to pass binding directives in domestic and foreign affairs or to play off the institutions of the Reich.

Nevertheless, a 'new course' was advocated, the 'socialist' laws were repealed and the Kaiser talked of a policy of 'togetherness' (*Sammlungspolitik*), based on a government-sponsored alliance between big business and big land owners. It was intended to mobilise patriotic elements and reduce the appeal of social democracy. This, however, failed to reconcile the labour force to the 'Social Empire'. Social conflicts came increasingly to the fore in which both the growing socialist movement and the liberals found themselves at odds with a government dominated by Junkers, industrialists, the military and bureaucrats. Document 1.5 is an example of officially approved propaganda intended to mythologise the new Emperor and unify the nation behind this image of a commanding Kaiser.

1.5 *Portrait of Wilhelm II* by Max Koner, 1890 (see p. 8)

This painting of Wilhelm II was completed by Max Koner in 1890, the year that Bismarck was dismissed. It is revealing for the manner in which Wilhelm wished to be portrayed. As an official representation, it would have required the Emperor's approval. Wilhelm had initially presented himself as the '*Volkskaiser*' ('People's Kaiser'). This idealised portrait of Wilhelm in an imperial pose with all his royal trappings is a far cry from the insecure, complex personality that would later be described by his biographers. Compare the statuesque figure represented here with the one that was concealed from the public – an Emperor with a stunted body and withered arm. The painting is therefore a good example of what might be referred to as the 'myth and reality' of historical evidence. It is obviously important for the historian to be aware of the myth that is being

Source: Bildarchiv Preussischer Kulturbesitz, Berlin

disseminated, but it is equally important to adopt a critical approach to sources in order to seek the reality beyond the myth.

The new policy of imperialism adopted by Wilhelm II represented the final attempt to conceal internal divisions by foreign policy successes. However, the hopes of liberal imperialists, who expected dynamic foreign and domestic policies, remained unfulfilled. Document 1.6 is a record of a revealing conversation between Chancellor Hohenlohe-Schillingsfürst and the Kaiser in March 1897.

1.6 Conversation between Chancellor Hohenlohe-Schillingsfürst and the Kaiser, March 1897

To my surprise H[is] M[ajesty] received me with great affability, listened assentingly to my explanation, and then indulged himself in a highly detailed lecture on the navy. ... He enumerated the ships we have and the ones we would need in order to survive a war; ... emphasised that we had to have an armoured fleet to protect our trade and keep ourselves supplied with provisions; and was of the opinion that our fleet would have to be strong enough to prevent the French fleet cutting off the food supplies we needed. In addition, he ... would have to find the means, and if the Reichstag didn't approve this, he would nevertheless carry on building and present the Reichstag with the bill later. Public opinion didn't concern him. He knew that people didn't love him, and cursed him; but that wouldn't deter him. I then reminded the Emperor of the difference between Prussia and the Empire; said that in Prussia he had old rights which continued to exist, so far as the Prussian constitution had not limited [them]. In the Empire the Emperor only had the rights which the Reichstag conceded to him. The Emperor interjected 'the Emperor hardly has any rights', which I attempted to refute. Besides, this was quite unimportant, said HM: the South German democratic states didn't worry him. He had 18 army corps and would make short work of the South Germans.

Source: **Fürst Chlodwig zu Hohenlohe-Schillingsfürst,** *Denkwürdigkeiten der Reichskanzlerzeit,* **ed. K. A. von Müller (Stuttgart, 1931), p. 310; quoted in I. Porter and I. Armour,** *Imperial Germany 1890–1918* **(Harlow, 1991), pp. 72–3**

The conversation revealed Wilhelm's obsession with strengthening the imperial navy even if this meant a further confrontation with the Reichstag. It also sheds some light on the historiographical debate over the origins of the First World War (see Chapter 4). As early as 1897, Wilhelm was referring to the number of ships that would be necessary in 'order to survive a war'. The manner of the Emperor is also revealing; he was clearly contemptuous of any form of parliamentary restraint and of non-Prussians, hinting that he would not be averse to employing his army corps in order to 'make short work of the South Germans'. Hohenlohe-Schillingsfürst diaries were not edited and published until 1931. We

have to be confident that this is a reliable memoir based on recorded conversation that took place and that they have not subsequently been 're-written' to
further discredit Wilhelm for starting and losing the war.

The Kaiser's motto was: '*Weltpolitik* as a task; to become a world power as an
aim; and the fleet as an instrument.' The building up of the fleet was a matter of
prestige for him and his advisers, in which account was taken of the collision
course that this inevitably meant with Great Britain. Some months after
Hohenlohe-Schillingsfürst recorded his conversation with the Emperor in 1897,
the Kaiser drew his own chart of German ships built between 1893 and 1899.

1.7 A naval chart drawn by Wilhelm II, 1897

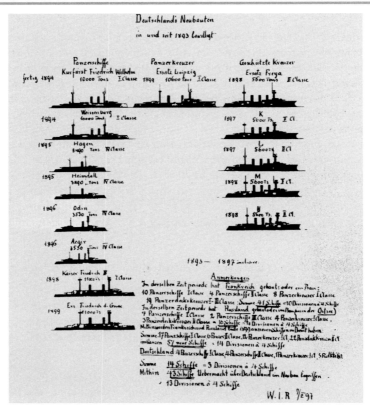

Source: Bildarchiv Preussischer Kulturbesitz, Berlin

The ships drawn by Wilhelm reveal considerable technical detail about tonnage
and fighting capacity. Below the chart, under the heading 'Observations',
Wilhelm compared the number of ships built in Germany during this period
with that of France and Russia and predicted that by 1899 France and Russia
would together have forty-three more ships than Germany. The inference is

clear; Germany would need greatly to increase its naval building programme. Admiral von Tirpitz had been appointed Secretary of State for the Navy in June 1897 with the aim of getting a new navy bill through the Reichstag. The 1898 Navy Law stipulated that Germany should create nineteen battleships by 1905. It is surely no coincidence that the Navy League (*Flotterverein*) was founded in 1898 by Admiral Tirpitz to promote naval expansion. It proved to be a great success, eventually attracting a membership of over a million people. Document 1.8 is an example of a 'press statement' from the Press Bureau of the Navy Office outlining the importance of maintaining a strong battle fleet.

1.8 Naval propaganda, *Nauticus*, 1900

… the concept of the navy has indeed, as *Prince Bismarck* once said, been the hearth around which the German attempts at unity have clustered and warmed themselves. Thus it has already helped to fulfil a great national mission. It has also, however, been allotted the further task of overcoming the discord between the parties in the united German Empire, and directing the minds of the disputants towards a higher goal: the greatness and glory of the Fatherland. Today millions of our compatriots are spiritually alienated from the state and the prevailing economic order; the concept of the navy possesses the power – that we have nowadays perceived – to revive the national spirit of the classes and fill them once again with patriotic loyalty and love for Kaiser and Reich.

Source: *Nauticus*, in *Jahrbuch für Deutschlands Seeinteressen* (1900), p. 225; reprinted in I. Porter and I. Armour, *Imperial Germany 1890–1918* (Harlow, 1991), p. 93

The new *Weltpolitik* strengthened the nationalist claims of the conservatives, who, especially in their propaganda campaigns for a strong German navy, were able to gain widespread support. Since its inception the Navy League had been disseminating propaganda in an attempt to mobilise public opinion in the navy's favour. This article appeared in the League's own journal *Nauticus*. It depicted the navy as the unifying force of the nation, referring to the millions who had become 'spiritually alienated from the state and the prevailing economic order'. This was a reference to the working class who, it was claimed, would benefit by identifying with a strong fleet. The strongly patriotic appeal used emotive terms such as 'loyalty and love', which were contrasted to 'party discord'. The Kaiser would make a similar appeal in 1914 when a *Burgfrieden* ('party truce') was evoked in an attempt to unify the nation behind the Emperor and German war aims.

On the defensive in domestic affairs, the middle-class forces pursued a line of aggressive imperialistic power politics. The Pan German League, the Navy League, and the Colonial League spread nationalist and anti-Semitic ideas. Interest and pressure groups not only dominated parliamentary lobbies, but because of the impotence of the Reichstag they gained a dangerously strong influence over German politics as a whole. Document 1.9 is taken from a Pan-German pamphlet of 1912 written by Heinrich Class.

1.9 German nationalism and the 'Jewish Question', 1912

The recuperation of our national existence ... *is only possible if Jewish influence is either completely eliminated, or pushed back to an acceptable and safe level.* ...

Nowadays *it is absolutely imperative* that the *frontiers should be closed totally and ruthlessly against any further Jewish immigration;* ... *those foreign Jews, who have still not acquired citizenship, should be ruthlessly and as fast as possible deported, down to the last man* – but even that is not enough.

However hard it will be for the German sense of justice: *we must generally limit the rights of resident Jews.* ...

The demand must be: *Jews resident in the country will be placed under aliens' law.*

The preliminary question runs: *Who is a Jew? ... A Jew, in the sense of the required aliens' law, is every person who, on 18 January 1871, belonged to the Jewish religious community, as are all descendants of persons who were Jews at that time, even if only one parent was or is Jewish.* ...

... but what should the aliens' law ordain? ...

All *public appointments* will remain *barred* to the Jews. ...

They will not be allowed to *serve in the army or in the navy.*

They will receive neither *active nor passive franchise.* The professions of *the law and teaching* will be prohibited to them; as will be the *management* of theatres.

Newspapers, where Jews work, will be labelled as such; the others, which we can call in general 'German' newspapers, will not be allowed either to be owned by Jews, nor to have Jewish managers.

Banks, which are not the purely personal businesses of individuals, will not be allowed to have Jewish managers.

Landed property will not be allowed in future either to be owned by Jews, or to be burdened by Jewish mortgages.

As recompense for the protection which Jews enjoy as aliens, they will pay twice the tax Germans do.

Source: Daniel Frymann [Heinrich Class], '*Wenn ich der Kaiser wär*' (Leipzig, 1912), p. 74; reprinted in I. Porter and I. Armour, *Imperial Germany 1890–1918* (Harlow, 1991), pp. 88–9

This was a vehemently anti-Semitic document that talked of recovering 'our national existence'. It attacked the Jewish influence in German society and called for Jews to be barred from positions of importance and in effect to become second-class citizens. From the historian's point of view this pamphlet reveals not only the existence of a 'Jewish question' in right-wing circles in 1912 and the 'solutions' sought; it also, of course, has historical parallels with the anti-Semitic propaganda that the National Socialists would disseminate in the 1920s and 1930s, culminating in the infamous Nuremberg Laws (1935), when these sentiments were backed up by the legal weight of the State (see Chapter 6). Evidence of anti-Semitism being propogated by powerful interest groups before 1914, such as the Pan-German League, helps to substantiate the argument put forward by historians that stresses the role of traditional elites and the continuities in social structures and ideology linking imperial Germany with the Nazi era.

Kaiser Wilhelm's claim that Germany had become a world power on the basis of an imperial fleet that could challenge the Royal Navy was enthusiastically received. However, his successes in foreign policy were limited, and the price paid was the self-inflicted isolation of Germany and the forming of an alliance by its rivals – Britain, France and Russia. The declaration of war in 1914 aroused apparent enthusiasm, and the political parties agreed to a 'truce' (*Burgfrieden*). The nation appeared united behind the banner of a fully justified war of self-defence. Even the Social Democrats voted in favour of the war credits which would finance the German war effort. Document 1.10 is a photographic record of scenes in Munich greeting the announcement of war.

1.10 Enthusiastic crowd in Munich, photographed on 2 August 1914

Source: Imperial War Museum, London

This photograph captured the enthusiasm for the announcement of war in the Odeon Platz in Munich on 2 August 1914. Among the crowd can be seen a young Adolf Hitler. Germany had declared war on Russia the previous day, and the crowd in the Odeon Platz would have been responding to the news that the German army had just invaded Luxembourg and that an ultimatum had been sent to Belgium demanding safe passage for German troops. Was enthusiasm for the war as great as photographs such as this appear to suggest? The citizens who cheered in Munich (and elsewhere) on 2 August were not to know that, two days later, Germany would be at war with both France and Great Britain. Surprisingly few studies have been undertaken about popular feeling in the belligerent nations in July and August 1914. We do know, however, that peace demonstrations designed to warn Austria-Hungary against a further escalation of the crisis had taken place in German cities a few days before the outbreak of war (see Chapter 4).

In recent years historians have begun to look beyond the photographs of crowds milling below the Imperial Palace in Berlin or the Odeon Platz in Munich and question just how widespread was the enthusiasm for the war. Peter Hanssen, a Reichstag deputy from Schleswig-Holstein, recorded vividly the mobilisation scenes on his way south to Berlin and the oppressed atmosphere in the capital.

1.11 Germany on the eve of war. A diary entry of 2 August 1914, written by Peter Hanssen

One can plainly see how nervous the people are becoming as they read. Time and time again they involuntarily gaze up at the sky. At the café a man I didn't know whispered to me: 'We are too late! Russia has a big headstart.'

'The mood is depressing', lamented a lady at the same table. Those around agreed with her.

I came through Wilhelmstrasse. People were standing close together on the side-walks of the Unter den Linden to catch a glimpse of the Kaiser when he would come speeding by from Potsdam in his automobile. But there was no rejoicing, no enthusiasm; over all hung that same heavy, sad, and depressed atmosphere.

Source: P. Hanssen, *Diary of a Dying Empire*, introduction by R. Lutz, ed. R. Lutz, M. Schofield and O.O. Winther (Indianapolis, 1955), p. 14

Such documents raise serious questions about the extent of popular enthusiasm. In August 1914, the Kaiser and his government claimed that the war had created a new sense of solidarity. In a speech to the Reichstag the Kaiser declared: 'From this day on, I recognise no parties, but only Germans.' The Chancellor, Bethmann Hollweg, spoke of Germany as the victim of unprovoked aggression. The cessation of party strife (*Burgfrieden*) could not, however, survive a long war, just as the reconciliation of class tensions was dependent on a swift military victory. In fact, the war increased internal political conflicts which became embroiled with foreign policy aims; some advocated a negotiated peace, others a victorious peace with annexations. The radicalisation of the Left and Right was demonstrated in 1917 by the founding of the German Fatherland Party on the one hand and the Spartakus League on the other. The political and military collapse of the Empire forced the Kaiser to abdicate. It also provided an opportunity for a new beginning and for the reconsideration of the liberal and democratic ideals which had been extolled in the early part of the nineteenth century.

CHRONOLOGY: IMPERIAL GERMANY 1871–1918

1871	January	German Empire founded and Wilhelm I of Prussia proclaimed German Emperor (Kaiser) at Versailles.
1871		*Kulturkampf* (cultural struggle) with Catholic Church begins.
1873	May	The first of the May Laws are introduced intended to weaken the influence of the clergy.
1875		Formation of the German Social Democratic Party.
1878	May–October	Two attempts to assassinate Wilhelm I provide Bismarck with the excuse to draft anti-socialist legislation.
1879		Passing of the Exceptional Law aimed at undermining the SPD and trade unions.
1888	March	Crown Prince Frederick succeeds Emperor on his death.
	June	Frederick dies and is succeeded by Crown Prince Wilhelm (Wilhelm II).
1890	March	Bismarck dismissed. Lapse of anti-socialist legislation. General Leo von Caprivi is appointed Chancellor and pledges a 'new orientation' in German politics.
1891–4		Caprivi signs series of trade treaties.
1893		Formation of the Agrarian League. Pan German League founded.
1894		Caprivi resigns, replaced by Prince Hohenlohe.
	October	Count Bernhard von Bülow becomes Foreign Minister.
1897	June	Admiral von Tirpitz appointed Secretary of State for the Navy.
	October	Count Bernhard von Bülow becomes Foreign Minister.
1898		Navy League founded. First Navy Bill.
1900		Bülow becomes Chancellor. Second Navy Bill.
1902		Bülow Tariff Law.
1904–7		Herero revolt in South-West Africa.
1907		Bülow Bloc formed.
1908		*Daily Telegraph* affair.
1909		Bethmann Hollweg appointed Chancellor.
1912		SPD becomes largest party in Reichstag.
1912–13		Balkan Wars.
1913		Large increases in army. Zabern incident.
1914		First World War begins.
1916		Hindenburg appointed Chief of the General Staff.
1917		United States declares war on Germany. Russian Revolution.
1918	March	Treaty of Brest-Litovsk.
	September	Army admits defeat.
	October	Naval mutinies begin.

	9 November	Wilhelm II flees to Holland and a German Republic is proclaimed in Berlin.
	11 November	Armistice, signed in Compiègne, ends the war.
1919	June	Treaty of Versailles signed.

BIBLIOGRAPHY

Sources and documents

W.N. Medlicott and D. Coveney, *Bismarck and Europe* (1971); L. Snyder, *Documents of German History* (1958); J.C.G. Rohl (ed.), *From Bismarck to Hitler: The Problem of Continuity in German History* (1970); and more recently see I. Porter and I. Armour, *Imperial Germany 1890–1918* (Longman, 1991), which contains several documentary sources.

Secondary works

Works which place this period in the wider context of modern German history include: W. Carr, *A History of Germany, 1815–1945* (rev. edn 1979); A. Ramm, *Germany, 1789–1919* (1967); G.A. Craig, *Germany, 1866–1945* (1978). See also M. Kitchen, *The Political Economy of Germany, 1815–1914* (1978). For distinctive interpretations of the Imperial period as a whole see H.-U. Wehler, *The German Empire, 1871–1914* (trans., Leamington Spa, 1984); G. Eley and D. Blackbourn, *The Peculiarities of German History: Bourgeois Society and Politics in Nineteenth Century Germany* (Oxford, 1984). See also J. Sheehan (ed.), *Imperial Germany* (New York, 1976). Studies of Bismarck can be found in L. Gall, *Bismarck* (vol. 2, 1990); D.G. Williamson, *Bismarck and Germany 1862–1890* (1986); B. Waller, *Bismarck* (1985); A.J.P. Taylor, *Bismarck* (1955); W. Richter, *Bismarck* (1964); W.N. Medlicott, *Bismarck and Modern Germany* (1965); E. Eyck, *Bismarck and the German Empire* (1950). E. Eyck, *Bismarck after Fifty Years* (Historical Association, 1965) examines historians' views of Bismarck. For an overview of the historiographical debates of the period see R. Chickering (ed.), *Imperial Germany: A Historiographical Companion* (1996).

For the Wilhelmine era, see M. Balfour, *The Kaiser and his Times* (1964) and the essay collection by R. Evans (ed.), *Society and Politics in Wilhelmine Germany* (1978). See also A. Nichols, *Germany after Bismarck* (1958); J.C.G. Rohl, *Germany without Bismarck* (1967). On personalities of the period, see J.C.G. Rohl and N. Sombart (eds), *Kaiser Wilhelm II: New Interpretations* (Cambridge, 1982); K. Jarausch, *The Enigmatic Chancellor: Bethmann Hollweg and the Hubris of Imperial Germany* (London, 1973); K. Lehman, *The Chancellor as Courtier: Bernhard von Bülow and the Governance of Germany 1900–09* (1990). For recent biographies of Wilhelm II see T. Kohut, *Wilhelm II and the Germans: A Study in Leadership* (1992); L. Cecil, *William II: Emperor and Exile, 1900–1941* (1996). The Kaiser's early life is traced in J. Röhl, *Young Wilhelm. The Kaiser's Early Life, 1859–1888* (1998).

On the role of the Right and its groupings, see R. Chickering, *We Men Who*

Feel Most German: A Cultural Study of the Pan-German League 1886–1914 (1984); P. Pulzer, *The Rise of Political Anti-Semitism in Germany and Austria* (1988); J. Retallack, *Notables of the Right: The Conservative Party and Political Mobilisation in Germany 1876–1918* (1989); G. Eley, *Reshaping the Right: Radical Nationalism and Political Change after Bismarck* (1980). On the military, see M. Kitchen, *The German Officer Corps: 1870–1914* (1968); G.A. Craig, *The Politics of the Prussian Army, 1640–1945* (1945); H.H. Herwig, *'Luxury Fleet': The Imperial German Navy 1888–1918* (1980). On the Left, see C.E. Schorske, *German Social Democracy, 1905–17* (1955); P. Gay, *The Dilemma of Democratic Socialism* (New York, 1952); R. Evans (ed.), *The German Working Class, 1888–1933* (1982); D. Geary, *European Labour Protest, 1848–1939* (1981); H. Grebing, *The German Labour Movement* (1969).

On economic development see the chapter in C.M. Cipolla (ed.), *The Fontana Economic History of Europe* (vol. 4, 1973); G. Stolper, *German Economy, 1870 to the Present* (2nd edn, 1967); and W.O. Henderson, *The Industrialisation of Europe, 1780–1914* (1969). On social and economic conditions, see Ashok V. Desai, *Real Wages in Germany, 1871–1913* (1968); S.H. Hickey, *Workers in Imperial Germany. The Miners of the Ruhr* (1985). For an interesting account of the role of women in the war see U. Daniel, *The War From Within: German Working-Class Women in the First World War* (1997).

An excellent general survey of foreign policy is I. Geiss, *German Foreign Policy, 1871–1914* (1976). Fundamental to an understanding of the historiographical debate is F. Fischer, *Germany's Aims in the First World War* (1967), a controversial critique of German foreign policy under the Kaiser, which Fischer followed up in *War of Illusion* (1972). For an analysis of the controversy see J.A. Moses, *The Politics of Illusion: The Fischer Controversy in German Historiography* (1975). On the period leading to war, see V.R. Berghann, *Germany and the Approach of War in 1914* (1973), which contains an excellent synthesis of the war aims debate. Still of interest is A.J.P. Taylor, *The Struggle for Mastery in Europe, 1848–1914* (1954). See also P.A. Kennedy, *The Rise of the Anglo-German Antagonism, 1860–1914* (1980). For an analysis of the interaction between propaganda and public opinion during the war, see D. Welch, *German Society, Propaganda and Total War, 1914–1918: The Sins of Omission* (1999). On the war itself see Roger Chickering's excellent textbook, *Imperial Germany and the Great War, 1914–1918* (Cambridge, 1998); H. Herweg's comparative analysis, *The First World War: Germany and Austria-Hungary, 1914–18* (1997); and the more 'popular' anecdotal account in V. Moyer, *Victory Must Be Ours: Germany in the Great War* (1995).

Articles

On Bismarck, see J.C. Rohl, 'The Politics of Bismarck's Fall', *H.J.* (1966). On the Kaiser, see W.J. Mommsen, 'Kaiser Wilhelm II and German Politics', *J.M.H.* (1990). See also D.J. Fraley, 'Government by Procrastination: Chancellor Hohenloe and Kaiser Wilhelm II 1894–1900', *C.E.H.* (1974); D. Blackbourn, 'Liberalism, Catholicism and the State in the Second Reich', *H.W.J.* (1988); R.J. Ross, 'Enforcing the Kulturkampf: The Bismarkian State and the Limits of

Coercion in Imperial Germany', *J.M.H.* (1984); J. Steinberg, 'The Tirpitz Plan', *H.J.* (1973). On the peace movement see J. Shand, 'Doves among the Eagles: German Pacifists and their Government during World War I', *J.C.H.* (1975); K. Jarausch, 'From Second Reich to Third Reich: The Problem of Continuity in German Foreign Policy', *C.E.H.* (1979).

2

France, 1871–1944

The surrender of Napoleon III and a large French army to the Germans at Sedan on 1 September 1870 led three days later to the proclamation of the Third Republic and to the formation of a Government of National Defence in Paris. However, despite the strength of republicanism, the wider desire for peace and stability was reflected in the republicans' defeat in the national parliamentary elections held in February 1871. The republican forces had been too closely identified with the continuation of the war, whereas the task of the new Assembly, which had a conservative and royalist majority, was to approve a peace settlement with Germany. The Assembly met in Versailles and elected a government which, by deliberate intent or through a series of tactless blunders, provoked public unrest. The insurrection of the Paris Commune was finally defeated in May 1871 after a long and bloody fight. France recovered rapidly from these disasters, and by September 1873 the war indemnity had been repaid and the German occupation army was withdrawn.

A republic divided

Although the French people had played an important part in the economic recovery, France was still polarised over the form of government it should adopt. For several years after 1871, during the government of the Duc de Broglie and the presidency of Marshal MacMahon, it looked as though the power of conservatism might be strong enough to produce a restoration of the Bourbon monarchy. But the monarchists were divided, and when the Comte de Chambord (grandson of Louis Philippe) insisted on replacing the tricolour with the white fleur-de-lis of the Bourbons as France's national flag, this was opposed. Also, the monarchists were divided between the Legitimists, who supported the claims to the French throne of the Comte de Chambord (grandson of Charles X), and the Orleanists, who supported the Comte de Paris (grandson of Louis Philippe). Consequently, some monarchists became convinced that a restoration of the monarchy was impossible.

The revival of republican feeling under the leadership of the fiery Léon Gambetta, together with the divisions in the ranks of the monarchists, led in 1875 to the adoption of constitutional laws which, without formally declaring France a republic, ushered in a republican regime. Thus, out of the defeat and humiliation of 1870–1, the Third Republic was born, albeit by a one-vote majority, and referred to as 'the regime which divides Frenchmen least'. Despite a series of scandals and short-lived governments it was to survive against all the odds, until an even greater humiliation would destroy it in 1940.

2.1 The Constitutional Laws of the Third Republic: Law on the Organisation of the Public Powers, 25 February 1875

1. The legislative power is exercised by two assemblies, the Chamber of Deputies and the Senate. The Chamber of Deputies is elected by universal suffrage. ... The composition, the method of election, and the powers of the Senate shall be regulated by a special law.

2. The President of the Republic is chosen by an absolute majority of votes of the Senate and Chamber of Deputies united to form a National Assembly. He is elected for seven years. He is re-eligible.

3. The President of the Republic shares the right to initiate legislation with members of the two Chambers. He promulgates the laws when they have been voted by the two Chambers; he superintends, and is responsible for, their execution. He can exercise a presidential prerogative of mercy: amnesties can be granted by law only. He is the supreme head of the armed forces. He is responsible for all civil and military appointments. He presides over national festivals. ... Every act of the President of the Republic must be countersigned by a Minister.

4. As vacancies occur ... the President of the Republic appoints, in the Council of Ministers, the Councillors of State ...

5. The President of the Republic may, with the advice of the Senate, dissolve the Chamber of Deputies before its term has legally expired.

6. The Ministers are collectively responsible to the Chambers for the general policy of the government, and individually for their personal acts. The President of the Republic is responsible in case of high treason only ...

8. The Chambers shall have the right by separate resolutions, taken in each by an absolute majority of votes, either upon their own initiative or upon the request of the President of the Republic, to declare a revision of the Constitutional Laws

necessary. After each of the two Chambers shall have come to this decision, they shall meet together as a National Assembly to proceed with the revision …

Source: *Annals of the American Academy of Political and Social Science*, vol. 3, March 1983; in G.A. Kertesz (ed.), *Documents in the Political History of the European Continent 1815–1939* (Oxford, 1968), p. 320

Document 2.1 formally established the Third Republic and set out the constitutional structure of government. It is a document that appears at first glance to be straightforward, even rather dull. However, on closer inspection it reveals a great deal about the prevailing uncertainty of the period and the hopes and expectations of the different political camps in France at this time. It should be noted that this was intended to be a *provisional* constitution. These so-called 'organic laws' provided for a republican form of government based on parliamentary rule and manhood suffrage, but they were drafted in such a way that they might equally apply to a constitutional monarchy as to a republic. In other words, they anticipated the possibility of replacing the President with a king.

Article 1 established that legislative power was to be exercised by two parliamentary assemblies: the Chamber of Deputies and the upper house, the Senate. In opting for a bicameral system, rather than a single National Assembly, the conservative majority hoped to counterbalance the Chamber of Deputies with the Senate. The 300 senators had to be at least 40 years old (radicalism was associated with youth): 225 were elected by the *départements* for a term of nine years, in a manner which meant that the rural conservative departments were over-represented, and the outgoing National Assembly elected a further 75 life senators. Article 2 is often referred to as the 'Wallon Amendment'. By a majority of one vote, the word 'republic' was here slipped into the title of 'President of the Republic', who was to be elected by an absolute majority of the National Assembly for a term of seven years. Under Article 5, the new President had the power to dissolve the Chamber of Deputies, while Article 6 introduced the concept of ministerial responsibility. Within a year both articles would be invoked in what was the first test of the new constitution. Elections in 1876 produced a Chamber of Deputies dominated by republicans with a moderate republican, Jules Simon, as Prime Minister. The President, Marshal MacMahon, considered the anti-clerical demands of the Left unacceptable and in May 1877 dismissed Simon with the consent of the Senate; he also dissolved the Chamber, which had refused to accept MacMahon's choice of prime minister. The newly elected Chamber, however, was firmly opposed to the President's policies and asserted once and for all the supremacy of its authority over the personal rule of the presidency.

In 1879 MacMahon was forced to resign, and after his succession by Jules Grévy, who had led the parliamentary revolt against him, the importance of the presidency began to decline; presidential power to dissolve parliament was never again invoked during the Third Republic. Unfortunately, however, the Chamber of Deputies was rarely able to produce a clear majority, and as a result government was notoriously unstable and crises were frequent. In the first forty years there were fifty changes of government.

On the surface, France, which remained the sole republican state among the great powers of Europe, presented a picture of political instability. At times of crisis, political groupings tended to polarise into two irreconcilable camps on the Right and Left. The social groups behind the monarchists were predominantly Catholic; so republicans, largely under the influence of Jules Ferry (a Protestant), implemented a series of anti-clerical measures, particularly in the field of education, designed to weaken the influence of the Church. The intention was to unite the country behind a secular republic. These anti-clerical measures, however, alienated large sections of the country. During the next thirty years, amidst frequent changes of government, there were to be numerous political crises and scandals that *appeared* to threaten the very survival of the republic.

The first major threat came from the so-called Boulanger affair between 1886 and 1889. General Georges Boulanger had been military governor in Tunis and was appointed Minister of War in 1886 because of his defiance of Bismarck and his progressive views (for a soldier). In fact, he became the centre of a new cult of personality that challenged the complexity of republican politics and united Catholics, monarchists and radicals, and also gained considerable popular support. 'Boulangism' thus attracted the discontented at a time when the people seemed to be losing confidence in republicanism. When the government fell in 1887 Boulanger lost his post but allowed himself to be elected to the Chamber of Deputies – although as a serving officer he was ineligible, and his election was declared invalid. Boulanger was now perceived as a new Napoleon who could bypass politicians, and the campaign he waged after his abortive 'election' to the Chamber for a revision of the constitution gained widespread support.

By 1889 'Boulangism' had become an expression of political conservatism, and was so serious a threat that in January 1889 he appeared to have successfully staged a *coup d'état* in Paris. At the last moment Boulanger lost his nerve, and this allowed the republicans to regroup and threaten him with a charge of treason. He fled to Belgium with his mistress and, in 1891, he committed suicide over her grave.

2.2 Boulanger's speech at Tours, 17 May 1889

... I call on all good Frenchmen to rally around me in order to strengthen the Republic by purifying it. In this appeal I don't ask anybody where he comes from. ... It does not matter to me whether he rallies to the Republican idea by enthusiasm or by reason. What is important is that he should rally without reservations, with a sincere desire to accomplish the common task ...

I have faith in the republican idea. I believe that when our institutions will correspond with our needs, with the aspirations of that fundamentally democratic society which constitutes France, all doubts which might still exist will vanish. I am sure that those who come to us today with the determination to help in our great enterprise without really daring to believe in it will become the most sincere, the most devoted republicans …

Republicans of long standing, who have fought and suffered for the Republic, are numerous in the national party … and nothing hinders those who have not yet joined us from coming to swell our ranks and thus to prove the vanity of the baseless fears of our enemies.

When I declared the Republic to be open, I did not say that it was open to the monarchists or closed to the republicans. I said that I would open it to all men of good will, and only those are excluded who systematically refuse to deny their sentiments of personal predilection in order to work exclusively for the unity, the greatness, and the prosperity of the fatherland …

I am marching … towards the Republic, but a non-parliamentary republic, a republic which gives the country a strong Government, a republic which will protect the humble and the small, a republic which takes passionate care of the interests of the people, a republic which, lastly, respects individual liberty, first of all the liberty of conscience which is the first and most important of all the liberties. Long live France! Long live the Republic! Long live Liberty!

Source: G.A. Kertesz (ed.), *Documents in the Political History of the European* *Continent 1815–1939* **(Oxford, 1968), pp. 322–3; translated by G.A. Kertesz from A. Zévaés,** *Au temps du Boulangisme* **(Paris, 1930), pp. 153–4**

Document 2.2 is an extract taken from General Boulanger's last speech in France. Boulanger had proved to be an effective and popular orator and this particular speech was intended to appeal to as wide an audience as possible. In it he appealed to *all* Frenchmen to 'purify the Republic'. What did he mean by this? First of all, he appeared to be suggesting that he did not wish to be closely associated with any particular sectional interest. He talked about the Republic being open to monarchists and republicans. Yet we know that he was financed by aristocrats and had largely become a tool for monarchists and clericals. Remember also that the humiliation of military defeat by Prussia in 1870 had not been forgotten in France. Indeed, nationalist sentiment had been aroused by the so-called Schnaebelé affair of 1887, when a French frontier official had been arrested by the Germans on the grounds of espionage.

For many, General Boulanger provided the focus for a new sense of nationalism based on military glory. It is no coincidence that he advocated that Alsace-Lorraine (surrendered by France to the German Empire in 1871) should be returned to France and that conditions in the army should be improved. His demand for a 'new type of republic' was intended to awaken nationalist sentiment to 'work exclusively for the unity, the greatness, and the prosperity of the fatherland'. Strong leadership and strong government are the key ideas here. Boulanger actually stated that he intended to 'march … towards … a non-parliamentary republic'. This speech, then, is an emotional appeal to overthrow the government and establish a dictatorship with mass support. Such sentiments would later be expressed by fascist leaders in Europe.

Even if it is true, as some historians have suggested, that the threat posed by Boulanger has been exaggerated, 'Boulangism' – the nationalist and right-wing challenge to the Republic – did not disappear with the General's death but continued to plague the Third Republic when tensions were exacerbated by successive crises. The most notorious of these was the Dreyfus affair, which divided the country and revealed its stability to be only superficial. In 1894 Captain Alfred Dreyfus, a young Alsatian Jewish army officer, was court-martialled and sentenced to life imprisonment on Devil's Island for selling military secrets to Germany through Colonel Schwartzkoppen, the German Military Attaché in Paris.

The conviction of Dreyfus did not immediately divide the nation. However, the case dragged on for twelve years and provoked bitter division between 'Dreyfusards' (supporters of Dreyfus, mainly the Left, intellectuals, and anti-clericals) and 'anti-Dreyfusards' (extreme nationalists, Catholics, anti-Semites and the army), who believed that the authority of the state, as represented by the army, should not be questioned. In many respects Dreyfus had become a symbol eclipsed by the clash of principles that forced many of the French to reappraise their political beliefs and to take sides for and against the Republic. Documents 2.3 and 2.4 illustrate the different positions adopted and the issues that were raised by the Dreyfus case.

2.3 Concluding paragraphs of Émile Zola's 'J'accuse', 13 January 1898

… I accuse Lieutenant-Colonel Du Paty de Clam of having been the diabolical contriver of the judicial error, unconscious I would fain believe; and of having afterwards defended his nefarious work for three years by machinations as ridiculous as they are guilty.

I accuse General Mercier of having made himself the accomplice, through his mere weakness of character, in one of the greatest iniquities of the century.

I accuse General Billot of having had in his hands the certain proofs of Dreyfus' innocence and of having stifled them; of having incurred the guilt of a betrayal of humanity, of a betrayal of justice, in order to serve political ends and to save a [General Staff] that was compromised.

I accuse Generals de Boisdeffre and Gonse of having made themselves accomplices in the same crime – the one, no doubt, led on by clerical passion, the other perhaps by that esprit de corps which makes of the War Office Bureau a holy ark and not to be touched.

I accuse General de Pellieux and Commandant Ravary of having turned their inquiry into a work of villainy, by which I mean that the inquiry was conducted with the most monstrous partiality; and that of this partiality the report of Ravary is an imperishable monument, brazen in its audacity.

I accuse the three handwriting experts – MM. Belhomme, Varinard, and Couard –

of having drawn up lying and fraudulent reports; unless, indeed, a medical examination shows them to be the victims of a diseased eyesight and judgement.

I accuse the War Office of having carried on in the press ... an abominable campaign intended to lead astray opinion and hide its misdoings.

Lastly, I accuse the first court-martial of having violated correct judicial procedures by condemning an accused man on a document which was kept secret, and I accuse the second court-martial of having shielded this illegality to order, committing in its turn the judicial crime of acquitting a man they knew to be guilty ...

Source: Émile Zola, 'J'accuse', *L'Aurore*, 13 January 1898

The military authorities refused to accept new evidence that Dreyfus had been convicted on forged evidence. When accumulated evidence began to point to the real traitor, Commander Esterhazy, political pressure led to his trial, at which he was acquitted on the forged evidence of Major Henry of the Intelligence Branch. The case of Dreyfus was taken up by the novelist Émile Zola, who in an open letter to President Faure, entitled 'J'accuse', made a series of damaging allegations against the army.

The first point to note is the newspaper in which Zola's accusations were published. This was *L'Aurore*, edited by the radical, Georges Clemenceau. Although the paper's circulation rose to 200,000 with the publication of 'J'accuse', this figure was dwarfed by the circulations of the anti-Dreyfusard press, which could boast a readership of 1,500,000 for *Le Petit Journal* and 500,000 for *La Libre Parole*, together with an unmatched network of provincial publications. The ensuing debate that took place in the newspapers is reminiscent of the newspaper 'circulation wars' with which we are familiar today. Zola's article ran to 3,000 words, however; the extract printed here is only the conclusion.

The accusations levelled by Zola were intended to achieve maximum effect. The distinguished writer pulled few punches, and the language employed was colloquial so that it could be understood by all. By naming individual officers engaged in prosecuting Dreyfus and acquitting Esterhazy, Zola believed that he could force the President to set up a full enquiry into the case: 'Truth is on the march; nothing will stop it.' General Boisdeffre, Chief of the General Staff, and General Gonse, his assistant, were responsible for the investigation of the crime and were accused by Zola of being 'led on by clerical passion' – a clear reference to the Catholic Church, which the author suggested was behind the prosecution of Dreyfus. The War Office was accused of stirring up the press 'to lead astray opinion and hide its misdoings', and the courts martial were accused of illegality. Zola concluded by stating that he willingly risked prosecution ('Let them take me to court'), in 'the name of truth and humanity'. He presented himself not simply as a supporter of Dreyfus but as the conscience of republican justice. The extent of Zola's accusations against the army proved so sensational that people could no longer remain indifferent to the affair.

2.4 'The Last Skittle', a cartoon in *Le Psst!*, February 1898

Source: Jean-Loup Charmet

Document 2.4 is a cartoon by Caran D'Ache that appeared in the anti-Dreyfusard journal *Le Psst!* on 5 February 1898. The caption reads: 'Go on Baron, another one like that and the game is ours.' It is interesting that the Jewish financier Rothschild was chosen to appear rather than Dreyfus. The cartoon suggested that Jews had destroyed the main agencies of the state with the exception of the army (the 'last skittle'), which was about to receive a fatal strike from the 'Zola bowl' being hurled by Baron Rothschild. The figure urging the Baron on was a Prussian officer, who would presumably gain most from the destruction of the French army.

The unflattering image of the Jew depicted in this cartoon as a physically repellent figure (note the large diamond ring sparkling on Rothschild's left hand) corresponded to the wider anti-Semitism that had developed in France in the 1880s. (It is not dissimilar to the images that were contained in the vehemently anti-Semitic Nazi journal, *Der Stürmer*.) The Jewish community in France during this period numbered only 80,000, and had been largely assimilated successfully into the liberal atmosphere of the Third Republic. Nevertheless, right-wing nationalistic groups, in their desire to find a scapegoat for their own misfortunes, identified Jews with the republic and the economy and disseminated a vigorous anti-Semitic campaign, claiming Jews were undermining French values. The extent of anti-Semitic feeling was revealed in the Panama Scandal of 1892, when it was claimed that Jewish financiers had dispensed bribes in order to secure contracts for the building of the Panama Canal.

The Dreyfus affair provided an opportunity not only for renewed anti-Semitism but also for the anti-republican Right. Indeed, the two forces came together in the foundation of Charles Maurras's radical royalist group, *Action Française*, which continued to propagate its nationalistic and anti-Semitic propaganda until the end of the Second World War.

In 1899 the Dreyfus trial verdict was annulled and a retrial ordered. Dreyfus was retried and condemned, but with 'extenuating circumstances'. This proved to be the last desperate self-justification of the army leadership. In 1906 Alfred Dreyfus was eventually declared innocent and reinstated in the army at the rank of major and decorated with the Legion of Honour. The tensions that the Dreyfus affair brought to the surface refused to subside, however, and continued to divide the Third Republic.

The historian John Roberts has stated that 'If history is the story of significant change France has little history between the wars.' France in the 1930s continued to reflect the cleavages between Right and Left in politics. The years before 1914 were often referred to as *la belle époque* (the good old days). Indeed, after a long depression lasting until 1897, France began to enjoy a period of unprecedented prosperity. France was also compensating for its defeat in 1871 by rapidly developing a vast colonial empire in North and West Africa and Indo-China. Nevertheless, this was also a period characterised by political instability and economic disturbances. Spurred on by the ideas of Georges Sorel (*Reflections on Violence*, 1908), syndicalism developed as a positive alternative to parliamentary democracy, and Sorel's call for direct violent action and a general strike to bring about a system of federated trade unionism attracted disillusioned workers. In 1905 disparate groups within the socialist movement ranging from sydicalists to orthodox Marxists eventually agreed upon the formation of a united socialist party.

2.5 The Union of French Socialist Parties, 30 December 1904

The delegates of the [following] French organizations: Workers Socialist Revolutionary Party, Socialist Party of France, French Socialist Party, and [six] autonomous [socialist regional] Federations, appointed by their respective Parties and Federations to establish unity … declare that their organizations are ready to collaborate immediately in the task of the unification of socialist forces on the basis of the following, determined and accepted by common agreement:

1. The Socialist Party is a class party, whose aim is the socialization of the means of production and exchange, that is, the transformation of capitalist society into a collective or communist society, by the means of the economic and political organization of the proletariat. In its aim, in its ideal, in the means it uses, the Socialist Party is not a party of reform – although it will endeavour to achieve the immediate reforms demanded by the working class – but a party of class war and revolution.

2. Those elected to Parliament shall form a single group opposed to all bourgeois political factions. The socialist group in Parliament must refuse to the Government all means which assure the domination of the bourgeoisie and its maintenance in power, it must refuse, therefore, [the granting of] military votes, votes for colonial conquest, secret funds, and the whole of the budget.

The deputies can not commit the Party without its agreement even in exceptional circumstances.

In Parliament, the socialist group must devote itself to the defence and extension of the political freedom and rights of the workers, and to the pursuit and realization of reforms which improve the conditions of life … of the working class …

4. Freedom of discussion in the press is complete in all questions of doctrine and method, but with respect to action, all socialist newspapers must conform strictly to the decision of the Congress, interpreted by the central organization of the party …

6. The party will take steps to ensure that its deputies shall respect their *mandat impératif.*

Source: P. Louis, *Le Parti socialiste en France* (Paris, 1930); reprinted in G.A. Kertesz (ed.), *Documents in the Political History of the European Continent 1815–1939* (Oxford University Press, 1968), p. 326

Previous attempts to unify the socialist movement had proved unsuccessful. However, by December 1904 there was widespread recognition that the existence of several socialist parties undermined the effectiveness of the socialist cause. Following four meetings in December the declaration cited above as Document 2.5 was finally agreed and accepted by all groups in January 1905 as the basis for a new united socialist party. The declaration is in line with the revisionist movement under Bernstein's influence that was taking place within the Social Democratic Party in Germany.

Although it reaffirmed its class roots and its commitment to 'socialising the means of production and exchange', the declaration nevertheless stated that the new party was prepared to work within the parliamentary system in order to achieve reforms. Indeed, in 1906 and again in 1910, limited reforms were introduced such as the ten-hour working day for factory workers and old-age pensions. But the period leading to 1914 was characterised by a wave of strikes and demonstrations and by bitter political divisions that led to the imprisonment of some trade-union leaders and to the murder of Jean Jaurès, the popular leader of the moderate socialists.

The outbreak of the First World War united the nation briefly under the strong leadership of Raymond Poincaré and, later, Georges Clemenceau (a Dreyfusard). Germany had declared war on France on 3 August 1914, after France had supported Russian mobilisation plans and refused to declare neutrality. Of all the major western nations, France was the first to experience the impact of 'total war', since the Schlieffen Plan involved a knockout strike against France before turning to confront the Russians (see Chapter 4). For the rest of the war, France's north-eastern region became a lost battle zone. However, the war also provided an opportunity for the nation to unite against an aggressor and to erase the memory of defeat in the Franco-Prussian War. Document 2.6 is one of the most famous of the wartime posters that summed up French patriotism during the Great War.

2.6 'We Will Get Them!', a poster of 1916 (see p. 30)

This was a poster designed by Jules Abel Faivre in 1916 to persuade French citizens to subscribe to the Second War Loan in order to sustain the war effort. In fact, it proved so successful that it was reissued. The phrase '*On les aura!*' ('We will get them!') was coined by General Pétain during the Battle of Verdun, and referred to the military offensive against Germany. The pose of the soldier recalled a sculptured group by François Rude on the Arc de Triomphe. The simplicity of the design and the restrained assertion of patriotic faith symbolised in the searching eyes and outstretched hand of the ordinary soldier, urging the people on, recorded the mood of the nation and shows the way posters could play an important role in mobilising nationalist sentiment.

Source: Imperial War Museum, London

The experience of war exposed the weaknesses of the French political structure. Had victory not been achieved, this political structure might well have collapsed. However, having flirted briefly with a virtual military dictatorship, parliamentary government was restored. But the perennial question as to how France could create a strong executive within a parliamentary framework remained. After the war, right-wing organisations gained in strength once again and continued to challenge the authority of the republic. Anti-republican forces began to clamour for a more authoritarian regime. Slogans like 'France for the French' appealed to a nationalistic sentiment that continued to identify the republic with Jews, socialists and communists. The Stavisky scandal (1933–4) was exploited by right-wing fascist and royalist groups and by the communists, who maintained that the affair exposed the web of political corruption that pervaded the whole system. (Stavisky was a Jew who massively defrauded the state pawnshop of Bayonne and died in suspicious circumstances.) After Stavisky's suicide in January 1934, a series of armed demonstrations were planned, mainly by right-wing groups who had come together to overthrow the government and replace it with one of their own choice.

2.7 Appeal of the *Jeunesses Patriotes*, February 1934

People of Paris!
You will join us … outside the Town Hall, the cradle of your civic rights, and proclaim with us that the country is in danger. Led by your own representative you will tell Parliament what you are thinking. …
Enough of scandals!
Enough of rottenness!
Oppose those who exploit the public savings;
Oppose the Ministers and Deputies who have sold out;
Oppose a corrupt regime which has failed.
The Young Patriots cry to you:
Join us to defeat a decadent regime;
Join us against collapse and to save the peace;
Join us for the rebirth of the homeland;
Join us to carry out the national revolution.
Hunt out the thieves!
Give a Leader to France and not a master
And give back to Frenchmen confidence in the destinies of their country.

Source: Quoted in M. Chavardres, *Le 6 Février 1934: La République en danger*
(Paris, 1966), pp. 161–2

Document 2.7 was an appeal by the 'Young Patriots' that appeared in right-wing newspapers and was used as a poster to mobilise support. It was part of the concerted action waged by the various Leagues on the far right of the political spectrum aimed at violent insurrection. Other groups included *Solidarité Française*, *Croix de Feu*, *Action Française*, and its militant wing, *Camelots du Roi*. The references to 'scandal', 'rottennesss' and a 'corrupt regime' allude to Stavisky and his fraudulent dealings with central and local government ('those who exploit the public savings'). The expressions of discontent with the government led the 'Young Patriots' to demand the violent overthrow of 'a decadent regime', the re-establishment of order and authority and 'national rebirth' under strong leadership ('Give a Leader to France'). The call for a strong leader ('not a master') was a common theme that linked extremist groups on the Right. Indeed, Charles Maurras demanded the restoration of the monarchy – which, he argued, symbolised past greatness and by transcending party strife would unite the nation. This nostalgic vision of aristocratic (Catholic) France was out of touch with more dynamic elements, such as the 'Young Patriots', who had abandoned Maurras's old fashioned exclusiveness.

The economic slump had hit France later than other countries and unemployment was rising. Since 1930 a number of coalition governments had been formed but they were unable to solve France's political and economic problems. For anti-republican groups, the coming to power of Hitler in Germany in 1933 on a manifesto of 'rebirth' and regneration (see Chapter 6) only served to confirm their belief in the paralysis of French politics. The demands of groups like the 'Young Patriots' led to serious riots, which were defeated after bitter street fighting, and the republic was only saved by a strong coalition government whose members had not been tarnished by the Stavisky scandal. Nevertheless, some historians, notably David Thomson, have claimed that the Stavisky affair, the subsequent riots, and the clamour by anti-republican forces for a more authoritarian regime had a lasting effect on French politics and anticipated the official doctrine of the Vichy regime.

From the Popular Front to Vichy France

The recurrent ministerial crises and the growth of anti-parliamentary organisations finally persuaded communists, socialists and radicals to come together (once again) under a Popular Front programme committed to 'Bread, Peace and Liberty', which was also designed to combat fascism.

2.8 The programme of the Popular Front, 10 January 1936

POLITICAL DEMANDS

I. Defence of Liberty

1   General amnesty.
2   Against the Fascist Leagues:

   (a)   Effective disarmament, and dissolution of para-military formations ...
   (b)   The initiation of legal proceedings in cases of incitement to murder or of violent action endangering the safety of the State.

3   The cleansing of public life, especially through the enforcement of parliamentary disqualifications (i.e. inability of a Deputy to hold certain offices).
4   The Press:

   (a)   Repeal of the infamous laws and decrees restricting freedom of opinion.
   (b)   Reform of the Press by ... legislative measures ...
   (c)   The re-organization of State broadcasting, with the aim of ensuring the accuracy of information and balanced treatment for different political and social organizations at the microphone.

5   Trade union liberties:

   (a)   Application and observance of trade union rights for all.
   (b)   Observance of factory legislation concerning women.

6   Education and freedom of conscience:

   (a)   To safeguard the development of public education, not only by the necessary grants, but also by reforms such as the extension of compulsory attendance at school up to the age of fourteen, and, in secondary education, the proper selection of pupils as an essential accompaniment of grants.
   (b)   To guarantee to all concerned, pupils and teachers, full freedom of conscience, particularly by ensuring the neutrality of education, its nonreligious character, and the civic rights of the teaching staff.

7   Colonial territories: The setting up of a Parliamentary Commission of Enquiry into the political, economic and cultural situation in France's overseas territories ...

II. Defence of Peace

1   Appeal to the people, and particularly to the working masses, for collaboration in the maintenance and organization of peace.
2   International collaboration within the framework of the League of Nations for collective security, by defining the aggressor and the automatic and joint application of sanctions in cases of aggression.
3   A ceaseless endeavour to pass from armed peace to disarmed peace, first by a convention of limitation, and then by the general, simultaneous, and effectively controlled reduction of armaments.
4   Nationalization of the war industries and suppression of private trade in arms.
5   Repudiation of secret diplomacy, international action, and public negotiations to bring back to Geneva the States which have left it, without weakening the constituent principles of the League of Nations: collective security and indivisible peace.
6   Simplification of the procedure provided in the League of Nations Covenant for the pacific adjustment of treaties which are dangerous to the peace of the world ...

ECONOMIC DEMANDS

I. Restoration of purchasing power destroyed or reduced by the crisis

Against unemployment and the crisis in industry

The establishment of a national unemployment fund.
Reduction of the working week without reduction of weekly wages.
Drawing young workers into employment by establishing a system of adequate pensions for retired workers.
The rapid execution of a scheme of large-scale public works ...

Against the agricultural and commercial crisis

Revision of prices of agricultural produce, combined with a fight against speculation and high prices, so as to reduce the gap between wholesale and retail prices.
In order to put an end to the levies taken by speculators from both producers and consumers, the setting up of a National Grain Board ...
Support for agricultural co-operatives, supply of fertilizers at cost price ... , extension of agricultural credits, reduction of leasehold rents.
Suspension of distraints and the regulation of debt repayments.
Pending the complete and earliest possible removal of all the injustices inflicted by the economy decrees, the immediate repeal of measures affecting those groups whose living standards have been most severely damaged by these decrees.

II. Against the robbery of savings and for a better organization of credit …

In order to remove credit and savings from the control of the economic oligarchy, to transform the *Banque de France*, now a privately owned Bank, into the *Banque de la France*. …

Source: G. Fraser and T. Natanson, *Léon Blum* (London, 1937), pp. 307–12; in G.A. Kertesz (ed.), *Documents in the Political History of the European Continent 1815–1939* (Oxford University Press, 1968), pp. 333–5

The publication of the Popular Front programme on 11 January 1936 symbolised the resolve of the forces of the Left to resist fascism and to provide the French electorate with a socialist alternative. The programme was divided into sections dealing with political and economic demands. Under the subsection 'Defence of Liberty', it called for the disarmament and dissolution of the fascist leagues, a cleansing of public life, freedom of the press, a guarantee of trade union liberties, and full freedom of conscience in schools, where the school leaving age was to be raised to 14. The subsection 'Defence of Peace' appealed for the support of the 'working masses' to uphold the principles of disarmament and collective security through the League of Nations and the repudiation of secret diplomacy. The section dealing with 'Economic Demands' was the most radical, demanding a fundamental reorganisation of the banking and credit system including the nationalisation of the Bank of France and an end to the economic oligarchy of the so-called 'two hundred families' that allegedly dominated French financial and economic life. It called for the reduction in the working week without a reduction in wages, better pensions and unemployment benefits, and a large-scale programme of public works.

The first Popular Front government in France came to power in June 1936 under the premiership of Léon Blum and represented a genuine expression of republican democracy. (A similar alliance gained power in Spain and led to the Spanish Civil War, see Chapter 8.) Domestically it began well by negotiating the Matignon Agreement that brought an end to violent strike action and the occupation of the factories by introducing wage increases, a forty-hour week and annual two-week holiday with pay. However, the radical reforms advocated by the Popular Front had alienated important sections of French society, which remained suspicious of the Left and, as a result, preferred to invest its finances abroad. The franc dropped in value, and the subsequent inflation undermined many of the gains that had been secured at Matignon.

The French establishment, supported by the fascist leagues, increasingly sabotaged the economic and social policies that Blum was struggling to implement. Moreover, in foreign affairs the government was immediately confronted by the German reoccupation of the Rhineland, in contravention of the Versailles Treaty, and with the outbreak of the Spanish Civil War. The failure of the

Popular Front government to resist Hitler in the Rhineland, or to provide meaningful support to the Republican government in Spain, led to bitter internal recriminations that fatally weakened its resolve. A second Popular Front was formed in 1938, by which time a combination of internal disputes and the growing crises in international affairs culminating in the signing of the Munich Agreement (see Chapter 8) had undermined its credibility. Although the Popular Front introduced an extensive programme of social reform, it failed to unite the country; and, when the test of war came, a polarised and weakened France capitulated in the face of the German advance.

2.9 'Greetings from Paris', a postcard of 1940

Source: Centre for the Study of Propaganda, University of Kent at Canterbury

The German armed forces entered Paris on 14 June 1940. Document 2.9 is a souvenir postcard showing unarmed German soldiers sightseeing in Paris, having occupied the French capital for the second time in seventy years (that is, within the living memory of some French people). On 22 June 1940, France signed an armistice with Germany at Compiègne and as a result the country was demilitarised and divided into the occupied northen region and unoccupied Vichy under Marshal Pétain. The terms of the armistice were not as punitive as many had feared, and the belief gained ground that under the autocratic leadership of Pétain, a regenerated France might gain a place in a new order in Europe.

2.10 'Maréchal, nous voilà' ('Here we are, Marshal'), poster and music, 6 July 1941 (see p. 38)

On 10 July 1940, the historic struggle between Dreyfusard and anti-Dreyfusard forces was finally resolved when the Third Republic was legally abolished. Pétain formed an authoritarian government in the spa town of Vichy that remained implacably anti-republican and collaborated extensively with the Germans. The motto of the Vichy regime was '*Travail, Famille, Patrie*' ('Work, Family, Nation'). The song, 'Here we are, Marshal', was adopted and became the new Vichy anthem. The final verse was:

> The war is inhuman
> What a sad horror
> Let's not listen to hatred anymore
> Let's exhalt work
> And let's retain confidence
> In a new destiny
> Because Pétain is France!
> And France is Pétain!!

The cover to the sheet music also became a poster and showed a cross section of the 'new' France, with the flags of the Legion of ex-Servicemen marching towards Pétain, the father-figure of the nation. Fascist parties throughout Europe similarly attempted to identify leader figures with the nation (see Chapters 5 and 6). Supporters of Vichy claimed that Pétain had no other choice and that his actions had brought an end to the war and spared the French empire. However, for those forces that had defended the republic, the real choice had been summed up in the slogan coined before the armistice: 'Better Hitler than Blum'.

Waiting in the wings was another, lesser-known, military figure who had taken up the anti-Vichy, 'Free French' cry. This was General Charles de Gaulle; and after the war he, more than anyone, would restore national pride and shape the post-war destiny of France.

Source: Centre for the Study of Propaganda, University of Kent at Canterbury

CHRONOLOGY: FRANCE 1870–1944

1870	1 September	French defeated at Sedan.
	4 September	Republic proclaimed in Paris. Formation of Government of National Defence.
1871	8 February	Elections held for National Assembly.
	18 March	Rising of the Paris Commune.
	28 March	Proclamation of the Paris Commune and first decrees issued the next day.
	31 August	Thiers elected President of France.
1873	24 May	Thiers resigns. Marshal MacMahon elected president of the National Assembly.
	20 November	French monarchists confer MacMahon with presidential powers for seven years.
1875	30 January	Republican Constitution in France passed by one vote.
	16 July	French constitution finalised.
1879	30 January	MacMahon resigns and is succeeded by Grévy.
1886	7 January	General Boulanger becomes Minister of War.
1887	20 April	Schnaebele incident. A French officer and spy is arrested by the Germans. Grévy is criticised for weak stance. Boulanger represents nationalist feeling over the incident.
	18 May	Boulanger excluded from the Rouvier Ministry.
	1 October	Boulanger attempts coup d'état amidst the growing scandals associated with Grévy's presidency.
1888	27 March	Boulanger retires from the French army, making him eligible for election to parliament.
	15 May	Boulanger elected to the Chamber, standing for several constituencies. He advocates a revision of the Constitution.
1889	27 January	Boulanger's attempt to provoke a 'crisis' in Paris fails.
	8 April	Flight of Boulanger, fearing arrest. Republicans remain the major party in the elections.
	17 July	French law forbids multiple candidatures in elections.
1891	September 30	Boulanger commits suicide in Brussels.
1892	10 November	Panama Canal Scandal.
1894	15 October	Dreyfus arrested on charge of spying for Germany.
	22 December	Dreyfus convicted by court martial and sentenced to imprisonment on Devil's Island.
1897	15 November	Discovery that the document on which Dreyfus had been convicted was produced by Major Esterhazy. Government enquiry into Dreyfus case.
1898	13 January	Acquittal of Esterhazy for forgery prompts Zola's 'J'accuse' letter to the President.
	23 February	Zola imprisoned for 'J'accuse' letter.
	30 August	Forgery admitted by Colonel Henry in the Dreyfus case.
1899	3 June	Dreyfus trial verdict annulled and retrial ordered.
	9 September	Dreyfus retried and condemned but 'with extenuating circumstances'.
	19 September	Dreyfus pardoned by Presidential decree.
1900	30 April	Republicans form bloc to defend Republic against anti-Dreyfusards.
1906	12 July	Dreyfus completely exonerated by French government.
1913	17 January	Poincaré elected President of France.
	20 November	Zabern incident, in which a German officer insults recruits in Alsace-Lorraine, inflames Franco-German relations.

1914	1 August	Mobilisation of French troops.
	3 August	Germany declares war on France.
	12 August	France declares war on Austria-Hungary.
	5–9 September	Battle of the Marne.
1915	3 December	Joffre becomes French Commander-in-Chief.
1917	29 April	Pétain becomes chief of French staff.
	16 November	Clemenceau forms cabinet on Painlevé's fall.
1919	28 June	Versailles Treaty signed.
1921	16 January	Briand becomes Prime Minister.
1922	15 January	Poincaré appointed Prime Minister and Foreign Minister.
1925	1 December	Locarno Treaties.
1928	27 August	France and sixty-four other states sign the Kellogg-Briand Pact, outlawing war as a means of solving international disputes.
1929	27 July	Poincaré resigns as Prime Minister and is succeeded by Briand.
1931	27 January	Laval becomes French Prime Minister.
1933	31 January	Daladier's Government formed.
	December	Flight of Stavisky brings about scandal of financial corruption in politics.
1934	7 February	Daladier resigns.
	8 February	Doumergue forms National Union ministry of centre and moderate parties.
1935	14 July	Mass demonstrations throughout France demanding the dissolution of right-wing Leagues.
	3 November	Socialist groups unite as Socialist and Republican Union under Léon Blum; later joined by Radical Socialists and Communists to form a Popular Front.
1936	January	Programme of the Popular Front set out.
	4 June	Blum forms first Popular Front government.
1938	13 March	Blum forms second Popular Front government, but Senate rejects financial reforms.
	10 April	Blum resigns and is replaced by Daladier.
1939	26–31 August	Negotiations by Daladier and Chamberlain with Hitler fail.
	3 September	Britain and France declare war on Germany.
1940		
	21 March	Daladier replaced by Reynaud as Premier.
	29 May	British forces evacuated from Dunkirk.
	10 June	Mussolini declares war on France.
	14 June	German forces enter Paris.
	16 June	Pétain replaces Reynaud, who resigns.
	22 June	Armistice signed in historic railway carriage at Compiègne.
	10 July	Deputies assemble at Vichy and Pétain given full powers as 'Head of the French State', thus ending the Third Republic.
1942	November	Geographical division of France comes to an end as German troops occupy Vichy, France.
1944	6 June	Allied landings in Normandy.
	25 August	Paris liberated.
	23 October	Allies recognise De Gaulle's provisional government.

BIBLIOGRAPHY

Sources and documents

There is very little source material on post-revolutionary France. The most important collection of documents can be found in W. Fortescue, *The Third Republic* (2000). Of some interest is J.S. McClelland (ed.), *The French Right: From de Maistre to Maurras* (1970). See also G. Sorel, *Reflections of Violence* (1915). R. Kedward, *The Dreyfus Affair* (1965), contains a few documentary sources. Considerable insight into the historical 'flavour' of the period can be gained by reading the novels of Émile Zola, including *Germinal* (1885) and *La Débâcle* (1892).

Secondary works

There are many general introductions to this period, including D.W. Brogan, *The Development of Modern France, 1870–1940* (1940); J.P.T. Bury, *France, 1814–1940* (1949); A. Cobban, *A History of Modern France* (vol.3, 1965); G. Wright, *France in Modern Times* (1960). More recently, see J.-D. Bredin, *'The Affair': The Case of Alfred Dreyfus* (1987); J.-M. Mayeur and M. Rebérioux, *The Third Republic, 1871–1914* (1984); R.D. Anderson, *France, 1870–1914* (1977); R. Magraw, *France 1815–1914: The Bourgeois Century* (1983); D. Thomson, *Democracy in France Since 1870* (1964); J.F. McMillan, *Dreyfus to de Gaulle: Politics and Society in France, 1898–1969* (1985). T. Zeldin, *France, 1848–1945* (2 vols, 1973) analyses social, intellectual and political life, whilst E. Weber, *Peasants into Frenchmen, 1870–1914* (1977) focuses on social change. For two recent general histories, see J.F. McMillan, *Twentieth-Century France* (1992) and A. Adamthwaite, *Grandeur and Decline, 1914–40* (1993).

For works on the early period, see A. Horne, *The Fall of Paris* (1983), which includes a discussion of the Commune, whilst the same author's *The French Army in Politics* (1984) covers the army's role over both the Commune and the Dreyfus Affair. On the Commune see E. Schulkind, *The Paris Commune of 1871* (Historical Association, 1971); R.L. Williams, *The French Revolution of 1870–1871* (1969); S. Edwards, *The Paris Commune, 1871* (1971); R. Tombs, *The War against Paris, 1871* (1981). The Dreyfus Affair is the subject of G. Chapman, *The Dreyfus Case* (1955) and D. Johnson, *France and the Dreyfus Affair* (1966). M. Marrus, *The Politics of Assimilation: a Study of the French Jewish Community at the Time of the Dreyfus Affair* (1971) looks at the case from the Jewish viewpoint. H. Holdberg, *The Life of Jean Jaurès* (1962) and J.P.T. Bury, *Gambetta and the Making of the Third Republic* (1973) look at two leading figures on the left in the period.

French foreign policy is discussed in C. Andrew, *Théophile Delcassé and the Making of the Entente Cordiale* (1968) and J. Keiger, *France and the Origins of the First World War* (1983). The impact of nationalism is examined in R. Tombs (ed.), *Nationhood and Nationalism in France: From Boulangism to the Great War 1889–1918* (1991). On France during the Great War see P. Friedenson, *The French Homefront*

1914–1918 (1995). See also A. Prost, *In the Wake of War. 'Les Anciens Combattants' and French Society* (1994).

The period leading to the collapse of the Third Republic, particularly from the military perspective, is covered in M.S. Alexander, *The Republic in Danger* (1993). The Popular Front administrations are analysed by J. Jackson, *The Popular Front in France: Defending Democracy 1934–38* (1990). The dilemma confronting the Popular Front and foreign policy is tackled in N. Jordon, *The Popular Front and Central Europe* (1992).

A general overview of Vichy France is provided by R. Aron *The Vichy Regime* (1958). Various aspects of Vichy are covered by the following: H.R. Kedward, *Resistance in Vichy France* (1978) and Kedward, *In Search of the Maquis. Rural Resistance in Southern France 1942–44* (1993); R.O. Paxton, *Vichy France: Old Guard and New Order* (1972); J.F. Sweets, *Choices in Vichy France: The French under Nazi Occupation* (1986); A. Milward, *The New Order and the French Economy* (1970).

For a perceptive analysis of France since 1936, see M. Larkin, *France Since the Popular Front, 1916–1986* (1988).

Articles

R. Tombs, 'The Thiers Government and the Outbreak of Civil War in France, 1871', *H.J.* (1980) analyses the political processes in 1871. P.H. Hutton, 'Boulangism and the Rise of Mass Politics', *J.C.H.* (1976) examines the impact of Boulangism on French politics. The Dreyfus Affair is discussed in S. Wilson, 'Ideology and Anti-Semitism in France at the time of the Dreyfus Affair', *J.C.H.* (1975).

An economic analysis of inter-war France can be found in A. Sauvy, 'The Economic Crisis of the 1930s in France', *J.C.H.* (1969) and the Left in the period immediately after the Great War is tackled in T. Judt, 'The French Socialists and the Cartel des Gauches of 1924', *J.C.H.* (1976). The role of Blum is the central focus of M.D. Gallagher, 'Léon Blum and the Spanish Civil War', *J.C.H.* (1971).

For an interesting account of patriotism in Vichy France, see H.R. Kedward, 'Patriots and Patriotism in Vichy France', *Transactions of the Royal Historical Society* (1982).

3

Russia in revolution, 1890–1918

Nineteenth-century imperial Russia was still dominated by tsarist autocracy. Successive tsars believed that they inherited the divine right to rule Russia without challenge or opposition. It was a country in which opportunities for social reform by constitutional means appeared small and in which hopes of change were repeatedly disappointed. The Napoleonic Wars, however, had allowed a large number of educated Russians, mainly army officers, to gain first-hand knowledge of western Europe for the first time. This brought home to them the comparative backwardness of imperial Russia and the need for reforms.

The end of tsardom

When Tsar Alexander II ('the Liberator') succeeded to the throne in 1855, he was burdened with the debt of the Crimean War and faced considerable unrest at home. As a result he was persuaded to implement a range of reforms. In 1861, for example, the serfs were emancipated, gaining legal but not economic freedom. This was viewed as a landmark, opening the door to western-style modernisation. In 1864, local government was reorganised and provincial assemblies (*zemstvos*) were established with limited authority over local issues.

Once reforms had been started, however, agitation grew for wider freedoms. Political and economic conditions appeared ripe for a revolutionary challenge to tsarism. In a country where the majority of the people were peasants, agricultural stagnation and poverty, and the emergence of a small industrial proletariat created as a result of the rapid industrialisation, provided conditions for widespread discontent and demands for constitutional change.

3.1 The Narodniki Programme, October 1881

We are above all things socialists and men of the people. We are convinced that mankind can only secure liberty, equality, and fraternity – the material prosperity of all, and the complete development of the individual – on socialistic principles; and that the development of a nation can only be permanent when it acts with independence and freedom. The food of the people and the will of the people are our most sacred and indivisible principles. The masses are living in a state of economic and political slavery. Their labour serves only to feed and maintain the parasitical classes of society. They are deprived of all the rights of citizens; nothing that exists in Russia has been created by their will, and they are not even allowed to say what they want. Over them stands a herd of plunderers, placed there and supported by the Government. All power is in its hands; and it is solely by brute force – by its soldiers, police and officials – that the empire is kept together. Yet, notwithstanding the oppression which still stifles them, the people still cling to their old ideas of the right of the peasants to the land, of communal self-government, and of freedom of speech and conscience. We, therefore, as socialists and friends of the people, consider it our first duty to liberate them from the oppression that destroys them, and to bring about a political revolution which shall place the powers of the state in their hands. By so doing we shall secure the free and independent development of the nation according to its own wishes and tendencies, and the recognition of those socialistic principles which we advocate in common with it. We believe that the people's will could only be intelligibly manifested in a constituent assembly, if such assembly were free and elected by universal suffrage, and if it acted under instructions from the electors. Our aim, therefore, is to deprive the existing Government of power in order to transfer it to a constituent assembly, elected for the purpose of revising and altering all our present political and social institutions. Our programme is:

1   A Government elected by the nation, and acting in pursuance of the national will.
2   Self-government on the widest basis, secured by all posts in the administration being made elective.
3   All the land to be given to the people.
4   All factories to become the property of the workmen.
5   Complete freedom of conscience, speech, the press, public meeting and election.
6   Replacement of the standing army by a territorial army.

Source: G.A. Kertesz (ed.), *Documents in the Political History of the European Continent 1815–1939* **(Oxford, 1968), pp. 288–9**

The *narodniki* was a secret Russian revolutionary movement that gained some influence in the 1870s despite being savagely suppressed. Its first supporters were university students who attempted to convert peasants to socialism in the 'going to the people' movement. The *narodniki* later fragmented into two groups, the *Narodnaya Volya* (People's Will), the terrorist branch, and the *Chernii Peredel* (Black

Partition), who strove to work within the system to achieve a comprehensive redistribution of the land.

In March 1881, before Tsar Alexander II could prepare a constitution, he was assassinated by a terrorist bomb reputedly planted by the *Narodnaya Volya*. He was succeeded by Alexander III. In October of the same year the two wings of the *narodniki* jointly issued a manifesto of demands. This became known as the Narodniki Programme and was intended for wide public dissemination. In the light of the assassination of the Tsar, however, the newspapers, while referring obliquely to the programme, censored all discussion of its controversial contents. It was therefore taken to the people of Russia by their 'representatives', who read it out in public.

The manifesto starts by reaffirming the ideas of the French Revolution ('liberty, equality, fraternity') and the belief that both the individual and the nation must develop along socialist principles. It refers to the masses 'living in a state of economic and political slavery' and calls on the people to liberate themselves 'and to bring about a political revolution which shall place the powers of the state in their hands'. This echoes the 1848 Communist Manifesto where Karl Marx called for 'workers of the world to unite, you have nothing to lose but your chains'.

Immediately after the assassination of Alexander II, the *Narodnaya Volya* issued a separate manifesto addressed to 'the peoples of Europe', defending its actions and calling on the working-class movement to organise on an international basis. Marx's first International Working-Men's Association (IWMA) had been disbanded in 1876. The Second International was formed in Paris in 1889 and consisted of a loose federation of national parties and trade unions. It rejected anarchist methods but reaffirmed the commitment to Marxist ideas of class struggle and was not therefore prepared to co-operate with non-socialist parties in power. Its overriding aim was to prevent war, but the Second International effectively collapsed in 1914.

Interestingly enough, the Narodniki Programme refers to the people's lack of freedom and the all-embracing power of government, but it does not mention either the assassination of Tsar Alexander II or the new Tsar. This might suggest an overture to Alexander III, or it may simply represent a pragmatic decision not to alienate the population, who still held the position of the Tsar in high esteem. Either way, the content of the manifesto and the fact that it was agreed by both wings of the *narodniki* suggests a compromise was reached. The document ends with a six-point programme which, in the context of 1881, represents a radical programme for political and economic change.

The demands of the *narodniki* were never met; instead the tsarist regime responded with even greater repression of revolutionary groups. Nevertheless, attempts towards the end of the nineteenth century to restrict the revolutionary activities of groups in Russia were only partially successful. The government's repressive measures only served to alienate a wide range of intellectual groups that began to take shape in opposition to tsarism.

Russian socialism developed in two broad movements from the 1880s onwards, and by the beginning of the twentieth century these had taken on clear form as the Socialist Revolutionary Party and the Russian Social Democratic Labour Party (Marxist). Marxism was introduced by Russian intellectuals like Georgy Plekhanov. (Russian was the first language into which Marx's *Das Kapital* was translated.) In 1898, Marxist delegates met at Minsk under Plekhanov and formed the Russian Social Democratic Labour Party, which was the forerunner of the Communist Party. The party would split into two groups in 1903: the Bolsheviks ('those in the majority') and the Mensheviks ('those in the minority').

3.2 Vladimir Ilyich Ulyanov (Lenin), *What is to be Done?*, 1902

We must take upon ourselves the task of organising a universal political struggle under the leadership of *our Party* in such a manner as to obtain all the support possible of all opposition strata for the struggle and for our Party. We must train our Social Democratic practical workers to become political leaders, able to guide all the manifestations of this universal struggle and at the right time to dictate a positive programme of action for the discontented students, for the discontented Zemstvo Councillors, for the discontented religious sects, for the offended elementary school teachers, etc., etc. ... *the Party* will carry on this universal political agitation, uniting into one inseparable whole the pressure upon the government in the name of the whole people, the revolutionary training of the proletariat – while preserving its political independence – the guidance of the economic struggle of the working class, the utilisation of all its spontaneous conflicts with its exploiters, which rouse and bring into our camp increasing numbers of the proletariat. ...

Both these tendencies, the opportunist and the 'revolutionary', bow to the prevailing primitiveness; neither believes that it can be eliminated, neither understands our primary and most imperative practical task, namely, to establish *an organisation of revolutionaries* capable of maintaining the energy, the stability and continuity of the political struggle. ... If we begin with the solid foundation of a strong organisation of revolutionaries, we can guarantee the stability of the movement as a whole and carry out the aims of both Social Democracy and of trade unionism. If, however, we begin with a wide workers' organisation, supposed to be most 'accessible' to the masses, when as a matter of fact it will be most accessible to the gendarmes and will make the revolutionaries most accessible to the police, we shall achieve the aims neither of Social Democracy nor of trade unionism; we shall not escape from our primitiveness. ...

I assert: (1) that no movement can be durable without a stable organisation of leaders to maintain continuity; (2) that the more widely the masses are spontaneously drawn into the struggle and form the basis of the movement and participate in it, the more necessary is it to have such an organisation and the more stable must it be (for it is much easier for demagogues to sidetrack the more backward sections of the masses); (3) that the organisation must consist chiefly of persons engaged in revolutionary activities as a profession; (4) that in a country with an autocratic government, the more we *restrict* the membership of this organisation to persons who are engaged in revolutionary activities as a profession and who have been professionally trained in the art of combating the political police, the more difficult will it be to catch the organisation; and (5) the *wider* will be the circle of men and women of the working class or of other classes of society able to join the movement and perform active work in it. ...

Source: V.I. Lenin, *What is to be Done?* (Martin Lawrence, 1933)

Document 3.2 is taken from one of the first and most famous pamphlets by Vladimir Ilyich Ulyanov (he used the pseudonym Lenin permanently from about 1901). In *What is to be Done?*, Lenin set out his beliefs about the nature and methods of revolution and the tactics that were to be applied. It can therefore be distinguished from the Narodniki Programme in that it was directed to a small group of intellectuals committed to revolutionary struggle. In 1900, Lenin had founded *Iskra* ('the Spark'), the masthead of which proudly proclaimed: 'From this spark there shall arise a flame'. *Iskra's* function was to rouse the mass to revolutionary class consciousness. In *What is to be Done?*, published two years after the founding of *Iskra*, Lenin challenged the orthodox Marxist policies of Russian socialist intellectuals like Plekhanov by suggesting that, although revolution would be made by the proletariat, it would not come spontaneously; rather, it would require a revolutionary elite in the socialist party to inspire and direct the workers' efforts.

The key to an understanding of this document is Lenin's phrase 'an organisation of revolutionaries'. Lenin contended that the party leadership should consist of a small group of 'professional revolutionaries', rather than a sort of accidental leadership that might develop out of a mass party. According to Lenin this 'organisation of revolutionaries' should be willing to sacrifice everything for the cause and in so doing would be 'capable of maintaining the energy, the stability and continuity of the political struggle'. Lenin's belief in the necessity of a strictly disciplined party, within which a small disciplined group would first of all rouse the consciousness of the masses and then take decisions on their behalf, led directly to the famous split in 1903 between the Bolsheviks, who supported Lenin, and the Mensheviks who continued to argue for a more loosely based, open party.

What is to be Done? therefore not only anticipates this split but is a document that reveals the intensity of Lenin's thoughts and demonstrates how he enhanced his reputation as a formidable theoretician within international socialist circles. It is *the* seminal document outlining Bolshevik strategy. From now on those who supported him (like the Bolsheviks) stood for total ruthlessness in the pursuit of revolutionary ends; they were to act as the vanguard of the revolution and the working class. The 'party of the new type' and the tactics they were to adopt thus represent an historic break with parliamentarianism and constitute a challenge to orthodox Marxism – or at least to the reality of a capitalist system that was proving more adaptable than Marx had originally conceived. As such, the writings of Lenin provide new impetus, not just for socialist thought in Russia, but for the political Left throughout Europe at the beginning of the twentieth century.

Political and economic unrest in Russia became even more serious after the outbreak of the Russo-Japanese War (1904), which severely strained the resources of the nation. The subsequent humiliating defeat suffered by Russia in the Far East undermined the confidence of the people in both Tsar Nicholas II (1894–1917) and his government. Peasant uprisings had already occurred in 1902 and broke out again in 1905 as a result of war-weariness and humiliation; only now they were joined by proletarian unrest in the cities. This rising tide of unrest reached a climax on 22 January 1905, when a largely peaceful demonstration (estimated as comprising between 150,000 and 200,000 people), led by the Orthodox priest Father Gapon (a part-time police agent), attempted to present a petition of grievances ('we have become beggars; we have been oppressed; we are burdened by toil beyond our powers … we are treated as slaves') to the Tsar at the Winter Palace in St Petersburg. The procession was fired upon by order of one of the grand dukes (Nicholas II was absent from the Palace), and approximately 1,000 people were killed, with a further 3,000 wounded. The incident became known as 'Bloody Sunday' and may be considered the beginning of the so-called revolution of 1905.

Russia in turmoil

The mood and events of 1905 in Russia – a combination of war-weariness after the humiliating defeat by the Japanese, peasant uprisings and proletarian unrest in the cities – produced revolutionary strains which would force the tsarist regime to make concessions. Matters were brought to a head by the great mutiny in June 1905 on the battleship *Potemkin*, ostensibly because of maggot-ridden meat (these events were later given mythological significance in Sergei Eisenstein's 1926 film, *Battleship Potemkin*). There had also been isolated army mutinies, and a general strike was threatened. Nicholas II recognised that, with his best troops in Manchuria retreating from the Japanese, he would have to attempt a policy of conciliation at home. Accordingly a manifesto was issued in October 1905, which is reproduced as Document 3.3.

3.3 The October Manifesto, 17 October 1905

The rioting and agitation in the capitals and in many localities of Our Empire fills Our heart with great and deep grief. The welfare of the Russian Emperor is bound up with the welfare of the people, and its sorrows are His sorrows. The turbulence which has broken out may confound the people and threaten the integrity and unity of Our Empire.

The great vow of service by the Tsar obligates Us to endeavour, with all Our strength, wisdom, and power, to put an end as quickly as possible to the disturbance so dangerous to the Empire. In commanding the responsible authorities to take measures to stop disorders, lawlessness, and violence, and to protect peaceful citizens in the quiet performance of their duties, We have found it necessary to unite the activities of the Supreme Government, so as to ensure the successful carrying out of the general measures laid down by Us for the peaceful life of the State.

We lay upon the Government the execution of Our unchangeable will:

1   To grant to the population the inviolable right of free citizenship, based on the principles of freedom of person, conscience, speech, assembly, and union.
2   Without postponing the intended elections for the State Duma and in so far as possible, in view of the short time that remains before the assembling of that body, to include in the participation of the work of the Duma those classes of the population that have been until now entirely deprived of the right to vote, and to extend in the future, by the newly created legislative way, the principles of the general right of election.
3   To establish as an unbreakable rule that no law shall go into force without its confirmation by the State Duma and that the persons elected by the people shall have the opportunity for actual participation in supervising the legality of the acts of authorities appointed by Us ...

Source: F.A. Golder, *Documents of Russian History, 1914–17* (New York, 1927),
pp. 627–8

The October Manifesto begins with a rather sorrowful diatribe that attempted to re-establish the trust in the old image of the Tsar as the 'father of his peoples'. Although Nicholas was bowing reluctantly to the inevitable, the manifesto expressed a sense of sorrow more than anger ('the rioting and agitation ... fills Our heart with great and deep grief'). The two most important concessions were: (a) freedom of conscience, speech, and assembly and (b) provision for a constitution and an elected parliament (Duma) with real legislative power. The Tsar ended with an appeal to 'all the true sons of Russia' to help restore order in the country.

Other sources reveal that before the manifesto was agreed, Nicholas was torn between using force and/or granting concessions. The advice of his minister, Count Witte, proved decisive. Compare Document 3.4, which is an extract from a letter Nicholas wrote to his mother describing the discussions that took place with Count Witte about possible solutions to Russia's problems in 1905.

3.4 Tsar Nicholas II, letter to his mother, 1905

We very often met in the early morning to part only in the evening when night fell. There were only two ways open: to find an energetic soldier to crush the rebellion by sheer force. There would be time to breathe then but, as likely as not, one would have to use force again in a few months, and that would mean rivers of blood and in the end we should be where we started.

The other way out would be to give the people their civil rights, freedom of speech, and Press, also to have all the laws confirmed by a State Duma or parliament – that of course would be a constitution. Witte defends this energetically. He says that while it is not without risk, it is the only way out at the present moment. Almost everybody I had an opportunity of consulting is of the same opinion. ... He ... drew up a Manifesto. We discussed it for two days and in the end, invoking God's help, I signed it. ... My only consolation is that such is the will of God and this grave decision will lead my dear Russia out of the intolerable chaos she has been in for nearly a year.

Source: Quoted in R. Tames, *Last of the Tsars* (London, 1972), p. 72

The letter reveals not only the intensity of the discussions between Nicholas and his minister ('we often met in the early morning to part only in the evening'), but also that Count Witte had convinced the Tsar that concessions were preferable to force ('Witte defends this energetically') and that it was Witte who actually drafted the October Manifesto, which Nicholas signed ('invoking God's help') after two further days' discussion. A source such as a letter to a relative or friend can often provide a candid insight into human action and a more intimate glimpse behind formal decision-making.

Whether or not you see the October Manifesto as a genuine policy of conciliation or an attempt to 'buy off' the revolutionary movement, it served to split the opposition. It proved too much for the conservatives and too little for the Social Democrats, who continued with their agitation and tried unsuccessfully to organise another strike in Moscow. Liberals were also divided between moderates, who professed satisfaction with the concessions, and became known as the Octobrist Party, and 'progressives' (the Constitutional Democratic Party or 'Cadets'), who continued to demand further parliamentary reforms. Above all, the Revolution of 1905 and its comparative failure forced all opponents of the tsarist regime to reappraise the nature of revolution and the tactics they should adopt in the future. As historian James Joll has stated, the Russian Revolution of 1905 was the most impressive revolutionary outbreak in Europe since the Paris Commune, and it naturally made an enormous impression on the international socialist movement.

However, before the First Duma met, its powers were curtailed when the government passed the Fundamental Laws in May 1906, which allowed the Tsar to retain his autocratic powers. The Duma was declared to be merely the lower house of a two-chambered legislative body, and the Tsar would be allowed to choose and dismiss ministers as he pleased. Much of the value, then, of the concessions made in the October Manifesto were undercut by the provisions of these laws. Nevertheless, the manifesto formed the basis for the 1906 Constitution, which remained the bedrock of Russian political life until the

Revolution of 1917. Indeed, it could be said that between 1906 and 1912 Russia experienced a period of relative tranquillity, due largely to reforms undertaken by Peter Stolypin, who was appointed Prime Minister in 1906.

The outbreak of war was initially supported with enthusiasm in Russia. Although the tsarist regime had survived the crisis of 1905, it was vulnerable to a long-drawn out military conflict. In economic terms, Russia's position in 1914 was characterised by low productivity in agriculture, and an uneven performance in industry. Starting from a low industrial base, some sectors had achieved considerable growth, but Russian industry was highly dependent on foreign capital, whose flow would now be interrupted by war. Moreover, Russia was ill prepared to fight a modern war; its superiority in numbers could not compensate for the fact that only 30 per cent of Russian troops were armed. As a result, Russia suffered greater casualties than any other belligerent nation. By the summer of 1917 the Russian war effort was spent. However, reports from within Russia reveal that discontent was mounting before 1917.

3.5 Police reports on the internal situation in Russia, October 1916

The mass of the population is at present in a very troubled mood ... an exceptional heightening of opposition and bitterness of feeling became very obvious amongst wide sections of the population of Petrograd. There were more and more frequent complaints about the administration and fierce and relentless criticism of government policies. ... Complaints were openly voiced about the venality of the government, the unbelievable burdens of the war, the unbearable conditions of everyday life. Calls from radical and left-wing elements on the need to 'first defeat the Germans here at home, and then deal with the enemy abroad' began to get a more and more sympathetic hearing ... a situation was created which was highly favourable to any sort of revolutionary propaganda and actions. ... It is difficult to discount the possibility that German secret agents were operating in such a conducive atmosphere ...

Without doubt, rumours of this type are greatly exaggerated in comparison with the real situation, but all the same, the position is so serious that attention should be paid to it without delay ... the conviction has been expressed, without exception, that 'we are on the eve of great events' in comparison with which '1905 was but a toy' ...

Kadet delegates paint no less sorry a picture of food purchase in Russia. In the words of one of them, 'there is absolute ruin everywhere': the peasantry, cowed by requisitions, unhappy with interference in trading deals by provincial governors and the police, has no desire to sell its grain and other stocks, fearing that they will get only the statutory price. ... As a result, prices are rising everywhere, and goods are disappearing ...

In the words of another delegate, 'the countryside is now passing through the most critical time, for the first time in Russian history demonstrating the antagonism of town and country. ... The attitude of the countryside to the war has, right from the outset, been extremely unfavourable, for conscription had a much greater effect there than in the towns. Now in the country there is no belief that the war will be successful. … The atmosphere in the country has become one of sharp opposition not only to the government, but to other classes of the population: workers, civil servants, the clergy, etc. …

In the words of other Kadets … 'across the whole of Russia the same thing is seen: everyone understands that under the old order the Germans cannot be beaten … that the nation itself must interfere in the war. … This movement, which was to begin with purely economic, has become political and in the future could turn into a serious movement with a definite programme.'

Source: Quoted in J. Laver, *Russia 1914–1941* (London, 1991), pp. 7–8

Document 3.5 paints a bleak picture of despair and demoralisation far removed from the patriotic hysteria that greeted the announcement of war. In fact, if the number of strikes is any indication, there had been a revival of popular discontent after 1912. Four years of war had eroded old traditions and destroyed any form of consensus. The police reports might exaggerate the position ('the venality of the government, the unbelievable burdens of the war, the unbearable conditions of everyday life'), but in the light of subsequent events, the Tsar and his advisers clearly failed to appreciate the gravity of the situation ('we are on the eve of great events in comparison with which 1905 was but a toy'). Furthermore, the reports suggest that it was not just the peasants in the countryside (15 million of whom had been conscripted by 1917) but all shades of opinion and rank who shared the view that the war could not be won 'under the old order' and were now opposed to the government.

The Tsar had fatally weakened his constitutional position by taking over the command of the army in 1915 and refusing to co-operate with the Duma. When a spontaneous revolution of war-weary workers erupted in Petrograd (formerly St Petersburg) in February 1917 (it actually took place in March, just as the October revolution took place in November, Russia's Julian calendar being thirteen days behind the Gregorian calendar used in the West), the Duma urged him to appoint a parliamentary government that would enjoy the support of the people. Virtually the Tsar's last act of state was to suspend the Duma; on the evening of 15 March after vainly attempting to reach Petrograd, Nicholas II was finally compelled to abdicate. The Duma had already effectively assumed power by forming a Provisional Government. At the same time, however, the workers and soldiers of Petrograd organised themselves into a soviet and established a rival centre of power based on the 1905 model. The two organisations coexisted uneasily for a time ('dual power'), but opposition to the government, and to the soviet participation in it, continued to grow from both the Left and Right.

By this time the exiled revolutionary leaders, who had been taken by surprise by the events, were returning to Petrograd. Lenin arrived at the Finland Station in Petrograd on 3 April, after his journey in the famous 'sealed train' which the

Germans had allowed to pass through in the hope that Lenin would weaken Russia's war effort. Unlike his socialist colleagues, Lenin wanted power to be transferred to the soviets immediately. In his April Theses (Document 3.6), he advocated the creation of 'a republic of Soviets of Workers', Agricultural Labourers' and Peasants' Deputies'.

3.6 Lenin's April Theses, 4 April 1917

1. In our attitude towards the war, which also under the new Government of Lvov and Co. unquestionably remains on Russia's part a predatory imperialist war owing to the capitalist nature of that Government, not the slightest concession to 'revolutionary defencism' is permissible.

The class-conscious proletariat can give its consent to a revolutionary war, which would really justify revolutionary defencism, only on condition: (a) that the power pass to the proletariat and the poorest sections of the peasants; ... (b) that all annexations be renounced in deed and not in word; (c) that a complete break be effected in actual fact with all capitalist interests.

In view of the undoubted honesty of the broad sections of the mass believers in revolutionary defencism, who accept the war only as a necessity, and not as a means of conquest, in view of the fact that they are being deceived by the bourgeoisie, it is necessary with particular thoroughness, persistence and patience to explain their error to them, to explain the inseparable connexion existing between capital and the imperialist war, and to prove that without overthrowing capital *it is impossible* to end the war by a truly democratic peace ...

2. It is a specific feature of the present situation in Russia that it represents a *transition* from the first stage of the revolution – which, owing to the insufficient class-consciousness and organization of the proletariat, placed power in the hands of the bourgeoisie – to its *second* stage, which must place power in the hands of the proletariat and the poorest sections of the peasants.

This transition is characterized, on the one hand, by a maximum of legally recognized rights (Russia is *now* the freest of all the belligerent countries in the world); on the other, by the absence of violence in relation to the people, and, finally, by the unreasoning confidence of the people in the Government of capitalists, the worst enemies of peace and socialism.

This peculiar situation demands of us an ability to adapt ourselves to the *special* conditions of Party work among unprecedentedly large masses of proletarians who have just awakened to political life.

3. No support for the Provisional Government; the utter falsity of all its promises should be explained, particularly those relating to the renunciation of annexations. Exposure in place of the impermissible, illusion-breeding 'demand' that *this* Government, a Government of capitalists, should cease to be an imperialist Government.

4. Recognition of the fact that in most of the Soviets of Workers' Deputies our Party is in a minority, and so far in a small minority, as against a *bloc of all* the petty-bourgeois opportunists …

It must be explained to the people that the Soviets of Workers' Deputies are the *only possible* form of revolutionary government, and that therefore our task is, as long as *this* government yields to the influence of the bourgeoisie, to present a patient, systematic, and persistent *explanation* of the errors of their tactics …

As long as we are in the minority we carry on the work of criticizing and exposing errors and at the same time we preach the necessity of transferring the entire state power to the Soviets … so that the people may overcome their mistakes by experience.

5. Not a parliamentary republic – to return to a parliamentary republic from the Soviets of Workers' Deputies would be a retrograde step – but a republic of Soviets of Workers', Agricultural Labourers' and Peasants' Deputies throughout the country, from top to bottom.

Abolition of the police, the army, and the bureaucracy.

The salaries of all officials, all of whom are to be elected and to be subject to recall at any time, not to exceed the average wage of a competent worker.

6. In the agrarian programme the most important part to be assigned to the Soviets of Agricultural Labourers' Deputies.

Confiscation of all landed estates.

Nationalization of *all* lands in the country, the disposal of the land to be put in the charge of the local Soviets of Agricultural Labourers' and Peasants' Deputies. The organization of separate Soviets of Deputies of Poor Peasants …

7. The immediate amalgamation of all banks in the country into a single national bank …

8. It is not our immediate task to 'introduce' socialism, but only to bring social production and distribution of products at once under the *control* of the Soviets of Workers' Deputies …

10. A new International. We must take the initiative in creating a revolutionary International, an International against the *social-chauvinists* …

Source: V.I. Lenin, *Selected Works in Three Volumes* (London, n.d.), vol. 2, pp. 45–8

Lenin defended his April Theses before a joint meeting of Bolsheviks, Mensheviks and independent socialists and it was eventually published in the Bolshevik newspaper *Pravda* on 7 April, when it immediately caused violent controversy even within Bolshevik ranks. Lenin argued that there should be no co-operation with the Provisional Government ('mass believers in revolutionary defencism') and in effect called for a second revolution that would destroy the existing state machinery. In his work *Imperialism: The Highest Stage of Capitalism*, written in 1916, Lenin had argued that the First World War was an 'imperialist war' and would remain so until the capitalist bourgeoisie of Europe was over-thrown. The April Theses were an attempt to assert his authority over the Bolshevik party and to use the soviets as the vanguard of revolution.

The Bolshevik revolution

Once Lenin had persuaded his party to adopt the April Theses as the basis of Bolshevik strategy, slogans such as 'All Power to the Soviets' and 'Bread, Peace and Land', immediately found favour with workers and soldiers and served to set the Bolsheviks apart from other left-wing parties. The Provisional Government's failure to take Russia out of the war and incidents such as the 'July days' and the Kornilov Revolt, demonstrated the weakness of the regime and allowed the Bolsheviks to exploit its failings. As a result, Bolshevik support in the urban centres increased and, by September 1917, they had a majority in the Petrograd and Moscow soviets. When the Congress of Soviets met on 25 October, Lenin declared that power was now in their hands. However, elections to a Constituent Assembly, first promised in February, took place in November and resulted in a victory for the moderate socialist parties (Mensheviks and right-wing Socialist Revolutionaries), who polled 62 per cent, whereas the Bolsheviks received a mere 25 per cent. The Constituent Assembly finally met on 18 January 1918 (5 January in the old calendar) in Petrograd, a hostile city dominated by Bolsheviks. The struggle inherent in the existence of dual power was finally resolved when the Bolsheviks cynically dissolved the Assembly after its first sitting, once it became clear that they could not persuade the majority to fall in with their wishes and support the soviets. The Decree dissolving the Constituent Assembly is set out as Document 3.7.

3.7 Decree dissolving Constituent Assembly, 19 January (new calendar) 1918

From the very beginning of the Russian Revolution the Soviets ... came to the front as a mass organization. It brought the toiling and exploited classes together and led them in the fight for full political and economic freedom. During the first period of the revolution the Soviets increased, developed, and grew strong. They learned by experience the futility of compromising with the bourgeoisie ...

The Constituent Assembly which was elected on the lists made out before the October Revolution represents the old order when the compromisers and Cadets were in power.

At the time of voting for the Socialist Revolutionary Party the people were not in a position to decide between the Right Wing – partisans of the bourgeoisie – and the Left Wing – partisans of socialism. This accounts for the fact that the

Constituent Assembly, the crown of the bourgeois-parliamentary republic, stands in the way of the October Revolution and the Soviet Government …

The labouring classes have learned by experience that the old bourgeois parliament has outlived its usefulness, that it is quite incompatible with the task of establishing socialism, and that the task of overcoming the propertied classes and of laying the basis of a socialistic society cannot be undertaken by a national institution but only by one representing a class such as the Soviet. To deny full power to the Soviets … in favour of a bourgeois parliamentarianism or the Constituent Assembly would be a step backward and the death blow of the October workers'-peasants' revolution.

The Constituent Assembly which opened on January 5 has … a majority of Socialist-Revolutionists of the Right, the party of Kerensky. … It is natural that this party should refuse to consider the … recommendation of the sovereign organ of the Soviet Government and should refuse to recognize the 'Declaration of the Rights of the Toiling and Exploited People', the October Revolution, and the Government of the Soviet. By these very acts the Constituent Assembly has cut every tie that bound it to the Soviet of the Russian Republic. Under the circumstances the Bolsheviks and Socialist-Revolutionists of the Left … had no choice but to withdraw from the Constituent Assembly.

The majority parties of the Constituent Assembly – the Socialist-Revolutionists and the Mensheviks – are carrying on an open war against the Soviet, calling … for its overthrow, and in this way helping the exploiters in their efforts to block the transfer of the land and factories to the toilers.

It is clear that this part of the Constituent Assembly can be of help only to the bourgeois counter-revolution in its efforts to crush the power of the Soviets.

In view of the above the Central Executive Committee hereby decrees: The Constituent Assembly is dissolved.

Source: Reprinted from J. Bunyan and H.H. Fisher, *The Bolshevik Revolution 1917–18*, pp. 384–6, with the permission of the publishers, Stanford University Press. Copyright 1934 by the Board of Trustees and the Leland Stanford Junior University

Note the justification employed by the Bolsheviks for dissolving the Assembly. Although in the minority, they refer to themselves as the authentic representatives of the masses ('the toiling and exploited classes'). The Assembly (majority), on the other hand, was accused of standing 'in the way of the October Revolution … [denying] full power to the Soviet … '. Consequently the Bolsheviks 'had no choice but to withdraw'. The Socialist-Revolutionaries and Mensheviks are depicted as reactionary 'partisans of the bourgeoisie' intent on waging 'an open war against the Soviets' and blocking all land and factory reforms. The Bolsheviks also claimed (with some justification) that, when the elections to the Constituent Assembly had been held in November, their radical policies on 'bread, peace and land' had not had sufficient time to affect the result. All those who opposed the Bolsheviks were now conveniently labelled 'enemies of the people' and thus began a reign of terror and recriminations, culminating in the Kronstadt Revolt of March 1921, which finally killed off all legal opposition to the Bolshevik Party. The foundations of the new Soviet State were formally set out in the 1918 constitution of the Russian Socialist Federated Soviet Republic (RSFSR).[*]

Having dissolved the Constituent Assembly, the Bolsheviks were faced with the immediate need to consolidate their power. This they achieved by taking Russia out of the war in March 1918 (the Treaty of Brest-Litovsk), albeit at the loss of a third of European Russia to the Germans, and instigating a civil war against their opponents.

The ensuing conflict was characterised by great savagery on both sides but also by the skilful use of propaganda on the part of the Bolsheviks. Bolshevik leaders like Lenin and Trotsky recognised the importance of propaganda and in particular the need to legitimise their actions and justify the sacrifices that were being demanded of the people, who had suffered so much in the Great War. Given that the population was still largely illiterate, posters proved an effective and relatively cheap means of disseminating Bolshevik propaganda.

3.8 'The Year of the Proletarian Dictatorship', Bolshevik poster, 1918 (see p. 58)

Document 3.8 is a poster designed by Alexander Apsit entitled 'The Year of the Proletarian Dictatorship. October 1917–October 1918'. It was distributed by the All-Union Central Executive Committee of Moscow. The Soviet political poster was an art form that has its origins in the October Revolution. The first posters were a predominant feature of revolutionary demonstrations. They would have been displayed wherever propaganda and agitation could disseminate to the masses the ideas of the Communist party . The poster was viewed by the party as an important ideological weapon that overcame the problem of educating an illiterate population in the spirit of communism. Artists were encouraged to look upon poster design as a revolutionary duty. This 'new' revolutionary art form embraced a range of artistic traditions including Russian folk art, the satirical art of the 1905 Revolution and newspaper and magazine cartoons. In spite of an acute shortage of capital and printing materials, it was indicative of the high estimation of the poster in Bolshevik Russia that posters were given first priority in the print shops and publishing houses and distributed in over seventy towns by different Communist organisations. A feature of these early political posters was their remarkable sense of period characterisation. All former ties with tsarist Russia and capitalism were cast aside, and the future was presented in bold,

[*]   The 'Union of Soviet Socialist Republics' (USSR) came into being in December 1922.

Source: *The Soviet Political Poster 1917–1980* (Penguin, 1985), p. 2

simplistic terms and images. The masses, who are presented as the defenders of the Revolution, become the central heroic figure.

The historical significance of Apsit's poster is the manner in which the October Revolution is portrayed as a victory for both the agricultural peasants (symbolised by the figure on the right, with sickle) and the industrial workers (figure on the left, with sledgehammer and rifle). In the foreground can be seen the discarded trappings of the old tsarist regime (the Russian double-headed eagle, the crown and chains), and the background is taken up with happy workers marching across the countryside to the factories and the 'new dawn' (symbolised by the sunrise over Russia). The poster is like a theatrical tapestry telling a story in very simple terms. In this particular poster there is no reference to Lenin or any other Bolshevik leader; the 'ordinary people' are portrayed as heroes of the Revolution (notice the small child being held aloft in the centre).

The potential of the political poster as a mass art medium – its lucidity and simplicity of form, the relative ease of large print runs, the vividness of its imagery and its genuine affinity with popular aspirations – was not fully realised in the formative years following the Revolution. However, after Lenin's death in 1924, his successor, Joseph Stalin, increasingly turned to propaganda, coercion and the propagation of the 'cult of the personality' in order to legitimise repressive policies that had little to do with either orthodox Marxist-Leninism or the ideals of the October Revolution (see Chapter 7).

CHRONOLOGY: RUSSIA IN REVOLUTION, 1881–1922

1881		General Melikov (Minister of Interior) releases political prisoners and calls for greater share in government to offset extremism.
1883–4		Plekhanov leads groups studying Marxism.
1891		Thousands of Jews evicted from Moscow and forced into ghettos under pogroms instigated by Alexander III. Construction of the Trans-Siberian railway begins.
1891–3		Major famine in Russia.
1892		Sergei de Witte appointed Minister of Finance and Commerce.
1894	1 November	Nicholas II becomes Tsar after death of Alexander III.
1895		Lenin organises the St Petersburg 'League of Struggle for the Emancipation of the Working Class', and is later arrested.
1897		Lenin exiled to Siberia.
1899		First national students' strike.
1900		Leninist newspaper *Iskra* (the 'Spark') founded. Russian troops move into southern Manchuria.
1901		Foundation of the Social Revolutionary Party, mainly to represent the peasantry.
1902		Further strikes and student disturbances. Publication of Lenin's *What is to be Done?*.
1903		Strikes and peasant disturbances throughout Russia. In London the Social Democratic Party splits into two groups, the Bolsheviks and the Mensheviks. Under Lenin's leadership, the Bolsheviks advocate a small disciplined party which could lead a revolution.
1904	10 February	The Russo-Japanese war breaks out.

	May	Lenin publishes *One Step Forward, Two Steps Back*. Japanese victory at the Yalu; Port Arthur under intense attack.
	November	The Zemstvos Conference requests a wider range of liberal reforms.
1905	1 January	Russians surrender Port Arthur.
	22 January	'Bloody Sunday'. Father Gapon leads a peaceful protest to the Winter Palace with a Petition for the Tsar: Troops open fire killing many protestors.
	April–May	The Third Congress of the Russian Social Democratic Labour Party meets in London.
	June	Mutiny on the battleship *Potemkin*. Armed rising at Lodz.
	6 August	The draft law on the establishment of the Consultative State Duma published.
	5 September	The Russo-Japanese war brought to an end by the signing of the Treaty of Portsmouth.
	7 October	Nationwide political strikes.
	17 October	Tsar issues 'October Manifesto' promising a constitution and an elected parliament with genuine legislative power. The Tsar also guarantees civil liberties. The Constitutional Democratic Party (the Cadets) is formed.
	October–December	Formation of Workers' Soviets in major Russian cities.
	24–8 October	Armed forces revolt at Kronstadt.
	21 November	First sitting of the Moscow Soviet.
	November	Formation of the moderate Octobrist Party.
	23 December	Moscow Soviet stages uprising that leads to widespread armed risings in Russia, but by the end of the month the Moscow rising is crushed.
1906	April	Elections boycotted by Social Democrats and Socialist Revolutionaries; Constitutional Democrats ('Cadets') win largest number of seats.
	6 May	Tsar issues Fundamental Law of the Empire by which the Tsar retained his autocratic power, thus reversing many of the earlier democratic concessions.
	10 May	First Duma assembles; vote of no confidence in the government.
	June	Stolypin appointed Prime Minister.
	21 July	Dissolution of the Duma. Cadet leaders issue Vyborg Manifesto calling for a refusal to pay taxes and enter military service.
	July	Soldiers and sailors rise in Kronstadt.
	25 August	Stolypin makes large tracts of land available to the peasants.
	October	Peasants are allowed to leave their village communes or to join others. Stolypin removes restrictions on the election of peasants to the Zemstvos.
	22 November	Stolypin's Agrarian Reform Act ends communal system of landholding. Peasants are allowed to leave the commune and claim their share of land.
1907	5 March	The Second Duma meets.
	November	Election of the Third Duma.
1911	September	Stolypin assassinated.
1913		Election of Fourth Duma.
1914	Summer	General Strike in St Petersburg.
	1 August	Germany declares war on Russia.
	26 August	Russia defeated at battle of Tannenberg.
1915	6 September	Tsar assumes supreme command of the armed forces.

1916	16 September	Tsar discontinues Duma without dissolving it.
	September–October	Widespread unrest and sporadic mutinies at the front.
1917	7 March	Tsar leaves Petrograd for army GHQ; beginnings of large-scale demonstrations in the capital.
	9–11 March	Police fire on crowds as strikes break out and soldiers join the people; police fire at demonstrators, but fail to stem increasing numbers of soldiers joining in protest. Sittings of Duma discontinued again by orders of Tsar.
	12 March	Formation of Committee of State Duma to replace Tsarist government. Formation of Petrograd Soviet of Workers' and Soldiers' Deputies.
	14 March	Appointment of Ministers of the Provisional Government. 'Army Order No. 1' issued by Petrograd Soviet puts armed forces under its authority and urges rank and file to elect representatives to the Soviet.
	15 March	Tsar abdicates in favour of his brother, Grand Duke Michael, at the same time confirming the new ministry and asking the country to support it. Grand Duke Michael chooses not to accept the throne unless he is requested to do so by the Assembly. The Provisional Government forbids the use of force against rioting peasants.
	16 March	Abdication of Grand Duke Michael.
	13 April	Lenin arrives back in Petrograd.
	3–5 May	Bolshevik-organised demonstrations by garrison in Petrograd against the Ministers Guchkov and Milyukov. Kornilov resigns command of forces in Petrograd, and Milyukov and Guchkov resign from the government.
	18 May	Kerensky helps to reorganise provisional government.
	16–18 July	Bolsheviks organise demonstrations by sailors and Red Guards but the unrest is put down by loyal troops.
	21 July	Formation of new government with Kerensky as Prime Minister.
	1 August	Kornilov appointed Commander-in-Chief.
	3 August	Kerensky resigns. Party leaders give him a free hand to form new government.
	25–8 August	Kerensky holds Moscow State Conference to find centrist forces on which to base a new government and to settle differences with Kornilov, but fails to reach agreement.
	8 September	Troops begin to move against Petrograd, and Kerensky denounces Kornilov 'plot' against the government. Collapse of movement followed by arrest of Kornilov and fellow generals.
	19 September	Bolshevik majority in Moscow Soviet.
	6 October	Trotsky becomes Chairman of Petrograd Soviet.
	2 November	Parliament refuses to give Kerensky powers to suppress the Bolsheviks.
	7 November	Bolsheviks seize power in Petrograd, taking key installations and services. The Winter Palace is cut off and ministers of provisional government are arrested. Kerensky flees. Lenin announces the transfer of power to the Military Revolutionary Committee and the victory of the socialist revolution.
	8 November	Lenin appeals for a just peace without annexations and indemnities, and announces Decree on Land, affirming that all land is the property of the people. A Bolshevik government is formed.
	13 November	Counter-offensive by Kerensky against Petrograd fails.

	15 November	Bolsheviks gain power in Moscow.
	17 December	Russia and Germany agree a ceasefire and start negotiations.
1918	18 January	Opening of Constituent Assembly.
	19 January	Constituent Assembly dissolved.
	3 March	Russians sign Treaty of Brest-Litovsk, giving up large areas of pre-Revolutionary Russia. German troops continue to advance into central Russia and the Crimea.
	29 May	Partial conscription introduced for Red Army.
	16 July	Execution of Imperial family at Ekaterinburg.
1921	February	Strikes in Petrograd. Red Army invades Georgia.
1922	March–April	11th Party Congress. Stalin becomes General Secretary. Lenin forced to convalesce after operation to remove two bullets, the result of Kaplan's attempted assassination in 1918.
	30 December	Formation of Union of Soviet Socialist Republics, federating Russia, the Ukraine, White Russia and Transcaucasia.

BIBLIOGRAPHY

Sources and documents

G. Plekhanov, *Selected Philosophical Works*, London (1961). Memoirs of revolutionary leaders include: J.D. Duff (ed.), *Memoirs of Alexander Herzen* (1923); M. Gorky, *Autobiography* (trans. 1953); Prince Kropotkin, *Memoirs of a Revolutionist* (1899). L. Trotsky, *1905* (1971) describes the thwarted revolution of that year by a leading participant. Of all Lenin's writings, *What is to be Done?* (1902) is the most important for outlining Bolshevik strategy. For an account of how Russian intellectuals viewed Bolshevism see J. Burbank, *Intelligentsia and Revolution* (1989). Two useful general sourcebooks are G. Freeze, *From Supplication to Revolution: A Documentary Social History of Imperial Russia* (1988) and B. Dmytryshyn (ed.), *Imperial Russia: A Source Book, 1700–1917* (1990 edn). For a comprehensive collection of sources on the Revolutionary period and a mature synthesis of recent scholarship see R. Kowalski, *The Russian Revolution 1917–1921* (1997).

Secondary works

General textbooks that attempt to place the period in a wider historical context include: M. Kochan and R. Abraham, *The Making of Modern Russia* (1983); H. Seton-Watson, *The Russian Empire* (1967); J.N. Westwood, *Endurance and Endeavour: Russian History, 1812–1992* (1993); E. Crankshaw, *The Shadow of the Winter Palace* (1978); R. Pipes, *Russia under the Old Regime* (1977). Somewhat older accounts can be found in B. Pares, *The Fall of the Russian Monarchy* (1955) and M.T. Florinsky, *Russia: A History and an Interpretation* (1947). L. Kochan, *Russia in Revolution, 1890–1918* (1966) is a more recent analysis. Highly recommended is M. McCauley and P. Waldron, *The Emergence of the Modern Russian State, 1855–81* (1988) and O. Fiques, *A People's Tragedy – The Russian Revolution 1891–1924* (1996).

On Alexander II, W.E. Mosse, *Alexander II and the Modernisation of Russia* (1959) provides a useful survey. See also the Historical Association pamphlet written by M. Perrie, *Alexander II: Emancipation and Reform in Russia, 1855–1881* (1989). For the problems of rural Russia see J. Blum, *Lord and Peasant in Russia* (1965); G.T. Robinson, *Rural Russia under the Old Regime* (1949); W.S. Vucinich (ed.), *The Peasant in Nineteenth Century Russia* (1968). An interesting comparative analysis can be found in P. Kolchin, *Unfree Labour: American Slavery and Russian Serfdom* (1987). On Witte, see T.H. von Laue, *Sergei Witte and the Industrialisation of Russia* (1963). On the Dumas, G.A. Hosking, *The Russian Constitutional Experiment: Government and Duma, 1907–1914* (Cambridge, 1973) and R.B. McKean, *The Russian Constitutional Monarchy, 1907–1917* (Historical Association, 1977) are very useful.

On economic development in general see E. Falkus, *The Industrialisation of Russia, 1700–1914* (1972); A. Nove, *An Economic History of the U.S.S.R.* (1969); W.O. Henderson, *The Industrial Revolution on the Continent, Germany, France and Russia, 1800–1914* (1961).

K. Fitzlyon and T. Browning, *Before the Revolution* (1977) surveys Russia under Nicholas II. On the 1905 revolution see H. Harcave, *First Blood: the Russian Revolution of 1905* (1965), while G. Katkov (ed.), *Russia Enters the Twentieth Century* (1972) has valuable essays.

Specific works dealing with the opposition to the old order are F. Venturi, *The Roots of Revolution: A History of the Populist and Socialist Movements in Nineteenth Century Russia* (1960); P. Avrich, *The Russian Anarchists* (1967); J.L.H. Keep, *The Rise of Social Democracy in Russia* (1963); A.B. Ulam, *Lenin and the Bolsheviks* (1965). For an in-depth study of revolutionary turmoil in Petrograd, see M. McAuley, *Bread and Justice. State and Society in Petrograd 1917–22* (1993). For a first-rate analysis of the poster as tool of propaganda, see S. White, *The Bolshevik Poster* (1991).

For an excellent collection of essays on Russian foreign policy, see H. Ragsdale (ed.), *Imperial Russian Foreign Policy* (1993). See also D. Lieven, *Russia and the Origins of the First World War* (1983). On the effects of the war see M.T. Florinsky, *The End of the Russian Empire* (1931); R. Pearson, *The Russian Moderates and the Crisis of Tsarism, 1914–17* (1977); N. Stone, *The Eastern Front, 1914–17* (1978). The wealth of specific works on the Bolshevik seizure of power include E. Acton, *Rethinking the Russian Revolution* (1990); S. Fitzpatrik, *The Russian Revolution* (1984); M. Ferro, *October 1917: A Social History of the Russian Revolution* (1980); A. Wood, *The Origins of the Russian Revolution 1861–1917* (1987); R. Service, *The Russian Revolution 1900–1927* (1991); J.D. White, *The Russian Revolution 1917–21* (1993); R. Pipes, *Russia under the Bolshevik Regime, 1919–1924* (1995); C. Read, *From Tsar to Soviets. The Russian People and their Revolution, 1917–1921* (1996).

Articles

On unrest, see F. Zuckerman, 'Vladimir Burtsev and the Tsarist Political Police in Conflict, 1907–14', *J.C.H.* (1977); M. Perrie, 'The Russian Peasant Movement, 1905–7', *P.P.* (1972); L.H. Harrison, 'Problems of Social Stability in Urban Russia', *S.R.* (1964 and 1965); A.P. Mendel, 'Peasant and Worker on the

Eve of the First World War', *S.R.* (1965). For an alternative interpretation based on the urban experience, see G.R. Swain, 'Bolsheviks and Metal Workers on the Eve of the First World War' *J.C.H.* (1981). On various other aspects see T.H. von Laue, 'The Chances for Liberal Constitutionalism', *S.R.* (1965). On economic expansion see P.W. Garnell, 'Industrial Expansion in Tsarist Russia 1908–1914', *E.H.R.* (1982) and G.L. Yaney, 'The Concept of the Stolypin Land Reform', *S.R.* (1964). For an interesting account of Lenin's doctrine, see J. Frankel, 'Lenin's Doctrinal Revolution of April 1917', *J.C.H.* (1969). For a perceptive reappraisal of events leading to the October Revolution see V.P. Buldakov, 'The October Revolution: Seventy-Five Years On', *E.H.Q.* (1992).

4

The origins of the First World War and its aftermath

On 28 June 1914 Archduke Franz Ferdinand, heir to the Austrian throne, was murdered in Sarajevo in Bosnia, which had been annexed by Austria in 1908. The assassin and his co-conspirators were members of a Serbian nationalist group called 'the Black Hand'. In less than five weeks the alliance systems of the great powers had turned this local incident into a European war. The origins of the First World War are a source of major historical controversy that has refused to disappear over the years. The historiographical debate must, therefore, inform any discussion about the events that 'triggered' a European and then a world war in 1914.

The origins of the war can be analysed in many different ways, but any attempt to explain its origins must take into account the immediate causes of the war and the long-standing reasons for instability and international tension in Europe. The list of general causes would include the colonial conflicts and the scramble for overseas possessions; the building up of new alliances and the formation of two power blocs; the escalation of the arms race; and the increasing conflicts in the Balkans. Although the documents included in the first part of this chapter are generally related to the immediate causes of the war, they are intended to illuminate some of the wider issues as well. The illusions with which the First World War began all stemmed from the belief that it would be a short, clinical and controllable war ('It'll all be over by Christmas'). These hopes were soon to be disappointed.

It may be helpful to set out below the events as they unfolded, both before and after the assassination of Franz Ferdinand.

Chronology

1912	7 February	Wilhelm II (Kaiser) announces Army and Navy bills.
	12 February	Haldane visits Germany but fails to halt naval race.
	13 March	Balkan League between Serbia and Bulgaria formed.
	29 May	Greece joins Balkan League.
	17 October	First Balkan War.
	8 December	Wilhelm II calls military conference at Potsdam.
1913	5 January	Jagow succeeds Kiderlen-Wächter in the German Foreign Office.
	30 June	Second Balkan War opens.

	7 August	French Army bill ratified.
	10 August	Peace of Bucharest ends Second Balkan War.
	18 October	Churchill again proposes 'Naval Holiday'.
	20 November	Zabern Affair.
1914	May	Anglo-Russian naval talks begin.
	28 June	Assassination of Franz Ferdinand and his wife at Sarajevo.
	5 July	Hovos Mission: Wilhelm II issues 'blank cheque'.
	6 July	Wilhelm II leaves for Norwegian cruise.
	7 July	Austro-Hungarian Ministerial Council meets.
	8 July	Ultimatum to Serbia prepared.
	19 July	Austro-Hungarian Ministerial Council approves ultimatum to be handed over on 23 July.
	21 July	Francis Joseph approves ultimatum. Text of ultimatum sent to Berlin.
	23 July	Austria-Hungary hands over ultimatum.
	24 July	Austria-Hungary informs France, Russia and Britain of ultimatum. German ambassadors transmit note in Paris, London and St Petersburg that conflict be localised. Grey's first proposal to mediate. Delbrück meets Reich and Prussian authorities. Russian Council of Ministers considers partial mobilisation.
	25 July	Serbia replies to ultimatum. Vienna breaks off diplomatic relations with Belgrade. Wilhelm II orders return of Fleet. Grey again proposes mediation. Jagow forwards Grey's proposal to Vienna. Tsar orders preparations for mobilisation to be made.
	26 July	Russia asks Germany to exert moderating influence on Austria-Hungary. Grey proposes Four-Power conference of ambassadors in London. Austria mobilises on Russian frontier. France takes precautionary military measures.
	27 July	France accepts Grey's proposals. Bethmann Hollweg rejects idea of Four-Power conference.
	28 July	Austria-Hungary declares war on Serbia and shells Belgrade. Russia orders mobilisation of four western military districts.
	29 July	Vienna refuses to enter into negotiations with Serbia. Germany warns Russia. Moltke demands general mobilisation. Grey informs Lichnowsky that Britain could not remain neutral in the event of a continental war; again he proposes mediation. Russian general mobilisation ordered, but revoked by Tsar late that same evening.
	30 July	Austria-Hungary agrees to negotiations with Russia, but refuses to delay operations against Serbia. Moltke presses for general mobilisation. Austria-Hungary orders general mobilisation for 31 July. Russian general mobilisation ordered for 31 July.
	31 July	Vienna rejects international conference and orders general mobilisation. Russian general mobilisation becomes known in Berlin at noon. Wilhelm II proclaims 'state of imminent war' one hour later. Germany refuses to mediate and issues ultimatum to Russia.

	France decides to order mobilisation for I August.
I August	German ultimatum to Russia expires; Germany declares war on Russia and mobilises.
2 August	German troops occupy Luxembourg.
	Berlin transmits ultimatum to Belgium.
	British fleet is mobilised.
3 August	Germany declares war on France.
	Belgium rejects German demands.
	Italy remains neutral.
	German-Turkish treaty concluded.
	Britain mobilises army; Cabinet decides to issue ultimatum to Germany.
4 August	German troops invade Belgium, and Germany declares war on Belgium.
	Britain declares war on Germany after ultimatum expires.
5 August	Austria-Hungary declares war on Russia.
10 August	France declares war on Austria-Hungary.
12 August	Britain declares war on Austria-Hungary.

Showdown with Serbia

The murder of Archduke Ferdinand in Sarajevo was immediately followed by allegations of Serbian complicity by the Austro-Hungarian government. On 4 July Emperor Franz Joseph wrote to the German Kaiser, Wilhelm II, claiming that the assassination was the direct result of Russian and Serbian pan-Slavist agitation, and proposed to 'eliminate Serbia as a factor of political power in the Balkans'. After discussions with his Chancellor, Bethmann Hollweg, the Kaiser urged the Emperor to make war on Serbia, issuing what has become known as the 'blank cheque' by offering Germany's unqualified support.

4.1 The German 'blank cheque' to Austria, 1914

[Count Szogyény, Austrian Ambassador in Berlin, to Count Leopold Berchtold, Austro-Hungarian Foreign Minister]

Berlin 5 July 1914   *Strictly Confidential*

... the Kaiser authorised me to inform our gracious majesty that we might in this case, as in all others, rely upon Germany's full support ... he did not doubt in the least that Herr von Bethmann Hollweg would agree with him. Especially as far as our action against Serbia was concerned. But it was his [Kaiser Wilhelm's] opinion that this action must not be delayed. Russia's attitude will no doubt be hostile, but for this he had for years prepared, and should a war between Austria-Hungary and Russia be unavoidable, we might be assured that Germany, our old faithful ally, would stand at our side. Russia at the present time was in no way prepared for war, and would think twice before it resorted to arms ... if we had really recognised the necessity of warlike action against Serbia, he [Kaiser Wilhelm] would regret if we did not make use of the present moment, which is all in our favour …

Source: I . Geiss (ed.), *July 1914: Selected Documents* (London, 1967) p. 77

This document is a report by Count Szogyény, the Austrian Ambassador in Berlin of the conversation with Wilhelm II, in which the Kaiser appeared to be promising Germany's unconditional support for Austria. The confidential report was sent by Szogyény to the Austro-Hungarian Foreign Minister in Vienna. It confirmed that the Austrians could 'rely upon Germany's full support' but referred to the Kaiser's belief that 'this action (against Serbia) must not be delayed'. It is clear from the conversation that Wilhelm did not believe that Russia would intervene ('she is unprepared and would think twice about resorting to arms'); and 'should a war between Austria-Hungary and Russia be unavoidable, we [Austria] might be assured that Germany, our old ally, would stand by our side'. This is a reference to the Triple Alliance, formed in 1883 by Germany, Austria and Italy, and developed out of the Dual Alliance of Germany and Austria that had been concluded in 1879.

In the conversation with Szogyény, Wilhelm and his Chancellor were so convinced of the justness of the Austrian claims that they appeared to be urging Austria to 'make use of the present moment which is all in our favour' and make war on Serbia. In other words, Germany was providing Austria-Hungary with a 'blank cheque' in its quarrel with Serbia even if this meant war with Russia, the supporter of pan-Slavism. Clearly, Wilhelm II and Bethmann Hollweg were offering more than simply a free hand to Austria-Hungary; they were urging their ally to start a war against Serbia and to risk the wider consequences. Historians have argued that, without this support, Austria-Hungary would not have served its ultimatum to Serbia, thus launching the chain of events which led to the European war. For many historians, then, this 'blank cheque' proved to be the key decision on the road to war.

4.2 The Austrian ultimatum to Serbia, 22 July 1914

[The Austro-Hungarian Minister for Foreign Affairs, Berchtold, to the Minister at Belgrade, von Giesl]

Your Excellency will present the following note to the Royal Government on the afternoon of Thursday, July 23: On the 31st of March, 1909, the Royal Serbian Minister at the Court of Vienna made, in the name of his Government, the following declaration to the Imperial and Royal Government:

Serbia recognizes that her rights were not affected by the state of affairs created in Bosnia,[*] and states that she will accordingly accommodate herself to the decisions to be reached by the Powers in connection with Article 25 of the Treaty of Berlin. Serbia, in accepting the advice of the Great Powers, binds herself to desist from the attitude of protest and opposition which she has assumed with regard to the annexation since October last, and she furthermore binds herself to alter the tendency of her present policy toward Austria-Hungary, and to live on the footing of friendly and neighborly relations with the latter in the future.

Now the history of the past few years, and particularly the painful events of the 28th of June, have proved the existence of a subversive movement in Serbia, whose object it is to separate certain portions of its territory from the Austro-Hungarian Monarchy. This movement, which came into being under the very eyes of the Serbian Government, subsequently found expression outside of the territory of the Kingdom in acts of terrorism, in a number of attempts at assassination, and in murders.

Far from fulfilling the formal obligations contained in its declaration of the 31st of March, 1909, the Royal Serbian Government has done nothing to suppress this movement. It has tolerated the criminal activities of the various unions and associations directed against the Monarchy, the unchecked utterances of the press, the glorification of the authors of assassinations, the participation of officers and officials in subversive intrigues; it has tolerated an unhealthy propaganda in its public instruction; and it has tolerated, finally, every manifestation which could betray the people of Serbia into hatred of the Monarchy and contempt for its institutions.

This toleration of which the Royal Serbian Government was guilty, was still in evidence at that moment when the events of the twenty-eighth of June exhibited to the whole world the dreadful consequences of such tolerance.

It is clear from the statements and confessions of the criminal authors of the assassination of the twenty-eighth of June, that the murder at Sarajevo was conceived at Belgrade, that the murderers received the weapons and the bombs with which they were equipped from Serbian officers and officials who belonged to the *Narodna Odbrana*, and, finally, that the dispatch of the criminals and of their weapons to Bosnia was arranged and effected under the conduct of Serbian frontier authorities.

The results brought out by the inquiry no longer permit the Imperial and Royal Government to maintain the attitude of patient tolerance which it has observed for years toward those agitations which center at Belgrade and are spread thence into the territories of the Monarchy. Instead, these results impose upon the Imperial and Royal Government the obligation to put an end to those intrigues, which constitute a standing menace to the peace of the Monarchy.

In order to attain this end, the Imperial and Royal Government finds itself compelled to demand that the Serbian Government give official assurance that it will condemn the propaganda directed against Austria-Hungary, that is to say, the

---

[*] This is a reference to the annexation of Bosnia-Herzegovina by Austria-Hungary in 1908.

whole body of the efforts whose ultimate object is to separate from the Monarchy territories that belong to it; and that it will obligate itself to suppress with all the means at its command this criminal and terroristic propaganda.

In order to give these assurances a character of solemnity, the Royal Serbian Government will publish on the first page of its official organ of July 26/13, the following declaration:

> 'The Royal Serbian Government condemns the propaganda directed against Austria-Hungary, that is to say, the whole body of the efforts whose ultimate object it is to separate from the Austro-Hungarian Monarchy territories that belong to it, and it most sincerely regrets the dreadful consequences of these criminal transactions.
>
> 'The Royal Serbian Government regrets that Serbian officers and officials should have taken part in the above-mentioned propaganda and thus have endangered the friendly and neighborly relations, to the cultivation of which the Royal Government has most solemnly pledged itself by its declarations of March 31, 1909.
>
> 'The Royal Government, which disapproves and repels every idea and every attempt to interfere in the destinies of the population of whatever portion of Austria-Hungary, regards it as its duty most expressly to call attention of the officers, officials and the whole population of the kingdom to the fact that for the future it will proceed with the utmost rigor against any persons who shall become guilty of any such activities, activities to prevent and to suppress which, the Government will bend every effort.'

This declaration shall be brought to the attention of the Royal army simultaneously by an order of the day from His Majesty the King, and by publication in the official organ of the army.

The Royal Serbian Government will furthermore pledge itself:

1   to suppress every publication which shall incite to hatred and contempt of the Monarchy, and the general tendency of which shall be directed against the territorial integrity of the latter;

2   to proceed at once to the dissolution of the *Narodna Odbrana*, to confiscate all of its means of propaganda, and in the same manner to proceed against the other unions and associations in Serbia which occupy themselves with propaganda against Austria-Hungary; the Royal Government will take such measures as are necessary to make sure that the dissolved associations may not continue their activities under other names or in other forms;

3   to eliminate without delay from public instruction in Serbia, everything, whether connected with the teaching corps or with the methods of teaching, that serves or may serve to nourish the propaganda against Austria-Hungary;

4   to remove from the military and administrative service in general all officers and officials who have been guilty of carrying on the propaganda against Austria-Hungary, whose names the Imperial and Royal Government reserves

the right to make known to the Royal Government when communicating the material evidence now in its possession;

5   to agree to the cooperation in Serbia of the organs of the Imperial and Royal Government in the suppression of the subversive movement directed against the integrity of the Monarchy;

6   to institute a judicial inquiry against every participant in the conspiracy of the twenty-eighth of June who may be found in Serbian territory; the organs of the Imperial and Royal Government delegated for this purpose will take part in the proceedings held for this purpose;

7   to undertake with all haste the arrest of Major Voislav Tankositch and of one Milan Ciganovitch, a Serbian official, who have been compromised by the results of the inquiry;

8   by efficient measure to prevent the participation of Serbian authorities in the smuggling of weapons and explosives across the frontier; to dismiss from the service and to punish severely those members of the Frontier Service at Schabats and Losnitza who assisted the authors of the crime of Sarajevo to cross the frontier;

9   to make explanations to the Imperial and Royal Government concerning the unjustifiable utterances of high Serbian functionaries in Serbia and abroad, who, without regard for their official position, have not hesitated to express themselves in a manner hostile toward Austria-Hungary since the assassination of the twenty-eighth of June;

10   to inform the Imperial and Royal Government without delay of the execution of the measures comprised in the foregoing points.

The Imperial and Royal Government awaits the reply of the Royal Government by Saturday, the twenty-fifth instant, at 6 p.m., at the latest.

Source: M. Montegelas and W. Schücking (eds), *Outbreak of the European War: German Documents Collected by Karl Kautsky* (New York, 1924), pp. 603–6

Although the Austro-Hungarian Government could not formally prove any links between the Serbian Government and the terrorist 'Black Hand' organisation, the assassination of Archduke Ferdinand provided Austria with the opportunity for a showdown with Serbia. On 23 July 1914, three weeks after the 'blank cheque' had been issued, the Austro-Hungarian government finally overcame opposition from the Hungarian Prime Minister, Count Tisza, and presented a Note to Serbia. The preamble to the ultimatum charged the Serbian government with complicity in the assassination because it tolerated the rise of a subversive movement within its territory and had done nothing to prevent its criminal activities. ('This movement, which developed under the eyes of the Serbian Government, has found expression subsequently beyond the territory of the kingdom, in acts of terrorism, a series of assassinations and murders'.) The Note contained far-reaching demands and required the Serbian Government to reply within forty-eight hours. Interestingly enough, the Austro-Hungarian government failed to consult its allies and neither Germany nor Italy (Austria's Triple Alliance partners) knew its contents. The Note contained ten demands, the most important of which (clauses 5 and 6) required Serbia to admit Austrian officials into Serbia for the suppression of the agitation against the Monarchy and to institute a judicial inquiry against persons allegedly involved in the murder of Franz Ferdinand.

The ultimatum and the humiliating manner in which it was presented were widely regarded as making this a document which no independent state could accept. To the surprise of the international community, the Serbian reply, delivered just before the expiry of the ultimatum on 25 July, was conciliatory and appeared to accept the Austrian demands except the crucial *sixth* point: Serbia could not allow Austria to participate in criminal proceedings held in Serbia. Despite the placatory tone of this reply, Austria severed diplomatic relations, mobilised its army and, on 28 July, war was declared on Serbia and Belgrade was shelled. According to the historian A.J.P. Taylor: 'The Austro-Hungarian declaration of war on Serbia was the decisive act; everything else followed from it'.

'Total war' erupts

As you can see from the chronology (pp. 65–7), events after 28 July took on a momentum of their own as European diplomacy began to break down. Within a week the alliance systems of the great powers had turned a conflict in the Balkans into a European war, despite a few last-minute attempts to prevent this happening. Once Austria-Hungary mobilised its army against Serbia on 28 July, the Serbian government appealed to Russia for help; and Russia, in turn, began partial mobilisation of its own army. On 30 July, following the Austrian shelling of Belgrade, Russia ordered a general mobilisation. From now on, German military planning, which had been taking shape for some years, began to dominate political decision-making in Europe, and this partly explains why events moved so fast and why the diplomacy that had prevented earlier Balkan conflicts from escalating failed to prevent a European war in 1914.

Count Alfred von Schlieffen was Chief of the German General Staff from 1891 to 1905. The military plan for offensive action named after him was first produced in 1905 and, in spite of constant revision (notably from Helmuth, Count von Moltke), formed the basis of the German attack in the west in August 1914. The Schlieffen Plan was based on the premise that Germany would have to fight both France and Russia in any future war. The plan contemplated a 'knockout blow' in the west against France before turning on Russia. The success of the plan depended on the ability of the German army to move through neutral Belgium at great speed in order to surprise France. Russia's decision to mobilise its troops on 30 July provided the 'trigger' that set in motion the Schlieffen Plan and the German decision to attack France (in the process violating Belgian neutrality), because it was felt that any delay might undermine Schlieffen's military strategy. Belgium's justified refusal to allow safe passage for the German army through its territory led to Britain declaring war on Germany

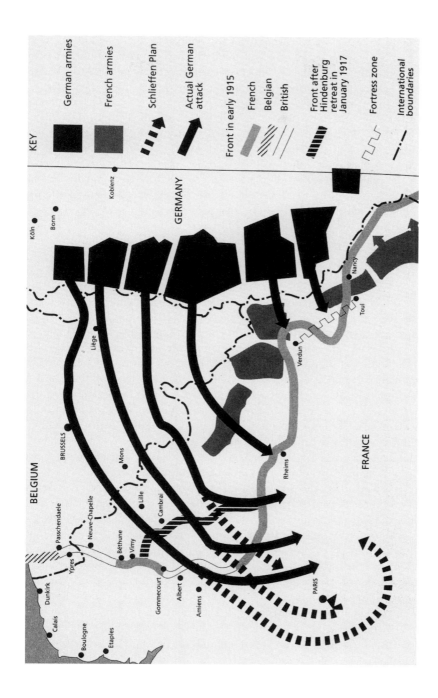

KEY

German armies

French armies

Schlieffen Plan

Actual German attack

Front in early 1915

French

Belgian

British

Front after Hindenburg retreat in January 1917

Fortress zone

International boundaries

GERMANY

BELGIUM

FRANCE

Köln

Bonn

Koblenz

Liège

BRUSSELS

Mons

Lille

Cambrai

Passchendaele

Neuve-Chapelle

Ypres

Béthune

Vimy

Gommecourt

Albert

Amiens

Dunkirk

Calais

Boulogne

Etaples

PARIS

Rheims

Verdun

Nancy

Toul

Map 2 The Schlieffen Plan

on 4 August (under a guarantee that Britain had given to Belgium in 1839), thus precipitating a general European war.

The military strategy that underpinned the Schlieffen Plan provides the clue to the speed with which events unfolded once the first fumbling political moves had been made. It also explains Wilhelm's encouragement to the Austrians to settle the Serbian question once and for all. From the German standpoint, a defeated Serbia would then allow Austria-Hungary to concentrate its forces against Russia. The Schlieffen Plan therefore reveals the importance of military strategy in 1914. The diagram of the actual German attack reveals that the strategy was never fully implemented; instead, German troops became bogged down in a long-drawn-out trench war. Nevertheless, as the chronology of events indicates, the politicians were sliding into war governed by Germany's desire to implement this plan. The Schlieffen Plan thus highlights the assumptions of international morality in the period and the general willingness of all powers to resort to force to carry out expansionist objectives. (The British Prime Minister, Lloyd George, later remarked that all the nations 'slithered over the brink into the boiling cauldron of war'.)

One of the most significant lessons to be learned from the experience of the First World War was that public opinion could no longer be ignored as a determining factor in the formulation of government policies. Unlike previous wars, the Great War was the first 'total war' in which whole nations, and not just professional armies were locked in mortal combat. The war served to increase the level of popular interest and participation in the affairs of state. The gap between the soldier at the front and civilian at home was narrowed substantially in that the entire resources of the state – military, economic and psychological – had to be mobilised. In 'total war', which required civilians to participate in the war effort, morale came to be recognised as a significant military factor, and propaganda began to emerge as the principle instrument of control over public opinion and an essential weapon in the national arsenal.

The implementation of the Schlieffen Plan involved Germany moving its troops through neutral Belgium. The subsequent invasion, which the Germans conceded was illegal, was the pretext for an anti-German propaganda campaign to mobilise support behind Britain's war aims. Belgium was depicted either as a defenceless child or a woman ravaged by brutal Prussian militarism. As well as state-sponsored propaganda, the British government was able to rely on individuals and groups to perpetuate the anti-German propaganda that had begun before 1914 with the escalation of the German naval programme, seen by many as a direct challenge to British naval supremacy. The theme of the 'Prussian Bully' was widely disseminated in newspapers, magazines, and animated cartoons in the cinemas. Document 4.3, a *Punch* cartoon by F.H. Townsend of August 1914, depicts a small shepherd boy heroically defending his country ('Bravo Belgium'), which can be seen behind the gate ('No thoroughfare'). German military aggression is symbolised by the 'Prussian Bully' brandishing his club, German sausages dangling carelessly from his pocket as he casts his ominous shadow towards the tranquil village and church spire that represent peaceful Belgium, in the field on the other side of the gate.

4.3 'The Prussian Bully invading Belgium', *Punch* cartoon, 12 August 1914

Source: *Punch* Publications

Britain emerged from the Great War with the doubtful distinction of having employed propaganda better than any other nation. Having entered the conflict with nothing that could be described as an official propaganda department, Britain finished the war with a highly respected Ministry of Information (established in 1918), which proved to be the model on which other governments were to base their own propaganda machinery. The emergence of propaganda as the chief instrument of control over public opinion was the inevitable consequence of 'total war'. In short, propaganda became an indispensable part of the equipment of the modern state at war.

The success of British propaganda in particular was not lost on a young corporal in the German imperial army. Writing some years later in *Mein Kampf* ('My Struggle'), Adolf Hitler observed: 'Germany had failed to recognise propaganda as a weapon of the first order whereas the British had employed it with great skill and ingenious deliberation'. As far as the Nazi party was concerned, the political importance of propaganda in post-war Europe was now fully recognised. In Britain, ordinary citizens emerged from the First World War feeling that they had been duped by their government, and with a deep mistrust of propaganda, which they now associated with lies and falsehood. In Germany, on the other hand, the first government ministry to be set up by the Nazis when they came to power in 1933 was the Ministry of Popular Enlightenment and Propaganda (see Chapter 6).

In 1961, the German historian, Fritz Fischer, published his controversial *Griff nach der Weltmacht* ('Germany's Bid for World Power'), which unleashed a debate that still refuses to die. Fischer argued that all the great powers were responsible for the outbreak of war in 1914, but that Germany must bear the greater part of the responsibility. Document 4.4 is Chancellor Bethmann Hollweg's September Programme, one of many documents cited by Fischer to substantiate his claim that economic expansion was the basis of Germany's political world diplomacy (*Weltpolitik*).

4.4 Bethmann Hollweg's September Programme, 1914

I FRANCE

The military to decide whether we should demand cession of Belfort and eastern slopes of the Vosges, razing of fortresses and cession of coastal strip from Dunkirk to Boulogne.

The ore-field of Briey, which is necessary for the supply of ore for our industry, to be ceded in any case.

Further, a war indemnity, to be paid in instalments; it must be high enough to prevent France from spending any considerable sums on armaments in the next fifteen to twenty years.

Furthermore: a commercial treaty which makes France economically dependent on

Germany, secures the French market for our exports and makes it possible to exclude British commerce from France. This treaty must secure for us financial and industrial freedom of movement in France in such fashion that German enterprises can no longer receive different treatment from French.

2 BELGIUM

Liège and Verviers to be attached to Prussia, a frontier strip of the province of Luxembourg to Luxembourg.

Question of whether Antwerp with a corridor to Liège, should also be annexed remains open.

At any rate Belgium, even if allowed to continue to exist as a state, must be reduced to a vassal state, must allow us to occupy any military important ports, must place her coast at our disposal in military respects, must become economically a German province. Given such a solution, which offers the advantages of annexation without its inescapable domestic political disadvantage, French Flanders with Dunkirk, Calais, and Boulogne, where most of the population is Flemish can without danger be attached to this unaltered Belgium. The competent quarters will have to judge the military value of this position against England.

3 LUXEMBOURG

Will become a German federal state and will receive a strip of the present Belgian province of Luxembourg and perhaps a corner of Longwy.

4 We must create a *central European economic association* through common customs treaties, to include France, Belgium, Holland, Denmark, Austria-Hungary, Poland and perhaps Italy, Sweden, and Norway. This association will not have any common constitutional supreme authority and all its members will be formally equal, but in practice will be under German leadership and must stabilise Germany's economic dominance over *Mitteleuropa*.

5 *The question of colonial acquisition*, where the first aim is the creation of a continuous Central African colonial empire, will be considered later, as will that of the aims to be realised *vis-à-vis* Russia.

6 A short provisional formula suitable for a possible preliminary peace to be found for a basis for the economic agreements to be concluded with France and Belgium.

7 HOLLAND

It will have to be considered by what means and methods Holland can be brought into closer relationship with the German empire.

In view of the Dutch character, this closer relationship must leave them free of any feeling of compulsion, must alter nothing in the Dutch way of life, and must also subject them to no new military obligations. Holland, then, must be left independent in externals, but be made internally dependent on us. Possibly one might consider an offensive and defensive alliance, to cover the colonies; in any case a close customs association, perhaps the cession of Antwerp to Holland in return for the right to keep a German garrison in the fortress of Antwerp and at the mouth of the Scheldt.

Source: Quoted in F. Fischer, *Germany's Aims in the First World War* (London, 1967), pp. 104–5

Drafted by Chancellor Bethmann Hollweg during the earlier stages of the Battle of the Marne, when the aims of the Schlieffen Plan still seemed likely to be fulfilled, the so-called September Programme of 1914 anticipated the speedy defeat of France and set out in an uncompromising fashion German objectives in the West. Germany's aims were motivated by economic factors and were aggressively expansionist. A weakened France was to become 'economically dependent on Germany', the Briey ore-field was to be annexed, and a war indemnity would be imposed so that France would be prevented 'from spending any considerable sums on armaments'. Belgium ('even if allowed to continue to exist') would be reduced to an occupied 'vassal state', while Luxembourg would become 'a German federal state'. According to this programme, Germany would also establish a 'central European economic association' that would 'stabilise Germany's economic dominance over *Mitteleuropa*'. No attempt was made in the notes to outline German aims in the east or in Africa but it did mention that the 'creation of a continuous Central African colonial empire' and the 'aims to be realised *vis-à-vis* Russia' would be considered later.

Critics of Fischer and his followers argue that too much emphasis is placed on the September Programme, which, they maintain, can be seen as a hasty reaction to meet an immediate situation. In other words, Bethmann Hollweg was simply anticipating a major military victory. However, Fischer crucially maintains that Germany's expansionist war aims were the symptoms of a planned drive for world power (*Weltpolitik*) that can be traced back to the 1890s. In particular, Fischer would point to the famous 'war council' meeting of 8 December 1912 between the Kaiser and his military advisers that appeared to postpone war until the navy had completed its submarine programme and the Kiel Canal had been opened. Thus the significance of the September Programme (according to Fischer) is that it was representative of the ideas and expansionist aspirations of political, economic and military elites in Germany in the period leading up to September 1914. If you agree with the Fischer thesis, then the assassination of Archduke Ferdinand that precipitated events in 1914 was not the cause of the war but merely a fortuitous pretext (a 'trigger') that allowed Germany to risk a war on two fronts in order to achieve its political, economic and military objectives.

When the European war did erupt in August 1914, it was for a long time conventionally depicted in glib images such as that of Document 4.5, a photograph of excited and enthusiastic reservists clamouring to participate in the conflict in the belief that they were defending their country.

4.5 French reservists reporting for duty, photographed in August 1914

Source: Hulton-Deutsch Collection

The scene in this photograph records French reservists, blissfully ignorant of the nature of industrialised warfare, leaving the Gare du Nord to report to military depots from where they would be taken to the western front. Few of those seen in this picture would survive the conflict. The declaration of war in 1914 was welcomed by many people in Europe, who gloried in the patriotic *élan* which it provoked. No doubt they imagined it would be another 1870-type war. However, as the war dragged on and the casualty figures multiplied, the reality of a long-drawn-out war of attrition became apparent. It was left to artists and poets to describe the solidarity of the front-line soldiers and to record the appalling conditions and the horror of 'total war'. The 'poetry of disillusionment' was universal and not confined to any one nation. I have chosen a poem by Wilfred Owen, written in 1917, to illustrate the experience of life in the front-line – in this case, the battle of the Somme.

4.6 Wilfred Owen, 'The Sentry', 1917

We'd found an old Boche dug-out, and he knew,
And gave us hell, for shell on frantic shell
Hammered on top, but never quite burst through.
Rain, guttering down in waterfalls of slime
Kept slush waist-high that, rising hour by hour,
Choked up the steps too thick with clay to climb.
What murk of air remained stank old, and sour
With fumes of whizz-bangs, and the smell of men
Who'd lived there years, and left their curse in the den,
If not their corpses...
     There we herded from the blast
Of whizz-bangs, but one found our door at last, –
Buffeting our eyes and breath, snuffing the candles.
And thud! flump! thud! down the steep steps came thumping
And splashing in the flood, deluging muck –
The sentry's body; then, his rifle, handles
Of old Boche bombs, and mud in ruck on ruck.
We dredged him up, for killed, until he whined
'O sir, my eyes – I'm blind – I'm blind, I'm blind!'
Coaxing, I held a flame against his lids
And said if he could see the least blurred light
He was not blind; in time he'd get all right.
'I can't,' he sobbed. Eyeballs, huge-bulged like squids',
Watch my dreams still; but I forgot him there
In posting next for duty, and sending a scout
To beg a stretcher somewhere, and floundering about
To other posts under the shrieking air.

Those other wretches, how they bled and spewed,
And one who would have drowned himself for good, –
I try not to remember these things now.
Let dread hark back for one word only: how
Half listening to that sentry's moans and jumps,
And the wild chattering of his broken teeth,
Renewed most horribly whenever crumps
Pummelled the roof and slogged the air beneath –
Through the dense din, I say, we heard him shout
'I see your lights!' But ours had long died out.

Source: E. Blunden (ed.), *The Poems of Wilfred Owen* (London, 1964), p.112,
by permission of Chatto and Windus on behalf of the Executors of the
Estate of Harold Owen

Wilfred Owen expressed the intense experience of industrialised warfare in a language and with an immediacy that a history textbook would find difficult to emulate. The poem distils the brutalising effects of war. Owen, who as an officer was responsible for sentry duty, described a wounded sentry horribly blinded by a German ('Boche') bomb, 'Eyeballs, huge-bulged like squids'. The poet tried 'not to see these things now'; however the suffering of this soldier clearly haunted him. Owen contrasted the soldier's desire to see again ('I see your lights!') with his own sense of futility and resignation after many years of fighting ('But ours had long died out'). The solitary experience of the soldier-poet attempting to come to terms with 'the shrieking air' of trench warfare, provides a sobering counterpoint to the patriotic scenes of cheering crowds in 1914 who believed that the war would be 'all over by Christmas'.

The poetry of the First World War – indeed the war's art in general – remains a moving memorial to those who died in the conflict. The memory of the war is also commemorated in the form of stone monuments that record the sacrifices of the fallen. Such a 'history of bereavement' continues to confront us in cities, towns and villages. When next you come across a war memorial, ask yourself whether or not the language of commemoration (referred to by one historian as a 'nation worshipping itself') retains any meaning for you – and if so, what precisely is its historical significance? For me, the poetry and art of the Great War convey a sense of sadness, loss and futility and also justified anger at the politicians and generals who sat around their tables while Europe bled. In the words of another Wilfred Owen poem ('The Parable of the Old Men and the Young'):

> …When lo! an angel called him out of heaven,
> Saying, Lay not thy hand upon the lad,
> Neither do anything to him. Behold,
> A ram, caught in a thicket by its horns;
> Offer the Ram of Pride instead of him.
> But the old man would not so, but slew his son, –
> And half the seed of Europe, one by one.

From Wilson's 'Fourteen Points' to the League of Nations

In December 1917, Germany secured a victory in the east, forcing the Russians to sue for peace at Brest-Litovsk. Shortly after the armistice had been signed by Germany and Russia, President Wilson enunciated his famous 'Fourteen Points', which constituted the most specific statement of war aims issued by the Allies.

4.7 President Woodrow Wilson's Fourteen Points speech, 8 January 1918

[Wilson begins by speaking of the failure so far of the negotiations between the Central Powers and the Russians at Brest-Litovsk.]

It is a reasonable conjecture that the general principles of settlement which [the Central Powers] at first suggested originated with the more liberal statesmen of Germany and Austria, the men who have begun to feel the force of their own peoples' thought and purpose, while the concrete terms of actual settlement came from the military leaders who have no thought but to keep what they have got. The negotiations have been broken off. The Russian representatives were sincere and in earnest. They cannot entertain such proposals of conquest and domination.

The whole incident is full of significance. It is also full of perplexity. With whom are the Russian representatives dealing? For whom are the representatives of the Central Empires speaking? Are they speaking for the majorities of their respective parliaments or for the minority parties, that military and imperialistic minority which has so far dominated their whole policy and controlled the affairs of Turkey and of the Balkan states which have felt obliged to become their associates in this war? The Russian representatives have insisted, very justly, very wisely, and in the true spirit of modern democracy, that the conferences they have been holding with the Teutonic and Turkish statesmen should be held within open, not closed, doors, and all the world has been audience, as was desired. To whom have we been listening, then? To those who speak the spirit and intention of the Resolutions of the German Reichstag of the ninth of July last, the spirit and intention of the liberal leaders and parties of Germany, or to those who resist and defy that spirit and intention, and insist upon conquest and subjugation? Or are we listening, in fact, to both, unreconciled and in open and hopeless contradiction? These are very serious and pregnant questions. Upon the answer to them depends the peace of the world.

But, whatever the results of the parleys at Brest-Litovsk, whatever the confusions of counsel and of purpose in the utterances of the spokesmen of the Central Empires, they have again attempted to acquaint the world with their objects in the war and have again challenged their adversaries to say what their objects are and what sort of settlement they would deem just and satisfactory. There is no good reason why that challenge should not be responded to, and responded to with the utmost candour. We did not wait for it. Not once, but again and again, we have laid our whole thought and purpose before the world, not in general terms only, but each time with sufficient definition to make it clear what sort of definitive terms of settlement must necessarily spring out of them. Within the last week Mr Lloyd George has spoken with admirable candour and in admirable spirit for the people and Government of Great Britain. There is no confusion of counsel among the adversaries of the Central Powers, no uncertainty of principle, no vagueness of detail. The only secrecy of counsel, the only lack of fearless frankness, the only failure to make definite statement of the objects of the war, lies with Germany and her Allies. The issues of life and death hang upon these definitions. No statesman who has the least conception of his responsibility ought for a moment to permit himself to continue this tragical and appalling outpouring of blood and treasure unless he is sure beyond a peradventure that the objects of the vital sacrifice are part and parcel of the very life of Society and that the people for whom he speaks think them right and imperative as he does.

There is, moreover, a voice calling for these definitions of principle and of purpose which is, it seems to me, more thrilling and more compelling than any of the many moving voices with which the troubled air of the world is filled. It is the voice of the Russian people. They are prostrate and all but helpless, it would seem, before the grim power of Germany, which has hitherto known no relenting and no pity. Their power, apparently, is shattered. And yet their soul is not subservient. They will not yield either in principle or in action. Their conception of what is right, of what it is humane and honourable for them to accept, has been stated with a frankness, a largeness of view, a generosity of spirit, and a universal human sympathy which must challenge the admiration of every friend of mankind; and they have refused to compound their ideals or desert others that they themselves may be safe. They call to us to say what it is that we desire, in what, if in anything, our purpose and our spirit differ from theirs; and I believe that the people of the United States would wish me to respond, with utter simplicity and frankness. Whether their present leaders believe it or not, it is our heartfelt desire and hope that some way may be opened whereby we may be privileged to assist the people of Russia to attain their utmost hope of liberty and ordered peace.

It will be our wish and purpose that the processes of peace, when they are begun, shall be absolutely open and that they shall involve and permit henceforth no secret understandings of any kind. The day of conquest and aggrandizement is gone by; so is also the day of secret covenants entered into in the interest of particular governments and likely at some unlooked-for moment to upset the peace of the world. It is this happy fact, now clear to the view of every public man whose thoughts do not still linger in an age that is dead and gone, which makes it possible for every nation whose purposes are consistent with justice and the peace of the world to avow now or at any other time the objects it has in view.

We entered this war because violations of right had occurred which touched us to the quick and made the life of our own people impossible unless they were corrected and the world secured once for all against their recurrence. What we demand in this war, therefore, is nothing peculiar to ourselves. It is that the world be made fit and safe to live in; and particularly that it be made safe for every peace-loving nation which, like our own, wishes to live its own life, determine its own institutions, be assured of justice and fair dealing by the other peoples of the world as against force and selfish aggression. All the peoples of the world are in effect partners in this interest, and for our own part we see very clearly that unless justice be done to others it will not be done to us. The programme of the world's peace, therefore, is our programme; and that programme, the only possible programme, as we see it, is this:

I. Open covenants of peace, openly arrived at, after which there shall be no private international understandings of any kind but diplomacy shall proceed always frankly and in the public view.

II. Absolute freedom of navigation upon the seas, outside territorial waters, alike in peace and war, except as the seas may be closed in whole or in part by international action for the enforcement of international covenants.

III. The removal, so far as possible, of all economic barriers and the establishment of an equality of trade conditions among all the nations consenting to the peace and associating themselves for its maintenance.

IV. Adequate guarantees given and taken that national armaments will be reduced to the lowest point consistent with domestic safety.

V. A free, open-minded, and absolutely impartial adjustment of all colonial claims, based upon a strict observance of the principle that in determining all such questions of sovereignty the interests of the populations concerned must have equal weight with the equitable claims of the government whose title is to be determined.

VI. The evacuation of all Russian territory and such a settlement of all questions affecting Russia as will secure the best and freest co-operation of the other nations of the world in obtaining for her an unhampered and unembarrassed opportunity for the independent determination of her own political development and national policy and assure her of a sincere welcome into the society of free nations under institutions of her own choosing; and, more than a welcome, assistance also of every kind that she may need and may herself desire. The treatment accorded Russia by her sister nations in the months to come will be the acid test of their good will, of their comprehension of her needs as distinguished from their own interests, and of their intelligent and unselfish sympathy.

VII. Belgium, the whole world will agree, must be evacuated and restored, without any attempt to limit the sovereignty which she enjoys in common with all other free nations. No other single act will serve as this will serve to restore confidence among the nations in the laws which they have themselves set and determined for the government of their relations with one another. Without this healing act the whole structure and validity of international law is forever impaired.

VIII. All French territory should be freed and the invaded portions restored, and the wrong done to France by Prussia in 1871 in the matter of Alsace-Lorraine, which has unsettled the peace of the world for nearly fifty years, should be righted, in order that peace may once more be made secure in the interest of all.

IX. A readjustment of the frontiers of Italy should be effected along clearly recognizable lines of nationality.

X. The peoples of Austria-Hungary, whose place among the nations we wish to see safeguarded and assured, should be accorded the freest opportunity of autonomous development.

XI. Rumania, Serbia, and Montenegro should be evacuated; occupied territories restored; Serbia accorded free and secure access to the sea; and the relations of the several Balkan states to another determined by friendly counsel along historically established lines of allegiance and nationality; and international guarantees of the political and economic independence and territorial integrity of the several Balkan states should be entered into.

XII. The Turkish portions of the present Ottoman Empire should be assured a secure sovereignty, but the other nationalities which are now under Turkish rule should be assured an undoubted security of life and an absolutely unmolested opportunity of autonomous development, and the Dardanelles should be permanently opened as a free passage to the ships and commerce of all nations under international guarantees.

XIII. An independent Polish state should be erected which should include the territories inhabited by indisputably Polish populations, which should be assured a free and secure access to the sea, and whose political and economic independence and territorial integrity should be guaranteed by international covenant.

XIV. A general association of nations must be formed under specific covenants for the purpose of affording mutual guarantees of political independence and territorial integrity to great and small states alike.

In regard to these essential rectifications of wrong and assertions of right we feel ourselves to be intimate partners of all the governments and peoples associated together against the Imperialists. We cannot be separated in interest or divided in purpose. We stand together until the end.

For such arrangements and covenants we are willing to fight and to continue to fight until they are achieved; but only because we wish the right to prevail and desire a just and stable peace such as can be secured only by removing the chief provocations to war, which this programme does remove. We have no jealousy of German greatness, and there is nothing in this programme that impairs it. We grudge her no achievement or distinction of learning or of pacific enterprise such as have made her record very bright and very enviable. We do not wish to injure her or to block in any way her legitimate influence or power. We do not wish to fight her either with arms or with hostile arrangements of trade if she is willing to associate herself with us and the other peace-loving nations of the world in covenants of justice and law and fair dealing. We wish her only to accept a place of equality among the peoples of the world – the new world in which we now live – instead of a place of mastery.

Neither do we presume to suggest to her any alteration or modification of her institutions. But it is necessary, we must frankly say, and necessary as a preliminary to any intelligent dealings with her on our part, that we should know whom her spokesmen speak for when they speak to us, whether for the Reichstag majority or for the military party and the men whose creed is imperial domination.

We have spoken now, surely, in terms too concrete to admit of any further doubt or question. An evident principle runs through the whole programme I have outlined. It is the principle of justice to all peoples and nationalities, and their right to live on equal terms of liberty and safety with one another, whether they be strong or weak. Unless this principle be made its foundation no part of the structure of international justice can stand. The people of the United States could act upon no other principle; and to the vindication of this principle they are ready to devote their lives, their honour, and everything that they possess. The moral climax of this the culminating and final war for human liberty has come, and they are ready to put their own strength, their own highest purpose, their own integrity and devotion to the test.

Source: *The Public Papers of Woodrow Wilson*, vol. I (New York, 1927), pp. 155–62

Wilson laid down his Fourteen Points in an address delivered at a joint session of the two Houses of Congress. Too often, the Fourteen Points are taken out of context and viewed in isolation. The preamble to them was equally important and revealed Wilson's concern that negotiations at Brest-Litovsk would end in a vindictive peace treaty. Wilson referred to the compelling 'voice of the Russian people' that lay helpless 'before the grim power of Germany'. The President hoped that his statement of war aims would provide the inspiration for Russia to continue to resist German demands. Wilson's 'programme for world peace' was a combination of lofty idealism and specific recommendations. The first five points outline general principles of peacemaking. These were followed by specific recommendations of the territorial changes required for a stable Europe. The final point called for the establishment of a 'general association of nations' to protect the 'political independence and territorial integrity' of 'great and small states alike'. It anticipated the establishment of the League of Nations.

Wilson's Fourteen Points were shaped by an implicit belief that European power rivalries had caused the war. His proposals provide a formula for peace, but the speech as a whole is far more interesting and revealing. Wilson not only revealed his deep-seated loathing for Germany, but by laying down an American 'new order of things', he also distanced the United States from the war aims of its European allies. Not suprisingly, the speech was largely unacceptable to Britain and France, who continued to view Wilson's proposals as vague and impractical.

The Germans, too, in their negotiations with Russia did not feel compelled by Wilson's notion of 'peace without annexations and indemnities'. When the terms of the Treaty of Brest-Litovsk were announced on 3 March 1918, Russia had lost Poland, the Ukraine, Finland and its Baltic provinces (see Chapter 7). Having seen his Fourteen Points ignored, President Wilson's negotiating position hardened, and he conceded to Allied demands for reparations and German disarmament. On 11 November, Germany signed an armistice with the Allies at Compiègne. The war had come to an end, but Wilson's Fourteen Points assumed greater significance when the Germans claimed that they had been duped into agreeing to an armistice on the basis of his proposals. In fact, during the armistice negotiations the German High Command was left in no doubt that the peace terms would be excessively harsh.

The European war ended in November 1918 and resulted in a European peace settlement in 1919. Document 4.8 is taken from the Treaty of Versailles, which consisted of 440 articles and is the most authoritative source for the manner in which the map of Europe was to be redrawn.

4.8 The Treaty of Versailles, June 1919

PART I THE COVENANT OF THE LEAGUE OF NATIONS

The High Contracting Parties,
In order to promote international co-operation and to achieve international peace and security
by the acceptance of obligations not to resort to war,
by the prescription of open, just and honourable relations between nations,
by the firm establishment of the understandings of international law as the actual rule of conduct among Governments,
and by the maintenance of justice and a scrupulous respect for all treaty obligations in the dealings of organised peoples with one another,
Agree to this Covenant of the League of Nations...

PART VII PENALTIES

Article 227 The Allied and Associated Powers publicly arraign William II of Hohenzollern, formerly German Emperor, for a supreme offence against international morality and the sanctity of treaties.

A special tribunal will be constituted to try the accused, thereby assuring him the guarantees essential to the right of defence. It will be composed of five judges, one appointed by each of the following Powers: namely, the United States of America, Great Britain, France, Italy and Japan.

In its decision the tribunal will be guided by the highest motives of international policy, with a view to vindicating the solemn obligations of international undertakings and the validity of international morality. It will be its duty to fix the punishment which it considers should be imposed.

The Allied and Associated Powers will address a request to the Government of the Netherlands for the surrender to them of the ex-Emperor in order that he may be put on trial.

Article 228 The German Government recognises the right of the Allied and Associated Powers to bring before military tribunals persons accused of having committed acts in violation of the laws and customs of war. Such persons shall, if found guilty, be sentenced to punishments laid down by law....

PART VIII REPARATION

[Selections. The whole takes up 20 pages.]

Section I: General Provisions

Article 231 The Allied and Associated Governments affirm and Germany accepts the responsibility of Germany and her allies for causing all the loss and damage to which the Allied and Associated Governments and their nationals have been subjected as a consequence of the war imposed upon them by the aggression of Germany and her allies.

Article 232 The Allied and Associated Governments recognize that the resources of Germany are not adequate, after taking into account permanent diminutions of such resources which will result from other provisions of the present Treaty, to make complete reparation for all such loss and damage.

The Allied and Associated Governments, however, require, and Germany undertakes, that she will make compensation for all damage done to the civilian population of the Allied and Associated Powers and to their property during the period of the belligerency of each as an Allied or Associated Power against Germany by such aggression by land, by sea and from the air, and in general all damage as defined in Annex I hereto.

In accordance with Germany's pledges, already given, as to complete restoration for Belgium, Germany undertakes, in addition to the compensation for damage elsewhere in this Part provided for, as a consequence of the violation of the Treaty of 1839, to make reimbursement of all sums which Belgium has borrowed from the Allied and Associated Governments up to November 11, 1918, together with interest at the rate of five per cent. (5%) per annum on such sums. This amount shall be determined by the Reparation Commission, and the German Government undertakes thereupon forthwith to make a special issue of bearer bonds to an equivalent amount payable in marks gold, on May 1, 1926, or, at the option of the German Government, on May 1 in any year up to 1926. Subject to the foregoing, the form of such bonds shall be determined by the Reparation Commission. Such bonds shall be handed over to the Reparation Commission, which has authority to take and acknowledge receipt thereof on behalf of Belgium. ...

PART XIV

Article 428 As a guarantee for the execution of the present Treaty by Germany, the

German territory situated to the west of the Rhine, together with the bridgeheads, will be occupied by Allied and Associated troops for a period of fifteen years. ...

Source: *Parliamentary Papers*, London, 1919, vol. LIII, Cmd 153, HMSO, pp. 127–357

Although the so-called 'peacemakers' reconstructed the map of the Middle East, Africa and Asia, these areas were viewed as less important than Europe. The statesmen who met at Versailles in January 1919 (Clemenceau representing France, Lloyd George of Britain and President Wilson of the United States) were confronted with the considerable task of establishing an immediate and lasting peace on a continent still recoiling from the aftermath of 'total war' and, at the same time, restoring political and economic stability. For all the propaganda about it being a 'war to end all wars', those who were engaged in the conflict were under no illusions and knew that it had been a struggle for mastery in Europe.

The Treaty of Versailles was only one of a number of settlements at the end of the war. The other treaties were as follows: Saint-Germain with Austria, Trianon with Hungary, Neuilly with Bulgaria. The Treaty of Sèvres with Turkey never came into operation, and was replaced by the Treaty of Lausanne in 1923.

Part I of the Treaty of Versailles is the Covenant of the League of Nations embracing the first twenty-six clauses. I have cited only the aims and objectives that were expressed at the beginning of the Covenant. It was believed at the time to be the supreme agency for maintaining international peace, and it is arguably the Treaty's most noble feature. The League of Nations was clearly an attempt to break away from the secret diplomacy that many believed had been partially responsible for the escalation of the Balkans conflict in 1914. The Covenant talked about establishing 'open, just and honourable relations between nations', and maintaining 'justice and scrupulous respect for all treaty obligations'. The League, however, could not prevent another war from breaking out in 1939 (see Chapter 8). This should not automatically lead to the conclusion that it failed, rather that member states (particularly the larger states) were not fully committed to carrying out their obligations under the Covenant. It was also weakened by the failure of the United States to ratify the Treaty of Versailles and to join the League of Nations.

The most controversial sections are Part VII and VIII, which dealt with 'penalties' and 'reparations'. Article 227 reflected the popular anti-German hysteria in Britain and France and called for the trial of the Kaiser (who had abdicated and fled to the Netherlands). Article 228 can be seen as enshrining the principle that international relations and war should be governed by moral considerations. Neither article was implemented, but the question of international morality and the conduct of war was raised again at the end of the Second World War, when the Nuremberg War Crimes Tribunal did prosecute individuals accused of committing war crimes.

The question of what reparations Germany should pay was an issue that divided the Allies. It was decided that Germany should be excluded from the discussions and presented with the terms: better a 'dictated' peace than a drawn-out wrangle that might allow Germany to exploit Allied differences. Reparations were justified legally by Article 231, the so-called 'war guilt' clause, which stated that Germany accepted responsibility for starting the war. The problem was: how much should they pay? The emotional effect of the war guilt clause, which was widely viewed in Germany as being 'imposed', obscured the fact that Article 232 represented a compromise between the Allies. Although Britain and France wished the Germans to pay for the whole cost of the war, Article 232 limits reparations to 'damage done to the civilian population ... and their property', thus representing a victory for President Wilson. British and French public opinion would have to be assuaged by the emotional 'war guilt' clause.

The Reparations Commission established by the treaty finally agreed in May 1921 on a figure of £6,600 million payable by Germany and its allies. The British economist John Maynard Keynes, who had been an observer at Versailles, wrote an influential book *The Economic Consequences of the Peace* that was highly critical of the financial thinking behind reparations and condemned the financial provisions. Germany's promise to pay reparations and its acceptance of a territorial settlement that resulted in the loss of 13 per cent of its territory and 6 million subjects had a profound effect on post-war politics. The decision to exclude Germany from the League of Nations only reinforced the claims of right-wing German nationalists, who condemned Versailles as a 'diktat' that should never have been signed in the first place.

In conclusion it can be said that the collection of peace treaties were not a lasting success. Map 3 shows the redrawn map of Europe in 1919. The German, Austro-Hungarian and Ottoman empires were destroyed and independent states such as Poland, Hungary, Yugoslavia and Czechoslovakia were formally recognised under the guiding principle of national self-determination. The result was that after 1919 nearly 30 million people now found themselves as national and racial minorities. The long-term consequences of allowing ethnic *irredentas* and minorities were to be a source of tension and simmering discontent in the late 1930s, just as they were tragically to become an issue once again in the 1990s.

BIBILIOGRAPHY

Sources and documents

Two useful collections of documents, but from different perspectives are: M. Hurst (ed.), *Key Treaties for the Great Powers, 1870–1914* (vol. 2, 1972); and I. Geiss, *July, 1914: Selected Documents* (1967), which provides sources on the diplomatic crisis of 1914.

P. Vansittart, *Voices from the Great War* (1983) contains eye-witness evidence on the war from all levels of society. Of the memoirs, see D. Lloyd George, *War Memoirs* (2 vols, 1928) and W.S. Churchill, *The World Crisis* (1928). Remember also, that literature provides an insight into the nature of the conflict. Highly

KEY

- Lost by Germany 1919
- Saar: League of Nations control 1919–1935
- Demilitarised Rhineland 1919–1936
- Austria-Hungary until 1918
- Plebiscite areas
- Former territory of imperial Russia

Map 3 European frontiers, 1919–37

recommended are: J. Reed, *The War in Eastern Europe* (1916); H. Barbusse, *Le Feu* (*Under Fire*) (1917); E. Junger, *The Storm of Steel* (1929); R. Graves, *Goodbye to All That* (1929); E.M. Remarque, *All Quiet on the Western Front* (1929). More recent works include: S. Faulkes, *Birdsong* (1997); P. Barker, the 'Regeneration' trilogy, comprising *Regeneration* (1991), *The Eye in the Door* (1993) and *The Ghost Road* (1995). For a survey of German wartime poetry see, P. Bridgewater, *German Poets of the First World War* (1985); for comparative collections see J. Silkin (ed.), *Poetry in World War One* (1983) and A. Powell (ed.), *A Deep Cry* (Sutton, 1998).

Secondary works

The literature on the 'origins' of the war appears never-ending. See J. Joll, *The Origins of the First World War* (1985); L.C.F. Turner, *The Origins of the First World War* (1970); F.R. Bridge, *The Coming of the First World War* (1984); J.A. Moses, *The Politics of Illusion* (1975). H.W. Koch (ed.), *The Origins of the First World War* (1984) contains essays from all the major contributors to the debate. Fundamental to the ongoing debate have been the contributions from F. Fischer, *Germany's War Aims in the First World War* (1967) and Fischer again with his modified *War of Illusions* (1975) and E. Kehr, *Battleship Building and Party Politics in Germany* (1975). A synthesis of the ongoing historiographical debate can be found in J.W. Langdon, *July 1914. The Long Debate, 1918–1990* (1991).

There is also a vast literature on the general history of the war: A.J.P. Taylor, *The First World War: An Illustrated History* (1966) – a moving photographic record of the conflict; B.H. Liddell-Hart, *History of the First World War* (1970). M. Ferro, *The Great War* (1963) is a short but brilliant introduction. See also J. Terraine, *The Western Front, 1914–18* (1964). For works which place the military aspects of the war in a broader context see K. Robbins, *The First World War* (Oxford, 1984); B. Bond, *War and Society in Europe, 1870–1970* (1984); G. Hardach, *The First World War* (1977); and more recently J. Keegan, *The First World War* (1998). The fateful first days of the conflict are evocatively captured in R. Wohl, *The Generation of 1914* (1979) and B. Tuchman, *August 1914. The First Month of the First World War* (1994).

The nature of 'total war' and the impact of technology is discussed in E. Kehr, *Economic Interests, Militarism and Foreign Policy* (1977); G. Krumeich, *Armaments and Politics in France on the Eve of the First World War* (1984); J. Ellis, *Eye-Deep in Hell* (1976); A.E. Ashworth, *The Trench Warfare* (1980); E. Leeds, *No Man's Land* (1979); while A. Horne, *The Price of Glory: Verdun, 1916* (1964); L. Macdonald, *They Called it Passchendaele* (1983); M. Middlebrook, *The First Day on the Somme* (1971) and *The Kaiser's Battle* (1983) (on Germany's 1918 offensive) give full treatment of individual battles, as does J. Keegan, *The Face of Battle* (1979).

The impact of the war on individual societies can be found in D. Welch, *German Society, Propaganda and Total War, 1914–18: The Sins of Omission* (1999); J. Kocka, *Facing Total War: German Society, 1914–1918* (1985); A. Rosenberg, *Imperial Germany: The Birth of the German Republic* (1931); A. Marwick, *The Deluge: British Society and the First World War* (1965); J. Winter, *The Great War and the British People*

(1985); B. Waites, *A Class Society at War, England 1914–1918* (1987); A.J. May, *The Passing of the Habsburg Monarchy* (2 vols, 1966); L. Kochan, *Russia in Revolution, 1890–1918* (1966); J.J. Becker, *The Great War and the French People* (1983); N. Stone, *The Eastern Front* (1978). General coverage of such issues is provided by A. Marwick, *War and Social Change in the Twentieth Century* (1974). A seductive but somewhat 'flawed' analysis can be found in N. Fergusan, *The Pity of War* (1998).

The revolutionary effects of the war are discussed in C.L. Bertrand (ed.,) *Revolutionary Situations in Europe, 1917–1922* (Montreal, 1977) and F.L. Carsten, *Revolution in Central Europe, 1918–1919* (1972). For Germany, see A.J. Ryder, *The German Revolution* (1966) and D. Geary, 'Radicalism and the Worker: Metalworkers and Revolution, 1914–1923', in R.J. Evans (ed.), *Society and Politics in Wilhelmine Germany* (1978). A first-rate compilation of recent scholarship on cultural trends can be found in J. Horne (ed.), *State, Society and Mobilization in Europe during the First World War* (1997). An excellent analysis of the use made by the British government of propaganda can be found in M. Sanders and P. Taylor, *British Propaganda During the First World War, 1914–18* (1982).

For a contemporary and powerful critique of the post-war peace settlements and the way they were implemented see J.M. Keynes, *The Economic Consequences of the Peace* (1919). More recently, see A. Sharp, *The Versailles Settlement: Peacemaking in Paris 1919* (1991); I.J. Lederer (ed.), *Versailles Settlement* (1974); V. Rothwell, *British War Aims and Peace Diplomacy* (1971); as well as A.J.P. Taylor, *The Struggle for Mastery in Europe, 1848–1918* (1954).

Articles

J.C.H. (July, 1966) is devoted to the 'origins' controversy. The interaction between domestic and foreign policy is taken up by M.R. Gordon, 'Domestic Conflict and the Origins of the First World War: The British and the German Cases' *J.M.H.* (1974). For accounts of film propaganda in Britain and Germany see N. Reeves, 'Film Propaganda and its Audience: The Example of Britain's Official Films During the First World War' *J.C.H.* (1983) and D. Welch, 'Cinema and Society in Imperial Germany 1905–1918', *German History* (1990). Different aspects of the press are tackled in D. Hopkin, 'Domestic Censorship in the First World War', *J.C.H.* (1970) and J.M. McEwen, 'The National Press During the First World War: Ownership and Circulation, *J.C.H.* (1982). Propaganda in general is given a comparative treatment in A.G. Marquis, 'Words as Weapons: Propaganda in Britain and Germany during the First World War', *J.C.H.* (1978). On the peace settlements, see A. Crozier, 'The Establishment of the Mandate Systems, 1919–25: Some Problems created by the Paris Peace Conference', *J.C.H.* (1979).

5

Fascist Italy

What is Fascism? In the aftermath of the First World War fascist dictators emerged in Italy, Germany, Portugal, Spain and, for a time during the Second World War, some of the occupied territories. Fascism varied from nation to nation, but in its simplest terms it was a doctrine that *sanctified the interests of the nation-state and minimised the rights of the individual*.

The roots and antecedents of fascism can be traced back to the French Revolution of 1789, which ushered in ideals of liberalism and representative government that eventually spread across Europe as the old political and social order was overturned. During the nineteenth century, liberalism went hand-in-hand with a wave of nationalism that resulted in the unification of Italy and Germany in the 1860s and 1870s. Many believed, however, that liberal democracy had failed to curb the excesses of capitalism, providing instead the conditions under which the strong could prey on the weak. The 1890s saw an intellectual revolt against the dominant ideology of liberalism and capitalism. As a result, two major doctrines gradually emerged in opposition to liberalism. On the Left it was challenged by Marxism, which burst onto the European scene in Russia; and on the Right it was attacked by a right-wing movement that came to be known as fascism.

Fascism therefore emerged in direct opposition to liberal democracy, because fascists contended that democracy had created class conflict and that individual rights undermined the authority state. Fascists opposed communism because they argued that communism (or socialism) deliberately inflamed class conflict for revolutionary purposes, and this also threatened the nation-state. What distinguished fascism from other right-wing political movements was its 'revolutionary' intention to replace the existing political structure with the 'one-party totalitarian state' that would eliminate class conflict by encouraging the people to place the nation-state before their own self-interests.

Mussolini and the rise of Italian fascism

It was in Italy that the first fascist dictatorship was established. Benito Mussolini's Fascist party had gained political power by the end of October 1922. The rise of fascism in Italy was a direct result of the strains produced by the First World War and the post-war economic fluctuations that successive liberal governments failed to resolve. The Versailles Treaty's failure to support Italy's territorial claims served only to exacerbate the country's crippling political and economic problems. A widespread belief gained ground that Italy's victory had been 'mutilated'. The subsequent rise to power of Mussolini was aided by the breakdown of the existing political system; both Giolitti's liberal government and the King, Victor Emmanuel III, lacked resolve, and the socialist camp was deeply divided.

Before the war, Mussolini had been on the far left of the socialist movement, which had supported Italian neutrality. In January 1919, he combined forces with the black-shirted *Arditi* (ex-servicemen who formed 'shock troops' armed with distinctive daggers), who supported the poet Gabriele D'Annunzio's illegal occupation of the Yugoslav port of Fiume. Having fallen out with the socialists over the question of Italian intervention in the war, Mussolini founded the Fascist party in 1919 with a radical and republican programme. In the summer of 1919 he circulated this programme in the form of a manifesto.

5.1 The original Fascist party programme, 1919

1   A Constituent National Assembly will proceed, as the Italian Section of the Constituent International Assembly of the peoples, to a radical transformation of the political and economic bases of the life of the community.
2   Proclamation of the Italian Republic. Decentralization of the executive power; autonomous administration of the regions and communes entrusted to their respective legislative organization. Sovereignty of the people, exercised by universal suffrage of all citizens of the two sexes; the people retaining the initiative of referendum and veto.
3   Abolition of the Senate. Abolition of the political police. The Magistrature to be elected independently of the executive power.
4   Abolition of all titles of nobility and all orders of knighthood.
5   Abolition of obligatory military service.
6   Liberty of opinion and conscience, of religion, of assembly, of the press.
7   A system of education in the schools, common and professional, open to all.
8   The greatest attention to social hygiene.
9   Suppression of incorporated joint stock companies, industrial or financial. Suppression of all speculation by banks and stock exchanges.
10 Control and taxation of private wealth. Confiscation of unproductive income.

11 Prohibition of work of children under the age of sixteen. An eight-hour work day.

12 Reorganization of production on a co-operative basis and direct participation of the workers in the profits.

13 Abolition of secret diplomacy.

14 An international policy based on the solidarity of the peoples and on their individual independence within the framework of a federation of States.

Source: Quoted in Count Carlo Sforza, *Contemporary Italy* (London, 1946), p. 244

As Mussolini was formulating this manifesto, he cemented his links with the *Arditi* by establishing the *fasci di combattimento* (combat action groups). The word *fasces* refers to the bundle of rods with a protruding axe which symbolised the authority and power of the Roman consuls. The term had a long tradition in Italian political life and had strong insurrectionary and left-wing overtones. The first fascist programme is of interest for the light its sheds on Mussolini's thinking during this period. Many of the demands are strongly nationalist and radical; it certainly represented a strong challenge to liberalism and the interests of the ruling class. The programme called for a republic, decentralisation of power to the regions and universal suffrage. There is also a call for the confiscation of war profits ('unproductive income'), which proved particularly popular with the working class. The programme was also anti-monarchist and anti-clerical, and in some respects posed a greater threat to the socialists than to the liberal parties.

Although Mussolini could not point to any firm political support in 1919 (he was humiliatingly defeated in elections in November), the programme, nevertheless, represented an attempt to lead revolutionary forces into the nationalist camp, thereby preventing any possible repeat of a Bolshevik-type revolution. The historian, Ernst Nolte, has talked about 'the origin of the Right' always lying 'in the challenge of the Left'. Fascism in Italy began to transform itself into a mass-movement when it took on a paramilitary character and attacked the socialists. By focusing on the threat posed (imagined or otherwise) by communism, the Fascists unquestionably tapped a latent fear on the part of many sections of Italian society. Above all, they offered the prospect of dynamic action in contrast to the inertia of parliamentary politics. However, by the time the Fascists gained power, the movement was largely middle-class and bourgeois.

In May 1920, in a new programme ('Postulates of the Fascist Programme'), Mussolini softened some of the more radical demands for reasons of expediency. He began to make conciliatory advances to the Roman Catholic Church and announced that he had also given up his republican ambitions, thus allowing the King to support him and his party. In fact, even after Mussolini came to power, very little of the original programme was implemented. What did remain was the sense of patriotic nationalism (fuelled by Versailles) and the notion of a corporate state (controlled by the Fascists) spearheading economic advancement and social reform.

The socialists for their part, were in disarray, and an attempted general strike called for July 1922 failed disastrously. This played into the hands of the Fascists, who announced that if the coalition government was unable to restore law and order then they would. Posing as the saviour of the state from communism, Mussolini felt confident enough in October 1922 to launch his famous 'march on Rome', when some 50,000 Blackshirts began to converge on the Italian capital. Although the Prime Minister (Luigi Facta) was prepared to resist, King Victor Emmanuel III refused to declare a state of emergency and instead *invited* Mussolini (who had remained in Milan!) to form a new government. Mussolini's first speech as Prime Minister of a Fascist-dominated coalition is set out as Document 5.2.

5.2 Mussolini's first speech as Prime Minister to the Chamber of Deputies, 16 November 1922

GENTLEMEN! What I am doing now in this hall is an act of formal deference to you, for which I ask no special sign of gratitude. ...

To the melancholy zealots of super-constitutionalism I shall leave the task of making their more or less pitiful lamentations about recent events. For my part, I insist that revolution has its rights. And so that everyone may know, I should like to add that I am here to defend and enforce in the highest degree the Blackshirts' revolution, and to inject it into the history of the nation as a force for development, progress, and equilibrium. [*Lively applause from the right.*]

I could have abused my victory, but I refused to do so. I imposed limits on myself. I told myself that the better wisdom is that which does not lose control of itself after victory. With 300,000 youths armed to the teeth, fully determined and almost mystically ready to act on any command of mine, I could have punished all those who defamed and tried to sully Fascism. [*Approval from the right.*] I could have transformed this drab, silent hall into a bivouac for my squads. ... [*Loud applause from the right; noise, comments; Modigliani:* 'Long live Parliament! Long live Parliament!' *Noise and shouts from the right; applause from the extreme left.*] ... I could have barred the doors of Parliament and formed a government exclusively of Fascists. I could have done so; but I chose not to, at least not for the present.

Our enemies have held on to their hiding places; and they have emerged from them without trouble and have enjoyed freedom of movement. And already they are profiting from this by spitting out poison again. ...

I have formed a coalition government, not indeed with the object of obtaining a parliamentary majority – which I can now get along very well without [*applause from the extreme right and extreme left; comments*] – but in order to rally to the support of this suffocating nation all those who, regardless of nuances of party, wish to save this nation.

From the bottom of my heart I thank my collaborators, ministers, and undersecretaries. ... And I cannot help recalling with pleasure the attitude of the laboring masses of Italians who have strengthened the Fascist motto by both their active and passive solidarity.

I believe that I also express the thought of a large part of this assembly, and certainly the majority of the Italian people, when I pay warm homage to the Sovereign who refused to take part in futile, last-minute reactionary maneuvers, who averted civil war and allowed the new and impetuous Fascist current, springing from the war and inspired by victory, to flow into the weakened arteries of the parliamentary state. [*Shouts of 'Long live the King!' Ministers and many deputies rise to their feet for warm, prolonged applause.*]

Before attaining this position I was asked on all sides for a programme. Alas! It is not programmes that are lacking in Italy; it is the men and the willingness to apply the programmes. All the problems of Italian life, all of them I say, have been solved on paper. What is lacking is the will to translate them into fact. Today the Government represents this firm and decisive will.

What preoccupies us most, especially at this moment, is foreign policy. I shall not deal here with all the problems, for in this field too I prefer action to words.

The fundamental guidelines of our foreign policy are the following things. Treaties of peace, whether good or bad, must be carried out once they have been signed and ratified. A self-respecting state can have no other doctrine. [*Lively approval.*] But treaties are not eternal; they are not irreparable. They are chapters of history, not its epilogue. Execution of them is the acid test. If in executing them their absurdity becomes evident, this may be the new fact that leads to a re-examination of the signatories' respective positions. Thus, I shall place before the Parliament the Treaty of Rapallo, as well as the agreements of Santa Margherita that derive from it.

... Let me now move on to establish another guideline of our foreign policy – viz., the repudiation of all 'revisionist' ideological smoke screens.

We agree that there is a kind of unity, or better yet, an inter-dependence in Europe's economic life. We agree that this economy must be reconstructed, but we deny that the methods hitherto adopted are working toward this end.

For the purpose of European economic reconstruction, bilateral commercial accords, based on the broadest kind of economic relations among peoples, are worth more than the bureaucratic and confused plenary conferences whose sad history everybody knows. As far as Italy is concerned, we intend to follow a policy of dignity and national self-interest. [*Lively approval from the right.*] ...

We do not indulge in the bad taste of exaggerating our power. But neither do we intend by excessive and false modesty to minimize it. My formula is simple: nothing for nothing. Whoever wants to have concrete evidence from us of friendship must also give us concrete evidence of friendship. [*Approval from the right.*]

Just as Fascist Italy has no intention of tearing up the peace treaties, so, for political, economic, and moral reasons, she also has no intention of abandoning her wartime allies. Rome is on the side of Paris and London, but Italy must show the Allies that it is embarking upon a courageous and severe examination of conscience such as has not been faced from the armistice to the present. [*Lively approval.*]

Does an Entente, in the real meaning of the word, still exist? What is the

Entente's position toward Germany, toward Russia, toward a Russo-German alliance? What is Italy's position in the Entente? ...

In the talks that I shall undertake with the prime ministers of France and England, I intend to face clearly the whole complex problem of the Entente and the resulting problem of Italy's position within the Entente. [*Lively applause.*]

... Either the Entente heals up its internal ills and contradictions and becomes a truly homogeneous bloc that is balanced and equal in strength, and with equal rights and equal duties; or else its end will have come, and Italy, resuming her freedom of action, will loyally adopt another policy that will safeguard her interests. [*Lively approval.*]

I hope that the first alternative takes place – for many reasons, including the outbreak of new turbulence throughout the Eastern world and the growing intimacy among the Russians, Turks, and Germans. But in order for that to be, it is necessary once for all to get away from hackneyed phrases. ...

A foreign policy such as ours – a policy of national self-interest, of respect for treaties, of equitable clarification of Italy's position within the Entente – cannot be passed off as adventurous or imperialistic in the vulgar sense of the word. We wish to pursue a policy of peace; but not one of suicide. ...

As for the economic and financial problem, Italy will argue at the forthcoming Brussels meeting that war debts and reparations are indivisible. For this policy of dignity and national well-being we must have in the [Ministry of Foreign Affairs] both central and subsidiary agencies that are adequate for the new needs of national life and the growing prestige of Italy in the world.

The guidelines of our domestic policy may be summarized in these words: economy, labor, discipline. The financial problem is basic. It is imperative to balance the budget with the greatest possible speed. We shall pursue a regime of austerity; we shall spend wisely; we shall assist all the productive forces of the nation; we shall put an end to all restrictions remaining from the war. [*Lively approval.*] ...

Whoever uses the word 'labor' means the productive bourgeoisie and the urban and rural working classes. We believe in no special privileges for the former, and none for the latter; but rather the safeguarding of the interests of all, so that they may be harmonized with those of production and of the entire nation. [*Loud applause.*]

The working proletariat, with whose status we are concerned, though not with demagogic or blameworthy indulgence, has nothing to fear and nothing to lose, but everything to gain from a financial policy that preserves the solvency of the state and prevents that bankruptcy that could make itself felt in a disastrous way, especially among the poorest strata of the population. ... The Italian citizen who emigrates must know that he will be carefully looked after by this nation's representatives abroad.

The increase of a nation's prestige in the world is proportionate to the discipline that the country displays at home. There is no doubt but that the domestic situation has improved, but not as much as I should like. ... The large cities and, in general, all our cities are calm; acts of violence are sporadic and peripheral, but they must come to an end. All citizens, regardless of party, must be able to move about freely.

All religious beliefs must be respected, with particular consideration for the dominant one, Catholicism. Fundamental freedoms must not be impaired; respect for the law must be exacted at whatever cost. The state is strong, and it intends to show its strength against everyone, even against any eventual Fascist illegality, for this would be an irresponsible and impure illegality wholly lacking in justification. [*Lively applause.*] I must add, however, that nearly all Fascists have given complete support to the new order of things. ... The state does not intend to abdicate its authority before anyone. Whoever defies the state will be punished. This explicit warning is addressed to all citizens. ... Since it is clear that sermons are not enough, the state will undertake to prune and perfect the armed forces that guard it ...

We ask for full powers because we wish to assume full responsibility. ... We propose to give discipline to the nation. ... Let none of our adversaries ... deceive themselves as to our stay in power. ... May God help me bring my arduous task to a victorious end!

Source: C.F. Delzell (ed.), *Mediterranean Fascism 1919–45* (London, 1971), pp. 45–51
(reprinted by permission of Macmillan Ltd)

This is a speech of two halves; the first is a conciliatory attempt to bring the nation together; the concluding section is very much a signal of intent. Remember that, despite the dramatic events and the propaganda value of the 'march on Rome', Mussolini assumed power constitutionally, and his first speech as Prime Minister suggested that he was prepared (at least in the first instance) to work within the parliamentary system, provided he is given 'full powers'. The speech began with a defiant defence of what Mussolini referred to as the 'Blackshirts' revolution' and his intention not to 'abuse' his victory, but to 'inject it into the history of the nation as a force for development, progress, and equilibrium'. Although the speech contained some ominous undertones ('300,000 youth armed to the teeth'), Mussolini claimed that he could have formed a government exclusively of Fascists, but chose instead a coalition in order to 'rally to the support of this suffocating nation'. The King was also warmly praised for 'averting' a civil-war, and (later in the speech) 'All religious beliefs must be respected', particularly Catholicism. Mussolini appeared to be already distancing himself from the radicalism of the Fascist party's 1919 programme.

Having shown himself to be a responsible politician and professed loyalty to the King and the constitution, Mussolini's next objective was to win over the nationalists. This he did by emphasising the importance of a strong foreign policy ('we intend to follow a policy of dignity and national self-interest'). Mussolini also referred to Italy's pre-war alliance with the Entente powers ('What is the Entente's position toward Germany, toward Russia, toward a Russo-German alliance?'). The Treaty of Rapallo whereby Italy dropped its claim to Dalmatia in favour of good relations with Yugoslavia, was also referred to. The speech concluded with an analysis of domestic policy that is summarised in the words 'economy, labor, discipline'. The key statement (earlier in the speech) is 'Today the Government represents … firm and decisive will'; but there is an ominous warning that 'Whoever defies the state will be punished.' It is in this spirit that Mussolini demanded 'full powers, because we wish to assume full responsibility'.

Steps to dictatorship

Although for the next two years Mussolini would maintain some semblance of constitutional legality, he was intent on consolidating his own position and eliminating all opponents. One of the means of achieving this was to recognise officially the paramilitary Blackshirt action squads that had helped him gain power. Accordingly Mussolini created a permanent fascist militia by means of the following Royal Decree.

5.3 Decree establishing the Fascist militia (MVSN), 14 January 1923

Art. 1: The Voluntary Militia for National Security is hereby established.

Art. 2: The Militia for National Security will serve God and the Italian fatherland, and will be under the orders of the Head of the Government. With the help of the Armed Corps of Public Security and the Royal Army, it will be responsible for maintaining public order within the nation; and it will train and organize citizens for the defense of Italy's interests in the world.

Art. 3: Recruitment will be voluntary, and all men between the ages of seventeen and fifty who apply may be admitted … , provided that in the judgment of the president of the Council of Ministers or of the hierarchical authorities designated by him they possess the physical and moral prerequisites.

Art. 4: Organic and disciplinary norms for the formation and operation of the Militia will be established by special regulations, to be prepared in harmony with existing laws by the president of the council. …

Art. 5: Nomination of officers and their promotion will be effected by royal decree upon recommendation of the Ministers of Interior and War.

Art. 6: The Militia for National Security offers its services free of charge. The state will pay for service performed outside the corps' commune of residence.

Art. 7: In case of partial or full mobilization of either the Army or the Navy, the Fascist Militia is to be absorbed by the Army and Navy, and in accordance with the obligations and military grades of its various members.

Art. 8: Expenses for establishment and operation of the Militia for National Security are to be charged to the budget of the Ministry of Interior.

Art. 9: All parties whatsoever shall be forbidden to have formations of a military character after the present decree goes into effect. Violators will be subject to punishment by law.

Art. 10: The present decree will be presented to Parliament for enactment into law and will go into force on February 1, 1923.

Source: Royal Decree no. 31, 14 January 1923, *Gazzetta Ufficiale del Regno,* **no. 16, 20 January 1923; quoted in C.F. Delzell (ed.)** *Mediterranean Fascism 1919–45,* **(London, 1971) pp. 52–3 (reprinted by permission of Macmillan Ltd)**

A major feature of the fascist dictatorships was the way in which they exploited political violence, while proclaiming their loyalty to constitutional legality. The decree establishing the Voluntary Militia for National Security (MVSN) went a long way in creating such a facade ('it will train and organize citizens for the defense of Italy's interests in the world'). The wording of the legislation appeared to suggest that the MVSN would swear allegiance to the King, whereas in reality it was separate from the armed forces and therefore under the control of Mussolini and the Fascist party, although paid by the state. One of the important features of twentieth-century dictatorships that distinguished them from previous autocratic regimes was the widespread use of paramilitary organisations that readily resorted to violence against their own people in order to sustain the one-party totalitarian state.

Not surprisingly, the use of political violence to suppress the opposition continued unabated after the MVSN had been established. In April 1924 elections were held amidst considerable intimidation from the MVSN, and the Fascists emerged with 65 per cent of the vote. Under the 'Acerbo Law' (1923) the party that gained the largest number of votes gained two-thirds of the seats in the Chamber. After the nature of the fascist victory was exposed in parliament by the outspoken socialist deputy, Giacomo Matteotti, he was abducted and murdered. His murder provoked public outrage and Mussolini even considered resignation. However, he was persuaded to adopt a hard line and between January 1925 and the middle of 1926 the foundations of a one-party totalitarian state were laid. Undoubtedly, the presence of the MVSN was a sustaining factor that enabled him to remain in power during this period of crisis.

An important aspect of Mussolini's consolidation of power was the use of propaganda. While the Italian Fascists recognised the importance of mass communications, they failed, in fact, systematically to co-ordinate their propaganda by means of a single ministry until 1937, when they followed the Nazi example and set up the Ministry of Popular Culture. Mussolini had been a journalist before he entered politics and regarded the press as the most important means of influencing public opinion. Censorship of the press was therefore the first measure that was introduced in July 1923. The decree regulating the press is set out in Document 5.4.

5.4 Decree regulating the press, 15 July 1923

Art. 1: In addition to the conditions prescribed by Articles 36 and 37 of the edict on the press dated March 26, 1848, the managing editor of a newspaper or other periodical publication must be either the director or one of the principal regular editors of this newspaper or publication, and he must obtain the recognition of the prefect of the province wherein the newspaper or publication is printed.

Senators and Deputies may not serve as managing editors. Anyone who has been sentenced on two occasions for crimes involving the press is ineligible to be managing editor, and he will lose this position if he has assumed it.

The decision of the prefect who refuses to recognize a managing editor must be based upon evidence. An appeal from this decision may be made to the Ministry of Interior. The decision of this minister may be appealed on legal grounds to the Fourth Section of the Council of State.

Art. 2: The prefect of a province is empowered, except where penal action prevents it, to address a warning to the managing editor of a newspaper or a periodical:

(a) If by means of false or tendentious news the newspaper or periodical impedes the diplomatic action of the Government in its foreign relations, or injures the national honor at home or abroad, or creates unjustifiable alarm in the population, or disturbs public order;

(b) If by means of articles, comments, notes, headlines, or illustrations it incites to crime or excites class hatred or disobedience to the laws and orders of public authorities, or compromises the discipline of public servants, or favors the interests of foreign states, societies, or individuals to the detriment of Italian interests, or holds up to opprobrium the King, the Royal Family, the Sovereign Pontiff, the religion of the state, or the institutions and organs of the state or of friendly powers.

This warning is to be issued by a decree resting upon evidence and in accordance with the recommendation of a committee that consists of the following people: a judge, who presides over it; a substitute for the King's procurator in the court of the locality or prefectural seat, appointed respectively by the first president and by the procurator general of the Court of Appeal; and a representative of the category of journalists, to be designated either by the local press association or, in its absence, by the president of the local tribunal. The committee will hold office for one year.

Art. 3: On the advice of the committee referred to above, the prefect may cancel the recognition of a managing editor who has received two warnings in one year.

The prefect may refuse to recognize a new managing editor whenever the previous one has been dismissed or condemned for any kind of press abuse twice in the space of two years to a penalty depriving him of his liberty for a period of six months or more; or whenever the newspapers or periodicals affected by the prefect's decisions have assumed new titles in order to continue their publication.

The decisions of the prefect are subject to the recourse set forth in Article 1.

Art. 4: Newspapers or other periodical publications printed in contravention of the previous regulations may be sequestered.

The sequestration is to be carried out by police authorities with no further need for special authorization.

Those who are guilty of abusive publication are to be punished in accordance with the laws in force. ...

Source: Royal Decree No. 3288, 15 July 1923, *Gazzetta Ufficiale*, no. 159, 18 July 1923; quoted in C.F. Delzell (ed.), *Mediterranean Fascism 1919–45* (London, 1971), pp. 53–6 (reprinted by permission of Macmillan Ltd)

As a result of this legislation, conditions were placed on those who wished to become editors. Moreover the responsibility for newspaper content now rested squarely with editors, whose freedom had been severely circumscribed. Under Article 2, newspapers could no longer publish 'false or tendentious news' or impede 'the diplomatic action of the Government' or create 'unjustifiable alarm in the population' or excite 'class hatred' or injure 'national honour'. The penalties for infringing the regulations governing newspaper content ranged from a warning to dismissal and finally the sequestration of a newspaper. By 1926 every newspaper in Italy required the permission of the government to continue publishing. Great newspapers like *La Stampa, Corriere della Sera* and *Il Messaggero* had their liberal-minded editors dismissed, and all criticism of the regime virtually ceased.

Having survived the Matteotti affair and muzzled the press, Mussolini embarked upon eliminating the remaining constitutional constraints imposed by parliament. In December 1925 legislation was passed which released Mussolini from parliamentary control, providing him with dictatorial power.

5.5 Decree on powers of the head of the government, 24 December 1925

Art. I: The executive power is exercised by His Majesty the King through his Government. The Government consists of the Prime Minister Secretary of State and the Ministers Secretaries of State.

The Prime Minister is the Head of the Government.

Art. II: The Head of the Government, who is Prime Minister and Secretary of State, is appointed and dismissed by the King, and is responsible to the King for the general policy of the Government.

The decree appointing the Head of the Government Prime Minister is countersigned by himself, and that of his dismissal by his successor.

The Ministers Secretaries of State are appointed and dismissed by the King upon proposal of the Head of the Government Prime Minister. They are responsible to the King and to the Head of the Government for all the acts and measures enforced by their Ministries.

The Undersecretaries of State are appointed and dismissed by the King upon the proposal of the Head of the Government in agreement with the Minister concerned.

Art. III: The Head of the Government Prime Minister directs and co-ordinates the work of the Ministers, decides whatever differences may arise among them, calls meetings of the Council of Ministers, and presides over them.

Art. IV: The number, constitution, and responsibilities of the Ministers are established by royal decree, upon proposal of the Head of the Government.

The Head of the Government may be entrusted by royal decree with the direction of one or more Ministries. In such cases, the Head of the Government by his own decree may delegate to the Undersecretaries of State a share of the responsibilities of the Minister.

Art. V: The Head of the Government is a member of the council for the guardianship of members of the Royal Family, and exercises the function of Notary of the Crown.

He is, furthermore, by right, Secretary of the Supreme Order of the Holy Annunciation.

Art. VI: No bill or motion may be placed on the agenda of either of the two Chambers without the consent of the Head of the Government.

The Head of the Government is empowered to request that a bill, rejected by one of the two Chambers, shall again be voted upon when at least three months have elapsed since the first vote. In such cases the bill is voted upon by secret ballot, without previous debate.

When, in submitting the bill for a second vote, the Government also submits amendments to the bill, there may be debate only upon the amendments, after which the bill will be voted upon by secret ballot.

The Head of the Government is also empowered to request that a bill, if rejected by one of the Chambers, be equally submitted to the other Chamber and voted upon, after due examination.

When a bill already passed by one Chamber is passed by the other with amendments, the debate in the Chamber to which it is submitted a second time is limited to the amendments, after which the vote on the measure will be by secret ballot.

Art. VII: The Head of the Government, during his tenure of office, takes precedence over the Knights of the Supreme Order of the Holy Annunciation at public functions and ceremonies.

He will receive from the State Treasury an annual appropriation to cover the expenses of his office, the sum being fixed by royal decree.

Art.VIII: The Head of the Government may designate from time to time the Minister who will substitute for him in case of absence or impediment; this designation is made separately for each given case.

Art. IX: Whosoever makes an attempt against the life, safety, or personal freedom of the Head of the Government is to be punished by a term of imprisonment of not less than fifteen years, and by life imprisonment if he succeeds in his attempt.

Whosoever offends the Head of the Government in words or deeds is to be punished by imprisonment or detention from six to thirty months, and by a fine of from 500 to 3,000 lire.*

Art. X: All regulations contrary to the present law are abrogated.

Source: Law No. 2263, 24 December 1925, 'Attributions and prerogatives of the Head of the Government Prime Minister Secretary of State', *Gazzetta Ufficiale del Regno,* **no. 301, 29 December 1925; quoted in C.F. Delzell (ed.),** *Mediterranean Fascism 1919–45,* **pp. 62–4 (reprinted by permission of Macmillan Ltd)**

This new legislation (outlined the day before Christmas!) set out the increased power of the Prime Minister (Mussolini) who was made Head of State. Although, under Article I, executive power was still nominally exercised through the King, it was Mussolini who gained from these new measures, as he alone was empowered to appoint and dismiss ministers. Article VI is particularly revealing, for it states that no bill can be discussed by Parliament 'without the consent of the Head of Government'. In other words, Mussolini could now prevent all political debate in Parliament.

How were the Fascists allowed to implement these totalitarian measures unchallenged, and what were the reactions of the King and parliament? Victor Emmanuel was reluctant to oppose the regime so long as it appeared strong enough to threaten the House of Savoy. As far as parliament was concerned, the repression of political dissidents certainly acted as a deterrent. It is estimated that 3,000 opponents were sentenced by the Fascist Special Council between 1926 and 1943 and over 10,000 dissidents were banished to remote areas.

In January 1926, legislation was passed which removed the need for parliamentary approval of legislation, and in December 1928 the parliamentary system was replaced by the Fascist Grand Council, which put the finishing

---

*   Modified by Law no. 2008, 25 November 1926, regarding 'Measures for the Defence of the State'. Article 1 of this latter law declared: 'Whosoever makes attempts against the life, safety or personal freedom of the King or the Regent is to be punished by death. The same applies if the attempt be made against the life, safety, or personal freedom of the Queen, the Crown Prince, or the Head of the Government.'

touches to the dictatorship and gave the Fascist party total political control. Mussolini claimed that through the Fascist Grand Council the people's views would be more accurately represented than in an elected assembly. In reality, the establishment of a *constitutional* dictatorship, meant that political power now resided with Mussolini and the party.

5.6 Establishment of the Fascist Grand Council, 9 December 1928

LAW RESPECTING THE CONSTITUTION AND FUNCTIONS OF THE GRAND COUNCIL OF FASCISM, 9 DECEMBER 1928

1   The Fascist Grand Council is the supreme organ which co-ordinates all the activities of the régime which emerged from the revolution of October 1922. It has deliberative functions in the cases determined by law, and, furthermore, gives opinions on any other political, economic or social question of national interest which may be put to it by the Head of the Government.

2   The Head of the Government, Prime Minister Secretary of State, is by right President of the Fascist Grand Council. He may summon it whenever he deems it necessary. ...

3   The Secretary of the National Fascist Party is also Secretary of the Grand Council. ...

5   The following are members of the Grand Council by reason of their duties, and for the entire duration of these duties:

   (1) The Presidents of the Senate and of the Chamber of Deputies.
   (2) The Ministers ...
   (3) The Under-Secretary of State to the President of the Council.
   (4) The Commandant-General of the Volunteer Militia for National Security.
   (5) The members of the Directorate of the National Fascist Party.
   (6) The Presidents of the Italian Academy and of the Fascist Cultural Institute.
   (7) The President of the National Balilla Organization.
   (8) The President of the Special Tribunal for the Defence of the State.
   (9) The Presidents of the National Fascist Confederations of Syndicates legally recognized.
   (10) The President of the National Co-Operative Organization. ...

11 The Grand Council takes decisions:

   (1) Upon the list of deputies ... .
   (2) Upon the statutes, orders and policy of the National Fascist Party.
   (3) Upon the appointment and dismissal of the ... members of the Directorate of the National Fascist Party.

12   The views of the Grand Council must be ascertained on all questions of a constitutional character:

(1)   The succession to the Throne, the powers and the prerogatives of the King.

(2)   The composition and functioning of the Grand Council, the Senate of the Kingdom and the Chamber of Deputies.

(3)   The attributes and prerogatives of the Head of Government. ...

(4)   The faculty of the Executive Power to issue juridical regulations.

(5)   The organization of the syndicates and corporations.

(6)   The relations between the State and the Holy See.

(7)   International treaties involving modifications of the territory of the State and the colonies, or renunciation of territorial acquisitions.

Source: *British and Foreign State Papers,* vol. cxxix (London, 1928), part 2, pp. 757–60, also quoted in G.A. Kertesz (ed.), *Documents in the Political History of the European Continent 1815–1939* (Oxford, 1968), pp. 396–7

Under Article 1, the Fascist Grand Council was in theory the supreme policy-making body of the Fascist Party. By means of this legislation, Italy became a one-party state. The Grand Council was now transformed from an organ of the party to an organ of the state, with wide-ranging powers (Article 11). In practice, it became little more than a 'rubber-stamp' for decisions that had already been taken by Mussolini. Its composition is set out in Articles 5 and 12, further diminishing the prerogatives of the King by assuming responsibility for the succession to the throne. This weakened Victor Emmanuel's position because the Grand Council could now replace him constitutionally with a more sympathetic sovereign.

Fascist propaganda and the corporative state

Propaganda also played an important role in the projection of the leader-figure in Fascist Italy. At the head of all fascist regimes stands a charismatic leader embodying the nation's will and aspirations. Italian propaganda depicted 'Il Duce' as a protean superman whose powers were unlimited. Mussolini was well aware of the importance of this role and played up to such an image. Documents 5.7 and 5.8 are two examples of the manner in which Mussolini was presented to different sections of the population.

5.7 Mussolini as depicted on a school textbook cover, undated

Source: A. Rhodes, *Propaganda: The Art of Persuasion in World War II*
(London, 1976), p. 71

Document 5.7 is a cover of an ordinary school textbook for young children. It states; 'Benito Mussolini loves children very much. Long live the Duce! I salute the Duce. To us!' The image of Mussolini presented here is of a stern but kindly father figure. It is interesting that Mussolini is not wearing his military uniform and that even young children were encouraged to refer to him as Il Duce. Fascist governments attempted to teach schoolchildren qualities of obedience and devotion to their leaders. When the Fascists took office in Italy they immediately reformed the school and university curricula, emphasising Italy's role in world affairs, the importance of strong leadership and the need for discipline and sacrifice.

Fascism claimed to be a movement of youth and correspondingly established a multiplicity of organisations for every age group. For children under the age of eight there was the Order of the Wolf, while those between eight and thirteen joined the *Balilla* and then moved on to the *Avanguardisti* until the age of nineteen, when they could belong to the Young Fascists. After twenty-one they were then eligible for admission into the party. These youth movements indoctrinated Italian youth and were compulsory, serving to qualify young people for eventual membership in the party. The emphasis on military values, comradeship and obedience also trained them for national service.

5.8 Mussolini in typical pose: 'Believe, Obey, Fight', a poster of 1938 (see p. 111)

Document 5.8 is a 1938 poster issued by the *fasci di combattimento* (combat action groups), who had been closely associated with Mussolini since the founding of the Fascist party. Mussolini is shown in a typically strutting pose, standing on a wall, addressing a mass rally, the symbol of the *fasci* axes protruding on either side. Il Duce is in formal fascist paramilitary uniform. This bombastic pose was struck in countless newsreels and photographs and at rallies – chin and stomach out, arm outstretched. Official posters like this, together with film propaganda, embodied the Fascists' own image of themselves. Fascism demanded authority from above, obedience from below and this is expressed in the Italian formula: 'Believe, Obey, Fight'. When the Ministry of Popular Culture (*Miniculpop*) was established in June 1937, the Italian Fascists were finally able to co-ordinate all the means of communication and disseminate propaganda tightly controlled by the party. Radio, cinema, press, theatre, literature and art were systematically employed to disseminate themes and images that reflected Fascist ideology and policy.

Central to this ideology was the corporative system that by February 1934 had introduced twenty-two official corporations (or 'cycles' of economic activity) representing professional and commercial groups with the aim of harmonising the interests of capital and labour with the all-embracing interests of the state. The influence of syndicalism as espoused by George Sorel at the turn of the

Source: Welch Collection, Canterbury

century can be found in Mussolini's much trumpeted economic doctrine. Trade unions were abolished and strikes and lock-outs prohibited; the state arbitrated between labour and capital by means of the new Labour Courts, and a Charter of Labour (1927) set out as Document 5.9, established the structure for collective contracts.

5.9 The Charter of Labour, 21 April 1927

THE CORPORATIVE STATE AND ITS ORGANIZATION

1. The Italian nation is an organism with objects, life and means of action superior in power and duration to those of the individuals or groups which compose it. It is a moral, political and economic unit which is integrally realized in the Fascist State.

2. Labour in all its organized and executive forms, intellectual, technical and manual, is a social duty. In this aspect, and in this aspect alone, it is under the protection of the State.

Production as a whole is a unit from the national point of view; its objectives are single and are summed up in the welfare of individuals and the development of the national power.

3. Syndical or professional organization is free. But only the syndicate which is legally recognized and subject to the control of the State has the right legally to represent the entire category of employers or workers for which it is constituted, to protect their interests as against the State and other professional associations, to conclude collective labour contracts binding upon all belongings to the category, to impose contributions upon them and to exercise in respect of them delegated functions of public interest.

4. In the collective labour contract the solidarity between the various factors of production finds its concrete expression, through the conciliation of the opposing interests of employers and workers and their subordination to the higher interests of production.

5. The Labour Magistracy is the organ by which the State intervenes to settle labour disputes, whether they turn upon the observance of agreements and of other existing regulations, or upon the establishment of new conditions of labour.

6. The legally recognized professional associations assure the juridical equality of employers and workers, maintain discipline in production and labour and promote their improvement.

The corporations form the unitary organization of the forces of production and integrally represent their interests.

In virtue of this integral representation, the interests of production being national interests, the corporations are recognized by law as organs of the State.

As representatives of the unitary interests of production, the corporations may issue regulations of an obligatory character governing labour relationships, and also on the co-ordination of production whenever they have had the necessary powers to that end from the component associations.

7. The corporative State considers private initiative in the field of production to be the most effective and most useful instrument in the national interest ...

9. The intervention of the State in economic production takes place only when

private initiative is lacking or is insufficient or when the political interests of the State are involved. Such intervention may take the form of control, encouragement and direct management.

10. In collective labour disputes judicial action may not be initiated unless the corporative organ has first made an attempt at conciliation ...

COLLECTIVE LABOUR CONTRACTS AND LABOUR GUARANTEES

11. The professional associations are obliged to regulate, by means of collective contracts, labour relations between the categories of employers and workers whom they represent ...

12. The action of the syndicate, the work of conciliation of the corporative organs and the decision of the Labour Magistracy guarantee the equivalence of wages to the normal requirements of life, the possibilities of production and the yield of the labour.

The decision of wages is withdrawn from the scope of any general regulation and is entrusted to agreements between the parties in collective contracts ...

15. The worker has the right to a weekly day of rest, falling on Sunday ...

16. After one year of uninterrupted service the worker, in undertakings which operate continuously, has the right to an annual period of holiday with pay ...

19. Breaches of discipline and acts which disturb the normal functioning of the business, committed by workers, shall be punished, according to the gravity of the offence, by fine, suspension from work, and, in serious cases, by immediate dismissal without indemnity ...

LABOUR EXCHANGES

22. The State alone ascertains and controls the phenomenon of employment and unemployment, the comprehensive index of the conditions of production and labour.

23. The Labour Exchanges are constituted on the basis of parity under the control of the corporative organs of the State. Employers must engage workmen through these offices. They have the privilege of selection within the limits of the persons enrolled in the registers of the Exchange, giving preference to members of the Fascist party and of the Fascist syndicates according to their seniority on the lists ...

WELFARE, ASSISTANCE, EDUCATION AND INSTRUCTION

26. Social measures are a further manifestation of the principle of collaboration towards which employers and employees must contribute proportionately. The

State, through the corporative organs and professional associations, will endeavour as far as possible to co-ordinate and unify the system and institutions providing for welfare work.

27. The Fascist State proposes to accomplish:

(1) The improvement of accident insurance.
(2) The improvement and extension of maternity insurance.
(3) Insurance against occupational illnesses and tuberculosis as the first step towards general insurance against all illness.
(4) Improvement of insurance against involuntary unemployment.
(5) The adoption of special endowment insurance for young workers …

Source: *British and Foreign State Papers*, vol. cxxvii (London, 1927) part 2, pp. 756–61, also quoted in G.A. Kertesz (ed.), *Documents in the Political History of the European Continent 1815–1939* (Oxford, 1968), pp. 393–6

Document 5.9 is important, for it embodies the philosophical principles of the corporative state. It sets out thirty measures by which the Italian state intended to achieve industrial peace and protect its economic interests (only a selection are included in this extract). These included extra pay for unsociable hours (Article 14), an annual holiday with pay (Article 16) and an extension of various welfare measures for workers (Article 27). April 21 was also significant, for it became the Fascist Labour Day.

At first glance the Charter of Labour appears to lay the foundations of the corporative state. However, the concessions made to industrialists made a mockery of the fascist claim that the state would play the role of arbiter between capital and labour. The Charter was therefore a propaganda exercise, an attempt to compensate workers for the loss of their old rights to join trades unions and undertake strike action. Under the guise of the corporative state, the regime went beyond the purely economic sphere and increasingly used state interventionsim as a (new) form of social and political control. The example of the Labour Charter was widely copied in other fascist states, including Spain and Portugal.

Having established industrial peace at the expense of workers' rights, the Italian Fascists continued to make great play of their alleged economic successes. Improvements in road and rail communications, the increase in electricity supply and the draining of the Pontine Marshes to reclaim land in the 'battle for grain' all made excellent propaganda as examples of fascist forward planning. Document 5.10 is a propaganda poster proclaiming the achievements of the 'battle for grain'.

5.10 'The Battle for Grain', a poster of 1928

Source: Salce Collection, Trevino

The poster is used here to extol the achievements of agricultural workers in increasing annual yields of wheat production and to encourage them to even greater efforts. In the top left-hand corner, below the symbol of the *fasci*, the poster stated that 1,500,000 lire worth of prizes are offered for greater yields. Below the smiling faces of the two peasants with their bundles of wheat, the poster announced a national competition – 'The Battle for Grain', to be sponsored by the government – and it urged agricultural workers to apply to their nearest Agricultural Office.

The history behind such propaganda lay in the government's desire to achieve national self-sufficiency, especially in food production. Mussolini had initiated a campaign to increase the production of wheat by reclaiming land and intensively cultivating existing land. Whereas by 1935 Italy had succeeded in reducing wheat imports by 75 per cent, the per capita consumption of wheat was actually declining, and dairy farming was also suffering as a result of the resources allocated to the 'battle for grain'. Furthermore, unemployment and underemployment continued to plague the regime. By 1932 one and a quarter million were unemployed, and almost half the labour force was underemployed. Mussolini's response was to reduce both the working week (to spread out employment) and wages, which only served to exacerbate the deflationary trend. In fact, no conspicuous economic improvements were made under fascism, and the Italian economy continued to deteriorate throughout the 1930s.

The policy of autarky (economic self-sufficiency) proved, however, to be an important rallying-point for people of frustrated nationalist leanings. Some historians have argued that the Italian corporative state became a smoke-screen for an increasingly aggressive imperial foreign policy that culminated in 1935 with the invasion of Abyssinia. Although it was intended to divert attention from genuine domestic grievances, the Abyssinian war revealed just how fragile the economy really was, as Italy simply could not afford to sustain a long military campaign. It served also to put an end to any further genuine social and economic reforms.

From the time Mussolini came to power he was prepared to compromise with traditional forces in order to consolidate his own position. One of the major breaches in fascist theoretical principles was the concordat with the Vatican. The Roman Catholic Church could not be disciplined in the same way as the labour movement. The Church had supported the Fascists for their stance against socialism and as a strike-breaking force of the Right. This relationship culminated in 1929 in the signing of the Lateran Treaty and the Concordat (Documents 5.11a and 5.11b).

5.11a The Treaty of the Lateran, 11 February 1929

1. Italy recognizes and reaffirms the principle embodied in article 1 of the statute of the Kingdom dated the 4th March 1848 (cf. No. 86) according to which the Roman Catholic Apostolic religion is the sole religion of the State.

2. Italy recognizes the sovereignty of the Holy See in the international domain ...

3. Italy recognizes the full ownership and the exclusive and absolute dominion ... of the Holy See over the Vatican ...

4. The sovereignty and exclusive jurisdiction over the Vatican City, which Italy recognizes as appertaining to the Holy See, precludes any intervention therein on the part of the Italian Government and any authority other than that of the Holy See ...

8. Considering the person of the Supreme Pontiff as sacred and inviolable, Italy declares any attempt against the same, and any incitement to commit such an attempt, to be punishable with the same penalties as are prescribed in the case of an attempt ... against the person of the King ...

11. The central bodies of the Catholic Church shall be exempt from any interference on the part of the Italian State ...

25. By a special convention, signed at the same time as the present treaty ... provision is made for the liquidation of the sums due to the Holy See by Italy ...

26. ... The law dated 13 May 1871 (No. 115) and any other provisions contrary to the present treaty are abrogated ...

Source: *British and Foreign State Papers*, vol. cxxx (London, 1929), part 1, pp. 791–814

5.11b Concordat between the Holy See and Italy, 11 February 1929

1. In accordance with article 1 of the treaty (No. 180(a)), Italy shall assure to the Catholic Church the free exercise of spiritual power and the free and public exercise of worship, as well as of its jurisdiction in ecclesiastical matters ...

2. The Holy See shall communicate and correspond freely with the bishops, the clergy, and the whole Catholic world without any interference on the part of the Italian Government ...

5. No ecclesiastic may be engaged or remain in an employment or office of the Italian State or of public bodies subordinate thereto without the consent of the diocesan ordinary ...

19. The selection of archbishops and bishops shall appertain to the Holy See.
    Before proceeding to the appointment ... the Holy See shall communicate to the Italian Government the name of the person selected in order to ensure that the

latter have no objections of a political nature to such appointment ...

20. Before taking over their dioceses bishops shall take an oath of allegiance to the Head of the State ...

21. The bestowal of ecclesiastical benefices shall devolve upon the ecclesiastical authorities ...

34. Desiring to restore to the institution of marriage, which is the basis of the family, a dignity in conformity with the Catholic traditions of its people, the Italian State recognizes the civil effects of the sacrament of marriage as governed by canon law ... Actions for the nullity of marriage and the annulment of marriages solemnized but not consummated shall be reserved to the competence of ecclesiastical courts and departments. ... As regards suits for personal separation, the Holy See agrees that these shall be justifiable by the civil judicial authority ...

Source: *British and Foreign State Papers,* vol. cxxx (London, 1929), part 1, pp. 791–814

In order to appreciate the significance of the Lateran Treaty and the Concordat one has to realise that the Papacy had continued to disassociate itself from the Italian State since 1870 and the unification of Italy. In order to gain greater political prestige, Mussolini was prepared to grant to the Holy See large-scale concessions that successive liberal governments had refused to consider. Article 1 of the treaty recognised Roman Catholicism as 'the sole religion of the State', while Article 4 acknowledged the Vatican City as an independent state within a state. Article 11 guaranteed the Catholic Church from any 'interference on the part of the Italian State'. The Papacy was also provided with a large endowment by way of an indemnity for its losses during the unification period (Article 25). Moreover, as a result of the Concordat, the Church now regained control of such matters as marriage and divorce (Article 34). For its part, the Papacy, while clearly receiving far more than it gave, finally accepted the existence of Italy. Mussolini, on the other hand, could justifiably claim to have reconciled Church and State, whose differences had been a source of conflict that had bedevilled Italian politics since the *Risorgimento.*

The continued prominence of the Church in Italy, together with the preservation of the monarchy, has persuaded some historians to claim that Italian fascism was not as totalitarian as Nazism in Germany or Bolshevism in Russia. The Church, big business and the King all retained considerable power at the price of acquiescence to the façade of fascist principles. It is important to distinguish therefore between fascist theory, which purported to offer a radical alternative to capitalism, and its practice. While the idea of the fascist corporative state remained a genuine political innovation, containing elements of anarcho-syndi-calist ideas that had been associated with the 'radical' Mussolini during his early political career, in practice this anti-capitalist stance failed to deliver the judicial equality between employers and employed that the Charter of Labour (Document 5.9) had guaranteed. Instead, it degenerated into an assault on the rights of workers. Economically, fascism failed to solve Italy's problems. The deterioration in economic conditions at home only exacerbated the growing resentment at what was perceived as the over-reliance on Germany, the latter resulting in the Rome–Berlin Axis of 1936 and the military 'pact of steel' of May 1939. Mussolini's foreign policy became inexorably linked to the fortunes of German military prowess in the subsequent war.

The history of Italian fascism is therefore closely identified with the personality of its leader, Benito Mussolini, whose dominance began to recede only when the Allied forces landed in Sicily in July 1943. The successful Allied invasion of his country led directly to Mussolini's fall. Even sections of his own Fascist party recognised that an end to the war could be achieved only by removing Mussolini and negotiating a separate peace with the Allies. On 25 July 1943 the Fascist Grand Council, in a unique act of independence, recommended that the King should take over supreme power and Mussolini be dismissed. Neither the Fascist party nor the MVSN opposed this move. Mussolini's only remaining source of support was Hitler and the Nazi German leadership, who attempted briefly to reinstate him in power in northern Italy. On 28 April 1945, Mussolini was eventually caught by the Italian Resistance and shot. In an extraordinary reversal of popular feeling, his body, together with that of his mistress, was taken to Milan and publicly reviled in front of an hysterically abusive crowd. The Mussolini myth was finally at an end.

CHRONOLOGY: FASCIST ITALY, 1919–45

1919	23 March	*Fascio di combattimento* formed by Mussolini in Milan.
	2 September	Franchise extended and proportional representation introduced.
	12 September	The poet Gabriele D'Annunzio seizes Fiume.
	16 November	Socialists and Catholics receive strong support in the elections; fascists make only small gains.
1920	9 June	Giovanni Giolitti replaces Nitti as Prime Minister.
	31 August–September	Strikes and lockouts
	12 November	Treaty of Rapallo resolves disputes between Italy and Yugoslavia. Fiume to become an independent state.
1921	15 May	Gains for Liberals and Democrats at the elections.
	26 June	Giolitti resigns and is replaced by Bonomi.
1922	25 February	Luigi Facta heads new government.
	28 October	The Fascist 'March on Rome'.
	31 October	King Victor Emmanuel III requests Mussolini to form a cabinet.
1923	21 July	Electoral law passed, guaranteeing two-thirds of the seats in the Chamber to the majority party.
1924	6 April	Fascists win almost two-thirds of votes in election.
	30 May	Giacomo Matteotti launches attack on the Fascist government.

	10 June	Matteotti murdered. Non-fascists resign from Chambers and condemn violence.
	July	Press censorship introduced.
1925	2 October	Palazzo Vidoni pact between industrialists' association (*Confindustria*) and the fascist syndicates paving the way for syndicates to issue collective contracts.
	24 December	Mussolini assumes dictatorial powers.
1926	31 January	Government decrees given the power of law.
	3 April	Workers lose right to strike.
1927	21 December	Exchange rate fixed at 'quota 90' (92.45 Lire to £1).
1929	11 February	Lateran Treaties with Papacy creating the Vatican City as a sovereign independent state.
1935	3 October	Italian invasion of Abyssinia (Ethiopia).
1936	24 October	Rome–Berlin Axis formed.
1939	19 January	*Camera del Fascie delle Corporazioni* replaces parliament.
	7 April	Italian invasion of Albania.
	22 May	Hitler and Mussolini sign the Pact of Steel.
1940	10 June	Mussolini declares war and invades France.
1943	25 July	Grand Council of Fascism votes Mussolini out of office. Pietro Badoglio assumes control of the Italian government.
	23 September	Mussolini announces creation of fascist social republic of Salo.
1945	28 April	Mussolini shot by partisans on the shore of Lake Como. His corpse is taken to Milan and hung in the Piazzale Loreto.

BIBLIOGRAPHY

Sources and documents

The most comprehensive documentary collection is C. F. Delzell (ed.), *Mediterranean Fascism 1919–45* (1971), which also contains interesting material on Franco's Spain. See also J. Pollard's skilful analysis of a wide range of sources in *The Fascist Experience in Italy* (1998). *Count Ciano's Diaries, 1937–8* (1952) and *1939–43* (1947) provide an insight to the inner workings of the fascist regime but must be used with considerable scepticism. Documentation about opponents of the regime who were forced into exile and subsequently provided their own critique can be found in G. Salvemini, *The Fascist Dictatorship in Italy* (1928) and *Under the Axe of Fascism* (1936). For a moving, autobiographical, account of political banishment to a remote part of southern Italy, see C. Levi, *Christ Stopped at Eboli* (1982 edn).

Secondary works

General texts dealing with the rise of fascism include: F.L. Carsten, *The Rise of Fascism* (1967); W. Laqueur (ed.), *Fascism: A Reader's Guide* (1975); M. Kitchen, *Fascism* (1976); R. De Felice, *Interpretations of Fascism* (1977); and, more recently, R. Griffin (ed.), *Fascism* (1995) and R. Eatwell, *Fascism – A History* (1996). For a general background to Italian history see D. Mack Smith *Italy: A Modern History*

(1959); and R. Albrecht-Carrié, *Italy from Napoleon to Mussolini* (New York, 1950) – both are rather outdated now. For a modern study, see M. Clark, *Modern Italy, 1870–1995* (1996). A helpful short outline is provided by G. Carocci, *Italian Fascism* (1974) and M. Blinkhorn, *Mussolini and Fascist Italy* (1994); see also A. Lyttelton, *The Seizure of Power, 1919–29* (1973). P. Morgan, *Italian Fascism, 1919–1945* (1995) and J. Whittam, *Fascist Italy* (1995) are both excellent, up-to-date surveys.

On the pre-Fascist period C. Seton-Watson, *Italy from Liberalism to Fascism* (1967) is the standard work, but R. Bosworth, *Italy and the Approach of the First World War* (1983) analyses the strains in Italian society in the period before 1914 together with foreign policy issues. J.A. Davis, *Conflict of Control: Law and Order in the Making of Modern Italy* (1984) analyses internal control.

The rise and development of fascism is discussed in A. Lyttelton, *Italian Fascism from Pareto to Gentile* (1973) and, more recently, in P. Morgan, *Italian Fascism 1919–1945* (1995). On the Fascist period see E. Wiskemann, *Fascism in Italy* (1970); F. Chabod, *A History of Italian Fascism* (1961) provides a general political survey, whilst E.R. Tannenbaum, *Fascism in Italy, 1922–45* (1972) looks at social and cultural aspects. The process of assuming political control is looked at by R. Sarti, *The Axe Within: Italian Fascism in Action* (1974). Church–state relations are covered in A. Jemolo, *Church and State in Italy, 1850–1950* (1960) and R.A. Webster, *The Cross and the Fasces: Christian Democracy in Italy, 1860–1960* (1960).

Of the biographies of Mussolini, see C. Hibbert, *Benito Mussolini* (1962); L. Fermi, *Mussolini* (1961); C.C. Bayne-Jardine, *Mussolini and Italy* (1966); I. Kirkpatrick, *Mussolini* (1976); D. Mack Smith, *Mussolini's Roman Empire* (1977) and *Mussolini* (1982); and E.M. Robertson, *Mussolini as Empire Builder* (1977). E. Wiskemann, *The Rome–Berlin Axis* (1949) concentrates on the German alliance, as does F.W. Deakin, *The Brutal Friendship* (2 vols, 1966). The economic performance of fascist Italy is examined in W.G. Welk, *Fascist Economic Policy: An Analysis of Italy's Economic Experiment* (1938) and R. Sarti, *Fascism and Industrial Leadership in Italy, 1919–1940* (1971).

Comparative studies of fascist Italy and Nazi Germany are to be found in R. Bessel (ed.), *Fascist Italy and Nazi Germany: Comparisons and Contrasts* (1996) and A. de Grand, *Fascist Italy and Nazi Germany: 'The Fascist Style of Rule'* (1996).

Articles

The background to the rise of fascism in Italy is discussed in J.J. Roth, 'The Roots of Italian Fascism', *J.M.H.* (1967). A. Aquarone, 'Italy: The Crisis and the Corporate Economy', *J.C.H.* (1969) looks at the economic failures. For Mussolini viewed as a radical, see S. Woolf, 'Mussolini as Revolutionary', *J.C.H.* (1966). The role of intellectuals in fascist Italy is discussed in E.P. Noether, 'Italian Intellectuals under Fascism', *J.M.H.* (1971). The importance of agriculture is analysed by P. Cohen, 'Fascism and Agriculture in Italy', *E.H.R.* (1979). The importance of propaganda in the dissemination of the 'Duce-myth' is analysed in P. Melograni, 'The Cult of the Duce in Italy', *J.C.H.* (1978). Fascist foreign policy is analysed by S. Marks, 'Mussolini and Locarno: Fascist Foreign Policy in Macrocosm', *J.C.H.* (1979). For a critical overview see, A. de Grand, 'Cracks in the Façade: The Failure of Fascist Totalitarianism in Italy, 1935–39', *E.H.R.* (1991).

6

Nazi Germany

Although fascism first manifested itself in Italy, it is Nazi Germany that is usually referred to as the textbook totalitarian state. The rise and fall of National Socialism is understandably one of the most closely studied issues in modern European history. Historians have been at great pains to explain why millions of Germans voted for the Nazi party in free elections and how such a regime could eventually acquire such an extensive European empire; five decades after the collapse of the Third Reich, fundamental disagreements about interpreting Nazism still exist. The popular image of German society under Nazi rule is a confusing one, ranging from the adoration of crowds surrounding Adolf Hitler, to the bestiality of the concentration camps and fear of the Gestapo. It is a picture that raises questions crucial to our understanding of National Socialism. What, for example, were the respective roles of consent and coercion in sustaining the regime, and what was the nature of that consent? Behind the facade of national unity was there any dissent or even 'resistance', and, if so, was it terror alone that rendered it so ineffectual?

Hitler and early Nazism

Like the Fascist party in Italy, the Nazis started their political life as a radical party opposed to both the Versailles Treaty (although for different reasons) and the prevailing parliamentary system. Indeed, there are numerous similarities between the rise of fascism in Italy and that of National Socialism in Germany. Document 6.1 is the first Nazi party programme, which was officially announced in Munich on 24 February 1920:

6.1 The first Nazi party programme, 24 February 1920

BASIC PROGRAMME OF THE NATIONAL SOCIALIST GERMAN WORKERS' PARTY

The programme of the German Workers' Party is a programme of the times. The leaders reject the idea of setting new goals after the initial aims laid down in the programme have been achieved simply in order to ensure the continued existence of the party by artificially increasing unrest amongst the masses.

1. We demand the uniting together of all Germans, on the basis of the people's right of self-determination, in a greater Germany.

2. We demand equal status for Germany vis à vis other nations and the annulling of the Peace treaties drawn up in Versailles and St. Germain.

3. We demand land and property (colonies) to provide food for our nations and settlement areas for our population surplus.

4. Only a fellow German can have right of citizenship. A fellow German can only be so if he is of German parentage, irrespective of religion. **Therefore no Jew can be considered to be a fellow German**.

5. Those people who have no right of citizenship should only be guests in Germany and must be subject to laws concerning foreigners.

6. Only citizens should have the right to decide the leadership and laws of the state. Therefore, we demand that only those with rights of citizenship should have access to employment in any public office, whether it be at national, Länder or local level – we oppose the corrupt parliamentary system in which people are employed only on the basis of which party they belong to and not according to their character or ability.

7. We demand that the first priority of the state should be to ensure that its citizens have a job and a decent life. If it should prove impossible to feed the whole population of the state, foreign nationals (with no right of citizenship) should be repatriated.

8. Any further immigration of non-Germans must be prevented. We demand that all non-Germans who have entered the Reich since 2nd August 1914 be forced to leave immediately.

9. All citizens must have equal rights and obligations.

10. The first duty of all fellow citizens must be to work, either physically or mentally. The actions of an individual must not run contrary to the general interest and must have consideration for the common good.

Therefore, we demand:

11. Abolition of income for unemployed people or for those making no effort.

The breaking of the dominance of invested capital.

12. With regard to the huge physical and personal sacrifice which all wars demand of the people, personal enrichment by means of war must be seen as a crime against

the nation. Therefore, we demand **the collection of all wartime profits**.

13. We demand the nationalisation of all publicly owned companies (Trusts).

14. We demand profit-sharing by large companies.

15. We demand that generous improvements be made in the old age pension system.

16. We demand the establishment and maintenance of a healthy middle class. The large department stores should be immediately placed under the control of the local authority and should be rented out to small businesses at low prices. All small businesses should have the keenest regard for their deliveries to the state, the Länder or the local authorities.

17. We demand a property reform, which is in line with our requirements, and the creation of a law, which would allow the confiscation of property without compensation if this were in the general interest of the nation. We demand the abolition of all ground rents and the banning of all property speculation.

18. We demand an all-out battle against those who damage the common interest by their actions – criminals against the nation, profiteers, racketeers etc. should be punished by death, without regard for religion or race.

19. We demand the replacement of the system of Roman law, which serves the materialistic world order, by a system of German common law.

20. In order to make it possible for all capable and diligent Germans to receive a good education, thus enabling them to take up leading positions of employment, the state must carry the burden of a thorough overhaul of the national education system. The curricula of all institutions of education must adapt to the practical requirements of life. We must aim to instil national ideas from the earliest age in school (lessons in citizenship). We demand that the brightest children of poor parents should be supported by the state irrespective of their class or job.

21. The state must ensure the general good health of its citizens, by providing for mothers and children, by banning child labour, by ensuring the development of physical fitness, by making it a legal obligation to participate in sport or gymnastics and by providing all possible support for associations involved in instructing the youth in physical fitness.

22. We demand the abolition of the Söldnerheer and its replacement by a people's army.

23. We demand a legal battle against **open political slander** and its publication in the press. In order to make possible the establishment of a German press, we demand that:

a)   Newspaper editors and employees whose work appears in German must have German citizenship rights.

b)   Non-German newspapers must have the express permission of the state before they can appear in Germany. They must not be printed in German.

c)   Any financial contributions to German newspapers or any influence at all by non-Germans should be banned by law. Furthermore, we demand that any contraventions of the above should lead to the closing down of the newspaper in question and to the immediate expulsion from the Reich of those non-Germans involved.

Newspapers which are deemed to be against the common good should be banned. We demand a legal battle against any art and literature which exerts a harmful influence on public life and we demand that all institutions which contravene the afore-mentioned standards be closed down.

24. We demand the freedom of religions in the Reich so long as they do not endanger the position of the state or adversely affect the moral standards of the German race. As such the Party represents a positively Christian position without binding itself to one particular faith. The Party opposes the materialistic Jewish spirit within and beyond us and is convinced that a lasting recovery of our people can only be achieved on the basis of:

Common Good before Personal Gain

25. In order to achieve all of the aforegoing we demand the setting up of a strong central administration for the Reich.

We demand unrestricted authority for the central parliament over the whole Reich and its organizations. We demand the establishment of professional and industrial chambers to assist the implementation of the laws of the Reich in the Länder.

The leaders of the party promise to commit themselves fully to the achievement of the above aims, and to sacrifice their lives if need be.

Munich, 24th February 1920   For the Party Committee: Anton Drexler
Contributions should be sent to the Head Office:
Corneliusstraße 12 (Tel. 23620)
Business Hours 9–12(am), 2–6(pm)

Source: Münchener Plakatdruckerei, Bundesarchiv, Koblenz

Adolf Hitler was born in 1889 at Braunau am Inn on the Austrian side of the border with Germany. In 1913 he left Vienna for Munich and in August 1914 he joined a Bavarian infantry batallion and spent the next four years of the First World War on the western front, where he was promoted to the rank of corporal and generally served with distinction. At the end of the war, amid considerable revolutionary fervour in Germany, he returned to Munich and joined the German Workers' Party, a counter-revolutionary movement dedicated to the principles of 'German national socialism', as opposed to 'Jewish Marxism' or Russian Bolshevism. In February 1920 the party took the name National Socilialist German Workers' Party (*Nationalsozialistische Deutsche Arbeiterpartei*, NSDAP, Nazi for short) and set out its 25-point party programme. The name at the bottom of the document is not Hitler's but that of Anton Drexler, who set up the German Workers' Party in Munich. Although Hitler had only been a member of the party for a year, the 'twenty-five points' reveal the influence of his ideas. The programme contained many of the policies that became associated with the Nazis when they gained power constitutionally in 1933.

Articles 1–3 referred to the treaties drawn up in Versailles and St Germain (the treaty with Austria) and reflected the widespread humiliation felt by many Germans over what they believed were 'dictated' terms and conditions for peace and the failure of the newly created Weimar Republic to uphold Germany's interests as a great industrial and political power. Article 4 was explicitly racist and sought to preclude Jews from becoming citizens of Germany. As we have seen from Document 1.9, German anti-Semitism was not invented by National Socialism, but was prevalent in right-wing German nationalist circles in the late nineteenth century. Articles 10 and 21 referred to the duty of the citizens and state to work for and ensure physical and mental fitness. These are early indications of the eugenics policy that would later be implemented by the Nazis. As such they anticipated a degree of state interventionism that goes beyond the anti-Semitism of other nationalist groups. The outstanding distinction that can be made at this juncture between the early Italian Fascists and the embryonic Nazi party is the paramount importance given to establishing an all-embracing racial state in German National Socialism.

After the fiasco of the Munich *putsch* in 1923, Hitler used his period of imprisonment to write *Mein Kampf* ('My Struggle'), a somewhat misleading autobiography whose ideas were based on crude social Darwinism, a struggle for survival in which the criterion for fitness was racial purity. In *Mein Kampf*, Hitler outlined his beliefs and his political programme and developed some of the themes in the early party programme, particularly his obsession with establishing the German Utopian community of the *Herrenvolk* (master race). Unlike the Italian Fascist programme of 1919 (see Document 5.1), most of which was never carried out, it is revealing to contrast the extent to which the Nazis implemented many of the ideas in both the 'twenty-five points' and *Mein Kampf*. Although historians continue to differ about the relevance of *Mein Kampf* as a blue-print of Hitler's future ambitions, it remains an important historical source. Unable to address his audience in person, Hitler dictated his ideas instead. The text of *Mein Kampf* is thus a piece of political demagogy in prose. Hitler did not write *Mein Kampf*, he spoke it! Historians should not therefore be put off by its turgid style and the total lack of orginality of the ideas to be found within its covers. Extracts such as Document 6.2 not only shed light on Hitler's personality, but also provide revealing insights into his early political thought.

6.2 Adolf Hitler, *Mein Kampf* ('My Struggle'), 1925

... If from the 'folkish' we try to peel out the innermost kernel of meaning, we arrive at the following:

Our present political world view, current in Germany, is based in general on the idea that creative, culture-creating force must indeed be attributed to the state, but that it has nothing to do with racial considerations, but is rather a product of economic necessities, or, at best, the natural result of a political urge for power. This underlying view, if logically developed, leads not only to a mistaken conception of basic racial forces, but also to an underestimation of the individual. For a denial of the difference between the various races with regard to their general culture-creating forces must necessarily be extended; this greatest of all errors then becomes a basis for a similar way of viewing peoples and finally individual men. And hence international Marxism itself is only the transference, by the Jew, Karl Marx, of a philosophical attitude and conception, which had actually long been in existence, into the form of a definite political creed. Without the subsoil of such generally existing poisoning, the amazing success of this doctrine would never have been possible. Actually Karl Marx was only the *one* among millions who, with the sure eye of the prophet, recognized in the morass of a slowly decomposing world the most essential poisons, extracted them, and, like a wizard, prepared them into a concentrated solution for the swifter annihilation of the independent existence of free nations on this earth. And all this in the service of his race.

His Marxist doctrine is a brief spiritual extract of the philosophy of life that is generally current today. And for this reason alone any struggle of our so-called bourgeois world against it is impossible, absurd in fact, since this bourgeois world is also essentially infected by these poisons, and worships a view of life which in general is distinguished from the Marxists only by degrees and personalities. The bourgeois world is Marxist, but believes in the possibility of the rule of certain groups of men (bourgeoisie), while Marxism itself systematically plans to hand the world over to the Jews.

In opposition to this, the folkish philosophy finds the importance of mankind in its basic racial elements. In the state it sees on principle only a means to an end and construes its end as the preservation of the racial existence of man. Thus, it by no means believes in an equality of the races, but along with their difference it recognizes their higher or lesser value and feels itself obligated, through this knowledge, to promote the victory of the better and stronger, and demand the subordination of the inferior and weaker in accordance with the eternal will that dominates this universe. Thus, in principle, it serves the basic aristocratic idea of Nature and believes in the validity of this law down to the last individual. It sees not only the different value of the races, but also the different value of individuals. From the mass it extracts the importance of the individual personality, and thus, in contrast to disorganizing Marxism, it has an organizing effect. It believes in the necessity of an idealization of humanity, in which alone it sees the premise for the existence of humanity. But it cannot grant the right to existence even to an ethical idea if this idea represents a danger for the racial life of the bearers of a higher ethics; for in a bastardized and niggerized world all the concepts of the humanly beautiful and sublime, as well as all ideas of an idealized future of our humanity, would be lost forever.

Human culture and civilization on this continent are inseparably bound up with the presence of the Aryan. If he dies out or declines, the dark veils of an age without culture will again descend on this globe.

The undermining of the existence of human culture by the destruction of its bearer seems in the eyes of a folkish philosophy the most execrable crime. Anyone who dares to lay hands on the highest image of the Lord commits sacrilege against the benevolent creator of this miracle and contributes to the expulsion from paradise.

And so the folkish philosophy of life corresponds to the innermost will of Nature, since it restores that free play of forces which must lead to a continuous mutual higher breeding, until at last the best of humanity, having achieved possession of this earth, will have a free path for activity in domains which will lie partly above it and partly outside it.

We all sense that in the distant future humanity must be faced by problems which only a highest race, become master people and supported by the means and possibilities of an entire globe, will be equipped to overcome.

Source: Adolf Hitler, *Mein Kampf* ('My Struggle'), translated by R. Mannheim, with an introduction by D.C. Watt (London, 1969), pp. 347–9

Here we discover Hitler expanding his view on the importance of bringing the German nation to a common awareness of its ethnic and political unity. He does this by distinguishing the German *völkish* philosophy of nineteenth-century Romanticism with Marxism. Hitler attacked Karl Marx ('a Jew') and international Marxism for its failure to recognise the value of race and 'for a denial of the *difference* (my italics) between the various races'. According to Hitler the 'bourgeois world' had been infected by these 'poisons', while 'Marxism itself systematically plans to hand the world over to the Jews'. By contrast, the *völkisch* philosophy embraced by National Socialism, 'finds the importance of mankind in its basic racial elements'. Such a belief, claimed Hitler, promotes 'the victory of the better and stronger, and demand[s] the subordination of the inferior and weaker in accordance with the eternal will that dominates this universe'. Nazi racial teaching preached hatred of Jews, Slavs and Negroes, and proclaimed the superiority of the so-called Aryan race. The extract ends with an ominous prediction that the future will be dominated by a 'master race', supported by 'the means and possibilities of an entire globe'.

Although such crude social Darwinism formed an important element in Hitler's thinking, recent studies have tended to confirm that National Socialist ideology was neither a hotchpot of racial nonsense nor merely a means of securing an electoral victory prior to 1933. On the contrary, the Nazis saw their *Machtergreifung* ('seizure of power') as more than simply a change of government;

it represented the start of a revolution that would transform German society in accordance with their ideology. The so-called 'Nazi revolution' was essentially compounded of three elements. First, the Nazis utilised the legal authority of the State and its machinery to legitimise their control over the civil service, the police and the armed forces; all those who were unwilling to submit to this new authority were either dismissed or liquidated. Second, there was the widespread use made of terror and coercion in the absence of law and order that allowed Nazi 'stormtroopers' to seize persons and property at will. The pervasive fear of violence should not be underestimated, for it undoubtedly inhibited the forces of opposition. Nevertheless, as in Italy, the failure of the communists and socialists to combine to defeat Nazism was also a major contributory factor. The menace of violence, was, to some extent, counter-balanced by the positive image of Nazi society presented in the mass-media on an unprecedented scale. Propaganda is thus the third element. A society that was still suffering from a deep sense of national humiliation, and weakened by inflation, economic depression and mass unemployment, was perhaps not surprisingly attracted to a National Socialist revival which proclaimed that it could integrate disparate elements under the banner of national rebirth for Germany.

The Third Reich

From its very beginning, the Third Reich set itself the ambitious task of 're-educating' the German people for a new society based upon what it saw as a 'revolutionary' value system. The NSDAP rejected the kind of liberal democracy that had evolved in most western European countries by the twentieth century. The Nazis had fought the 1932 elections by offering what they termed the *volkischer staat* (people's state) as an alternative to the 'degeneracy' and conflict associated by the political Right with the Weimar Republic. Coupled with this rejection of democracy, which had failed Germany, was a growing belief that strong leadership was needed to transcend class and sectarian interests and provide a new start.

As a result of having emerged from the elections of July and November 1932 as leader of the largest single party, Hitler was eventually appointed Chancellor on 30 January 1933. In his first radio broadcast as Chancellor, Hitler condemned the shortcomings of the Weimar Republic and promised, in no uncertain terms, a complete break with the past. On 27 February the destruction of the Reichstag by fire was used by Hitler as a pretext to introduce an Emergency Decree signed by president Paul von Hindenburg placing restrictions on individual liberty, including freedom of opinion and freedom of the press. Over the next two years the Nazis consolidated their position by a process known as *Gleichschaltung* (co-ordination), which referred to the obligatory assimilation within the state of all political, economic and cultural activities. In practice this meant that all political parties, trades unions, youth organisations and churches were either dissolved or brought under state and party control. The final constitutional check on Hitler's dictatorial position disappeared when Hindenburg died in August 1934 and Hitler assumed the office of head of state as well as that of Chancellor.

In the elections held on 5 March 1933, the Nazi share of the vote increased to 43.9 per cent, but they never secured a clear majority in freely contested elections. On 13 March, Dr Joseph Goebbels was appointed Minister for Popular Enlightenment and Propaganda. It is not surprising that propaganda should warrant an entire government ministry; indeed, the story of the Nazi rise to power is often seen as a classic example of political achievement by means of propaganda. Two days after his appointment as Minister for Propaganda Goebbels outlined his view of the role of the new ministry in a revealing speech to representatives of the German press.

6.3 Goebbels on the task of the Ministry for Propaganda, 15 March 1933

Gentlemen! First of all I should like to thank the previous speaker for the kind words of greeting with which he welcomed me here. I believe that I can present myself to you as a colleague, as it were, because I do not come to the press field as an innocent but am myself from the press. In addition it has been my most heartfelt wish that the press above all might be drawn into this new Ministry of Popular Enlightenment and Propaganda that is being formed, because I know very well the very important role that the press plays nowadays in public life. This instrument is the seventh great power that is better suited than any other to shape and to influence public opinion for or against a government.

There can no longer be any doubt that since 30th January a National Revolution has been carried through in Germany, a Revolution that in a single bound has moulded historical events in the course of six to eight weeks in a way that in normal times would require ten or twenty or even thirty years. No-one can be in any doubt either that none of these events can be reversed and that, on the contrary, everyone, both in Germany and the world at large, must come to terms with the National Revolution and the events that it has brought about. Whether one supports or opposes this revolution and these consequences is in this context a matter of absolutely no importance. I see the establishment of this new Ministry of Popular Enlightenment and Propaganda as a revolutionary act of government because the new government has no intention of abandoning the people to their own devices and locking them up in an airless room. This government is, in the truest sense of the word, a people's government. It derives from the people and it will always execute the people's will ...

I see in the newly established Ministry for Popular Enlightenment and Propaganda a link between government and people, the living contact between the national government as the expression of the popular will and the people itself. ...

The name of the new Ministry tells us quite clearly what we mean by this. We have founded a Ministry for Popular Enlightenment and Propaganda. These two titles do not convey the same thing. Popular enlightenment is essentially something passive: propaganda, on the other hand, is something active. We cannot therefore be satisfied with just telling the people what we want and enlightening them as to how we are doing it. We must rather replace this enlightenment with an active government propaganda, a propaganda that aims at winning people over. It is not enough to reconcile people more or less to our regime, to move them towards a position of neutrality towards us, we want rather to work on people until they are addicted to us, until they realise, in the ideological sense as well, that what is happening now in Germany not only must be allowed, but can be allowed. ...

Propaganda is a much maligned and often misunderstood word. The layman uses it to mean something inferior or even despicable. The word 'propaganda' always has a bitter after-taste. But, if you examine propaganda's most secret causes, you will come to different conclusions; then there will be no more doubting that the propagandist must be the man with the greatest knowledge of souls. I cannot convince a single person of the necessity of something unless I have got to know the soul of that person, unless I understand how to pluck the string in the harp of his soul that must be made to sound. It is not true that propaganda presents merely a rough blueprint; it is not true that the propagandist does no more than administer complex thought processes in rough form, in a raw state, to the mass. Rather the propagandist must know not just the soul of the people in general but he must also understand the secret swings of the popular soul from one side to another. The propagandist must understand not only how to speak to the people in their totality but also to individual sections of the population: to the worker, the peasant, the middle-class: he must understand how to speak to both the South German and the North German, he must be able to speak to different professions and to different faiths. The propagandist must always be in a position to speak to people in the language that they understand. These capacities are the essential preconditions for success. ...

Now I come to a field that you yourselves represent: the *press*. I make no secret of it: I do not regard the banning of newspapers as a normal or an ideal state of affairs although I was the first among us to have the right to ban certain sections of the press. If opposition papers complain today that their issues have been forbidden, they can talk to me as a fellow-sufferer. There is, I think, no representative of any newspaper who can claim to have had his newspaper banned fifteen times as mine was. Nonetheless, as I say, the banning of papers is neither a normal nor an ideal state of affairs. On the contrary, I am of the opinion that the press must help the Government. The press may also criticise the Government but it should not do it in order to misrepresent the Government to the people. ... As I have already said, the press must not merely *inform*: it must also *instruct*. I turn first of all to the explicitly national press. Gentlemen! You too will consider ideal a situation in which the press is so finely tuned that it is, as it were, like a piano in the hands of the Government and on which the Government can play, a situation in which it is an enormously important and significant instrument of mass influence that the Government can make use of in the work for which it is responsible. It is quite possible that the Government and the press can work with and through one another in mutual confidence. I see it as one of my principal tasks to achieve that aim. I recognise the importance of the press and I know what it means to a government to have a good or a bad press. ...

If you will co-operate with us in trust I promise you that the Government will co-operate with you in trust. I also promise you that I shall stand up for the rights of the press everywhere and at all times but also on one condition: that the press stands up not just for the rights of the Government but also for the rights of the German people. If you do that, we shall do our bit. ...

Source: D. Welch, *The Third Reich: Politics and Propaganda* (London, 1993), pp. 136–46

This speech by the Propaganda Minister was not simply to explain the Government's intentions in setting-up the new Ministry for Popular Enlightenment and Propaganda – the first of its kind in Germany. It also afforded Goebbels the opportunity to introduce himself to the German press as a fellow journalist as well as a politician and to allay the fears of his audience. Not for the first time, Goebbels ingratiated himself by flattering his audience, referring to them as the 'seventh great power that is better suited than any other to shape and influence public opinion'. By presenting himself as one of them he hoped to gain a sympathetic understanding for some of the measures that he was about to outline. Bearing in mind that on 5 March 1933 the Nazis had made electoral gains but had failed to gain an overall majority, Goebbels began by asserting the legitimacy of both the government ('This government is, in the truest sense of the word, a people's government') and his ministry and its claim to represent the 'link between government and people ... the expression of the popular will'. According to Goebbels, propaganda would be the active force cementing the nation together. Goebbels then returned to the specific functions of the press which, he argued, should 'not merely *inform*; it must also *instruct*'. Clearly, greater emphasis would be placed on instruction and, as stated elsewhere in the speech, 'explaining Government policy to its readers in accordance with government instructions'. By the autumn of 1933 journalists would have little doubt that government directives were to be regarded as binding. Although Goebbels maintained that the press would have freedom to criticise, such freedom remained illusory.

The 'revolutionary' aims of the Nazi regime highlight the remarkably ambitious nature of propaganda. Although Nazism is often thought of as a temporary aberration in the history of a nation, it was in fact based upon various strands of intellectual thought which go back at least a century and which constitute the *völkisch* doctrine, essentially a product of late eighteenth-century romanticism (see Document 6.2). The major themes and policies associated with the Third Reich reflect the roots and antecedents of *völkisch* thought: (1) the appeal to national unity based upon the principle 'the community before the individual' (*Volksgemeinschaft*); (2) the belief in the innate superiority of the Teutonic race and the need for racial purity; (3) a hatred of enemies which increasingly centred on Jews and Bolsheviks; and (4) charismatic leadership

(*Führerprinzip*). Both the original doctrine and and the manner in which it was disseminated by Nazi propaganda led inexorably to the mobilisation of the German people for a future war.

The primary goal of Nazi propaganda was radically to restructure German society so that prevailing class, religious and sectional loyalties would be replaced by a new heightened national awareness. A considerable degree of mysticism was involved in the displacement of such deeply held yet conflicting values by means of a 'national' or 'people's' community (*Volksgemeinschaft*). In the years leading up to the Second World War, partly as an antidote to the increasing use of coercion and the subsequent loss of liberty, the Nazi regime eulogised its own achievements. The press, radio and film newsreels concentrated on the more prominent schemes: the impact of Nazi welfare services, 'Strength through Joy' (the Labour Front's agency for programmed leisure) and Winter Help. Posters proclaimed the benefits of 'socialism of the deed'; newsreels showed happy workers enjoying cruise holidays and visiting the 'people's theatre' for the first time; the radio bombarded the public's social conscience with charitable appeals; and the press stressed the value of belonging to a 'national community' and the need for self-sacrifice in the interests of the state. Cheap theatre and cinema tickets, along with cheap radio sets, a cheap 'people's car' (*Volkswagen*), even the 'people's court' (*Volksgerichtshof*) – all were intended to symbolise the achievements of the 'people's community'.

6.4 'Your Own KdF Car', a poster of 1939 (see p. 135)

This poster is advertising the benefits of saving for 'your own KdF car'. 'KdF' referred to the 'Strength through Joy' organisation and the car is the Volkswagen. In May 1933 most of the trade unions were replaced by the German Labour Front (*Deutsche Arbeitsfront* – DAF), and strikes were banned. In order to win over the support of the working class, the Labour Front established two new organisations: 'Beauty of Labour' (*Schönheit der Arbeit*) and 'Strength through Joy' (*Kraft durch Freude* –KdF). Both can be seen as an attempt to improve status and working conditions as a substitute for wage increases. Called at first 'After Work', Strength through Joy was to organise the leisure time and activities of the German labour force for the one purpose of enhancing the workers' productivity. The reduction of leisure to a mere auxiliary of work was the official philosophy of the Labour Front, although it preferred to concentrate on the achievements of organisations like KdF in providing workers with the prospect of owning one of the new 'people's cars' shown in the poster. Similar posters urged workers: 'Save five marks a week and get your own car.' Workers responded enthusiastically and payed in millions of marks to the saving scheme, but they received no cars.

One section of the population which proved particularly receptive to the notion of a 'national community' was German youth. From June 1933 all youth

Source: Bildarchiv Preussischer Kulturbesitz, Berlin

organisations were replaced by the Hitler Youth (*Hitlerjugend* – HJ) and its female counterpart, the League of German Girls (*Bund deutscher Mädel* – BdM). Writing in 1937, the Australian historian Stephen Roberts, who had spent over a year in Germany observing the system, referred to the 'triumph of Nazi propaganda over teaching'.

6.5 Stephen Roberts: a contemporary view of the Hitler Youth Movement, 1937

It would be foolish to underestimate the enthusiasm of young Germany for the *Führer*. All other interests are disappearing, and it would be misleading to think that the religious bodies which are so vocal abroad are holding their own with the children. Again and again in Germany, even in Catholic Bavaria and the Black Forest, I found cases of children whose Roman Catholic parents tried to keep them in the few struggling Church societies that still exist for children. The brown shirt or the drab blouse of Hitler won every time; the children wanted to follow the drums and fifes of their playfellows' bands, and, as they saw it, be normal. In every case the children wanted to join the *Hitler Jugend*. To be outside Hitler's organisation was the worst form of punishment.

The resultant worship was too distressing. ... Their attitude of mind is absolutely uncritical. They do not see in Hitler a statesman with good and bad points; to them he is more than a demigod. ... It is this utter lack of any objective or critical attitude on the part of youth, even with the university students, that made me fear most for the future of Germany. They are nothing but vessels for State propaganda ...

Source: S. Roberts, *The House that Hitler Built* (London, 1937), p. 208

Document 6.5 is an extract from Roberts' book *The House that Hitler Built*, first published in 1937 and written (according to the preface) 'for the man-in-the-street who wishes to have some idea of the German experiment'. Although this contemporary impression was intended to be 'objectively critical', some of the observations made here on the fanaticism of German youth for their Führer would not have unduly upset the Nazis, who viewed this as an 'achievement'. The assault on the individual, so characteristic of fascist regimes, was directed primarily at youth, with the intention of enveloping the individual at every stage of development within a single organisation by subjecting him or her to a planned course of indoctrination. In *Mein Kampf*, Hitler laid great stress on organisation, and this included the organisation of leisure time as well. Indoctrination in schools was therefore reinforced by the 'new comradeship' of the Hitler Youth movement.

However, although Roberts' impressions reflected accurately the overall position of German youth, the belief that the Hitler Youth had successfully mobilised all young people is clearly an exaggeration. Recent evidence, which would not have been available to Roberts, suggests that by the late 1930s the growing regimentation and militarism of the HJ was alienating some young Germans, who were forming independent gangs. The two most documented 'nonconformist' groups who rejected the Hitler Youth were the 'Swing Youth' (*Swing-Jugend*) and the 'Edelweiss Pirates' (*Edelweisspiraten*). Nevertheless, they represent a very small group of youth who rebelled against regimented leisure and who remained unimpressed by the propaganda eulogising a *Volksgemeinschaft*.

The Holocaust

Intrinsic to the idea of a 'national community' was the Nazi belief in the need for racial purity, an issue dominated by the 'Jewish question' but one that really encompassed two main 'enemies': the threat posed by the Jews from within Germany; and the danger of the *Slav Untermenschen* ('sub-human Slavs') in Poland and Russia. As we have seen from Document 6.2, the underlying drive behind Nazi 'racial teaching' was the obsessive desire to bring the Germans to a common awareness of their 'ethnic and political unity'. Nazi racial teaching within the educational system, and Nazi propaganda in general, preached hatred of Jews and Slavs and proclaimed the superiority of the so-called Aryan race. The desire for 'racial purity' centred on two interrelated themes; one was *Blut und Boden* ('blood and soil'), and the other was *Volk und Heimat* ('a people and a homeland'). The concept of 'a people and a homeland' sprang directly from the doctrine of *Blut und Boden*, which attempted to define the source of strength of the *Herrenvolk* (master race) in terms of peasant virtues, the Nordic past, the warrior hero, and the 'sacredness' of German soil – the last of which could not be confined by artificial boundaries imposed arbitrarily by a document such as the Versailles Treaty.

Only a few months after coming to power, the Nazis set about justifying the eradication of 'inferior' human beings. The first people to be exterminated were not Jews but 'unhealthy' Germans. Having successfully concluded a concordat with the Holy See on 20 July 1933, the new government announced the 'Law for the Prevention of Hereditarily Diseased Offspring', which permitted the compulsory sterilisation of people suffering from a number of allegedly 'hereditary' illnesses. Anti-Semitism was at the core of Nazi ideology, however, and the Jewish stereotype that developed from it provided the focal point for the feelings of aggression inherent in the ideology. Before 1939, anti-Semitism was propagated chiefly by means of the educational system and the press. Three major campaigns were waged in 1933, 1935 and 1938. Immediately after the Nazi electoral victory in March 1933 rank-and-file party activists went on the rampage, assaulting Jews, damaging Jewish shops and demanding a 'Jewish-free' economy. Despite continued harrassment at a local level there were no further official moves against Jews until September 1935, when, at the party rally in Nuremberg, Hitler announced a further batch of anti-Jewish legislation.

6.6 The Nuremberg Laws, 1935

I THE REICH CITIZENSHIP LAW OF 15 SEPTEMBER, 1935

The Reichstag has adopted by unanimous vote the following law which is herewith promulgated.

ARTICLE I: (1) A subject of the state is one who belongs to the protective union of the German Reich, and who, therefore, has specific obligations to the Reich.

(2) The status of subject is to be acquired in accordance with the provisions of the Reich and the state Citizenship Law.

ARTICLE II: (1) A citizen of the Reich may be only one who is of German or kindred blood, and who, through his behaviour, shows that he is both desirous and personally fit to serve loyally the German people and the Reich.

(2) The right to citizenship is obtained by the grant of Reich citizenship papers.

(3) Only the citizen of the Reich may enjoy full political rights in consonance with the provisions of the laws.

ARTICLE III: The Reich Minister of the Interior, in conjunction with the Deputy to the Führer, will issue the required legal and administrative decrees for the implementation and amplification of this law.

Promulgated: September 16, 1935. *In force:* September 30, 1935.

II FIRST SUPPLEMENTARY DECREE OF 14 NOVEMBER, 1935

On the basis of Article III of the Reich Citizenship Law of September 15, 1935, the following is hereby decreed:

ARTICLE I: (1) Until further provisions concerning citizenship papers, all subjects of German or kindred blood who possessed the right to vote in the Reichstag elections when the Citizenship Law came into effect, shall, for the present, possess the rights of Reich citizens. The same shall be true of those upon whom the Reich Minister of the Interior, in conjunction with the Deputy to the Führer, shall confer citizenship.

(2) The Reich Minister of the Interior, in conjunction with the Deputy to the Führer, may revoke citizenship.

ARTICLE II: (1) The provisions of Article I shall apply also to subjects who are of mixed Jewish blood.

(2) An individual of mixed Jewish blood is one who is descended from one or two grandparents who, racially, were full Jews, insofar that he is not a Jew according to Section 2 of Article V. Full-blooded Jewish grandparents are those who belonged to the Jewish religious community.

ARTICLE III: Only citizens of the Reich, as bearers of full political rights, can exercise the right of voting in political matters, and have the right to hold public office. The Reich Minister of the Interior, or any agency he empowers, can make exceptions during the transition period on the matter of holding public office. These measures do not apply to matters concerning religious organizations.

ARTICLE IV: (1) A Jew cannot be a citizen of the Reich. He cannot exercise the right to vote; he cannot occupy public office.

(2) Jewish officials will be retired as of December 31, 1935. In the event that such officials served at the front in the World War either for Germany or her allies, they shall receive as pension, until they reach the age limit, the full salary last received, on the basis of which their pension would have been computed. They shall not, however, be promoted according to their seniority in rank. When they reach the age limit, their pension will be computed again, according to the salary last received on which their pension was to be calculated.

(3) These provisions do not concern the affairs of religious organizations.

(4) The conditions regarding service of teachers in public Jewish schools remain unchanged until the promulgation of new regulations on the Jewish school system.

ARTICLE V: (1) A Jew is an individual who is descended from at least three grand-parents who were, racially, full Jews. ...

(2) A Jew is also an individual who is descended from two full-Jewish grandparents if:

(a) he was a member of the Jewish religious community when this law was issued, or joined the community later;
(b) when the law was issued, he was married to a person who was a Jew, or was subsequently married to a Jew;
(c) he is the issue from a marriage with a Jew, in the sense of Section I, which was contracted after the coming into effect of the Law for the Protection of German Blood and Honour of September 15, 1935;
(d) he is the issue of an extramarital relationship with a Jew, according to Section I, and born out of wedlock after July 31, 1936.

ARTICLE VI: (1) Insofar as there are, in the laws of the Reich or in the decrees of the National Socialist Labor party and its affiliates, certain requirements for the purity of German blood which extend beyond Article V, the same remain untouched. ...

ARTICLE VII: The Führer and Chancellor of the Reich is empowered to release anyone from the provisions of these administrative decrees.

III THE LAW FOR THE PROTECTION OF GERMAN BLOOD AND HONOUR, 15 SEPTEMBER, 1935

Imbued with the knowledge that the purity of German blood is the necessary prerequisite for the existence of the German nation, and inspired by an inflexible will to maintain the existence of the German nation for all future times, the Reichstag has unanimously adopted the following law, which is now enacted:

ARTICLE I: (1) Any marriages between Jews and citizens of German or kindred blood are herewith forbidden. Marriages entered into despite this law are invalid, even if they are arranged abroad as a means of circumventing this law.

(2) Annulment proceedings for marriages may be initiated only by the Public Prosecutor.

ARTICLE II: Extramarital relations between Jews and citizens of German or kindred blood are herewith forbidden.

ARTICLE III: Jews are forbidden to employ as servants in their households female subjects of German or kindred blood who are under the age of forty-five years.

ARTICLE IV: (1) Jews are prohibited from displaying the Reich and national flag and from showing the national colors.

(2) However, they may display the Jewish colors. The exercise of this right is under state protection.

ARTICLE V: (1) Anyone who acts contrary to the prohibition noted in Article I renders himself liable to penal servitude.

(2) The man who acts contrary to the prohibition of Article II will be punished by sentence to either a jail or penitentiary.

(3) Anyone who acts contrary to the provisions of Articles III and IV will be punished with a jail sentence up to a year and with a fine, or with one of these penalties.

ARTICLE VI: The Reich Minister of Interior, in conjunction with the Deputy to the Führer and the Reich Minister of Justice, will issue the required legal and administrative decrees for the implementation and amplification of this law.

ARTICLE VII: This law shall go into effect on the day following its promulgation, with the exception of Article III, which shall go into effect on January 1, 1936.

IV FIRST SUPPLEMENTARY DECREE FOR THE EXECUTION OF THE LAW FOR THE PROTECTION OF GERMAN BLOOD AND GERMAN HONOUR, 14 NOVEMBER 1935

ARTICLE II: ... Marriages between Jews and nationals of mixed Jewish blood who have only one fully Jewish grandparent shall also belong to the category of marriages forbidden. ...

ARTICLE III: (1) Nationals of mixed Jewish blood with two grandparents who are full Jews require the permission of the Reich Minister for the Interior and the Deputy Leader ... in order to contract a marriage with nationals of German or similar blood or with nationals of mixed Jewish blood who have only one full Jewish grandparent. ...

ARTICLE IV: A marriage shall not be contracted between nationals of mixed Jewish blood who have only one full Jewish grandparent ...

Source: *Reichsgesetzblatt*, I, 1935, pp. 1146ff.

The Nuremberg Laws were divided into two sections and the ordinances (supplementary decrees) based on them followed in November 1935. The Reich Citizenship Law denied Jews the right of citizenship, the right to vote and to hold public office. In effect, Jews had been named *personae non gratae*. Interestingly enough, there appears to be a compromise over the classification of a Jew. The ordinance to the Citizenship Law states (article II, 2) that those of mixed blood, i.e. with one or two non-Jewish grandparents, were entitled to German citizenship, albeit with certain restrictions. This represented a minor victory for 'moderates' within the Nazi party who had successfully resisted attempts to restrict classification to one Jewish grandparent. The Law for the Protection of German Blood and Honour outlawed marriage between Jews and gentiles and forbade sexual relations between them outside marriage. The law, which also denied Jews the right to fly the German flag, provided wide scope for the legal interpretation of 'miscegenation' and laid Jews open to denunciation and framing. The fascination of many anti-Semites with the sexual aspect of the legislation was an important feature of Nazi and anti-Semitic propaganda and found its most pornographic expression in Julius Streicher's semi-official broadsheet *Der Stürmer*, which specialised in denunciations of alleged Jewish moral and sexual practices. The preamble to the law referred to the Reichstag 'unanimously' adopting the legislation. Hitler obviously felt confident by September 1935 to pass such a racist law. Hindenburg, who had earlier emasculated attempts to prevent Jews from working in the civil service, was now dead, and the SA (*Sturm Abteilungen* or 'Stormtroopers'), the NSDAP paramilitaries, had been culled in the 'Night of the Long Knives'.

By the late 1930s the increasingly fanatical tone of propaganda reflected the growing radicalisation of the regime's anti-Semitic policies. The *Anschluss* (union) with Austria in March 1938 served to accelerate the unlawful seizure of Jewish property. The position of German Jews deteriorated further still with the *Kristallnacht* ('Crystal Night' or 'Night of the Broken Glass') of 9–10 November 1938, when party activists unleashed by Goebbels and the Propaganda Ministry burned down synagogues and vandalised thousands of Jewish shops. The 'final solution' to the 'Jewish problem' coincided with the radicalisation of Nazi foreign policy and the German invasion of the Soviet Union in June 1941. However, the systematic genocide of Jews was not implemented until after the Wannsee Conference of 20 January 1942 eventually co-ordinated measures for mass extermination. The process which Hans Mommesen refers to as 'cumulative radicalisation', which started with intimidation and persecution, culminated in a network of concentration camps (all outside Germany in occupied Poland) and the slaughter of 6 million Jews (and over a quarter of a million Gypsies) during the Second World War. Similarly, Hitler's obsessive anti-Bolshevism led to some 3 million Russian POWs dying – mostly of disease and starvation.

In attempting to explain the Holocaust it cannot be argued rationally that anti-Semitism was a result of National Socialism or that propaganda made Germans anti-Semitic (cf. the Dreyfus case in France, Chapter 2), but the fact remains that the Third Reich was responsible for an attempt at genocide of unparalleled scope and brutality. In order to illustrate the manner in which the Jewish stereotype was depicted, I have included two examples of vehemently anti-Semitic propaganda. The first consists of three extracts from the commentary of the most notorious of all anti-Semitic films, *Der ewige Jude* ('The Eternal/Wandering Jew'), which was released in November 1940.

6.7 Extracts from *Der ewige Jude* ('The Eternal/Wandering Jew'), Nazi propaganda film of 1940

The civilized Jew that we know in Germany only gives us half the picture of their racial character. This film shows genuine shots of the Polish ghettoes. … We recognize that here there lies a plague spot which threatens the health of the Aryan people. Richard Wagner once said: 'The Jew is the evil force behind the decay of man!' And these pictures confirm the accuracy of his statement. …

Rarely will you find a Jew engaged in useful work. … The uninitiated will at first feel inclined to view these haggling children as a sign of great poverty. But to the experienced observer it soon becomes clear that they are proud of behaving like their parents. These children see no ideals before them like our own youth. … For the Jews, business is a kind of holy transaction. How he earns his living is a matter of complete indifference to him. … Those things that are valued by the creative Aryan have been reduced by the Jew to the level of a mere piece of merchandise, which he buys and sells but cannot produce himself. … The Jews are a race without farmers and without manual workers – a race of parasites! …

Comparable with the Jewish wanderings through history are the mass migrations of an equally restless animal, the rat. … Wherever rats appear they bring ruin, they ravage human property and foodstuffs. In this way they spread disease: plague, leprosy, typhoid, cholera, dysentery, etc. They are cunning, cowardly, and cruel and

are found mostly in packs. In the animal world they represent the element of crafti-
ness and subterranean destruction – no different from the Jews among mankind!

Source: D. Welch, *Propaganda and the German Cinema, 1933–45*
(Oxford, 1983), pp. 294–5

The film was produced as part of a sustained propaganda campaign in 1940 to
convince the population that a 'Jewish Question' existed and needed to be
'solved'. Made by the Nazi Party and directed by Fritz Hippler (head of the film
section of the Propaganda Ministry) it was a full-scale documentary, and as such
would have been shown in all the cinemas. Although only three brief extracts
from the commentary are cited here, the film runs through the whole gamut of
Nazi allegations against Jews. These can be seen as a five-pronged attack, which
begins with scenes of the Warsaw ghetto, designed to show the reluctance of
Jews to undertake creative labour; it continues with the migration of Jews and
their attempts to assimilate with European peoples; the development of Jewish
banking houses; the destructive influence of Jews in the Weimar Republic; and
an attack on the nature of Jewish religion and its teaching, culminating in the
slaughter of animals for kosher meat.

The concept of the 'eternal or wandering Jew' was older than National
Socialism; it derived from the Christian legend of Ahasver, a Jew who prevented
Jesus from resting while he was carrying the cross. Thereafter he had to travel
the world without the release of death. Nazi propaganda saw in this that other
races had already persecuted the Jews. In 1937 the Nazi Party set up a touring
exhibition of 'degenerate art' under the heading of the 'Eternal Jew'. The poster
for the exhibition is shown as Document 6.8.

6.8 Nazi poster for the 'Eternal Jew' exhibition, 1937 (see p. 144)

By contrasting Jewish individualism and 'self-seeking' with the National Socialist
ideal of a 'people's community', and by showing Jews as motivated only by
money (in the right hand) and governed by bolshevism and the whip (in the left
hand), in this poster the Nazis hoped to demonstrate that Judaism was the total
antithesis of the cherished values of the German cultural tradition as interpreted
by Nazi ideology. But more importantly, the constant analogy made with rats
and parasites (as in the film of 'The Eternal/Wandering Jew') suggested that the
Jew differed from the Aryan physically and spiritually. The implication was that
here was a menace which had to be 'resisted'. Thus the conclusion to be drawn
from such films and posters was that the killing of Jews was not a crime but a
necessity: Jews, after all, were not human beings but pests which had to be exterminated.

At precisely the time that Jewish persecution was being intensified and final

Source: Bildarchiv Preussischer Kulturbesitz, Berlin

details of the solution arrived at (that is, towards the end of 1941), Nazi secret police reports were noting either boredom with or massive indifference to the 'Jewish Question'. Such indifference proved fatal to the victims. Interest in the fate of Jews had in fact rapidly evaporated after the *Kristallnacht*. The historian Ian Kershaw has written that the 'road to Auschwitz was built by hate, but paved with indifference'. The conditions that allowed for apathy and indifference may be attributed partly to the effects of Nazi propaganda itself, which could depend upon widespread latent anti-Jewish feeling (see Document 1.9), and partly also to a closed political environment, cut off from the outside world, within which that propaganda was working.

Thus when the Nazis came to power they chose the Jew as the permanent scapegoat on which those in the movement could work off their resentment; and their propaganda used the historical predisposition of the population towards an anti-Semitic explanation for Germany's cultural, economic and political grievances. Therefore an important negative function of anti-Semitic propaganda was to divert public attention from the economic and social measures that the regime had promised but had failed to deliver. Nevertheless, while it remains important for the historian to attempt to explain the route that led to Auschwitz, that is not the same as providing an apology for such abhorrent policies. The Holocaust can have no apologists.

Nazi ideology and propaganda

Just as National Socialism needed its enemies, so it also required its heroes. For their concept of the heroic leader the Nazis turned once again to *völkisch* thought and the notion of the *Führerprinzip* (leadership principle), centred on a mystical figure embodying and guiding the nation's destiny in a similar fashion to Il Duce in Fascist Italy. The *Führerprinzip* was to be based on a very special personality who had the will and power to actualise the *Volksstaat*. This would be achieved by the man of destiny – resolute, dynamic and radical – who would destroy the old privileged and class-ridden society and replace it by the ethnically pure and socially harmonious 'national community'. By implication the *Führer*-figure would be the antithesis of democracy. The extreme fragmentation of Weimar politics, which was increasingly seen in terms of a failure to govern, served only to make such leadership qualities appear all the more attractive.

Following the 'seizure of power', the authority associated with charismatic leadership was transferred from the NSDAP to the state and nation. On 1 August 1934, the Law Concerning the Head of State of the German Reich merged the offices of Reich President and Reich Chancellor into the new office of 'Fuhrer and Reich Chancellor', which became quickly abbreviated to 'Fuhrer'. A plebiscite was held in order to confirm Hitler's new position. The results were an impressive victory for Hitler, with almost 90 per cent voting 'yes'.

While in theory the Weimar Constitution was never abandoned, Hitler's position as Führer and exclusive representative of the nation's will was quickly consolidated. In order to achieve a position of unrestricted power, the Nazi state set up a judiciary that sanctioned what was happening and, by its total subservience to the 'will of the Führer', sacrificed its traditional function as an independent third force of the State. The basis for the interpretation of all laws was now the National Socialist ideology, as expressed in the party programme, and the speeches of the Führer. This was made explicit in a speech by Hans Frank, the head of the Nazi Association of Lawyers and of the Academy of German Law, in 1938.

6.9 'Führer Power', a speech by Hans Frank, 1938

1. At the head of the Reich stands the leader of the NSDAP as the leader of the German Reich for life.

2. He is, on the strength of being leader of the NSDAP, leader and Chancellor of the Reich. As such he embodies simultaneously, as Head of State, supreme State power and, as chief of the Government, the central functions of the whole Reich adminis-tration. He is Head of State and chief of the Government in one person. He is Commander-in-Chief of all the armed forces of the Reich.

3. The Führer and Reich Chancellor is the constituent delegate of the German people, who without regard for formal pre-conditions decides the outward form of the Reich, its structure and general policy.

4. The Führer is supreme judge of the nation. … There is no position in the area of constitutional law in the Third Reich independent of this elemental will of the Führer. …

The Führer is not backed by constitutional clauses, but by outstanding achieve-ments which are based on the combination of a calling and of his devotion to the people. … Whether the Führer governs according to a formal written Constitution is not a legal question. … The legal question is only whether through his activity the Führer guarantees the existence of his people.

Source: D. Welch, *The Third Reich: Politics and Propaganda* (London, 1993), p. 85

Hitler's position of absolute power was justified not in legal-rational terms as Chancellor and Head of State but in charismatic terms as *Führer* of the German *Volk* – not a state, but a German nation as a racially determined entity. As the custodian of the nation's will, constitutional limitations could not be imposed on his authority. The legal system and individual judges had no right to question the decisions of the Führer, which were increasingly disguised as laws or decrees, and thus given the facade of 'normality'. There was therefore no legal means of appeal against decisions of the 'people's court' (*Volksgerichtshof*), which had been set up in 1934 to deal with cases of high treason and treachery. Such 'normality' could, however, be violated at any time by individuals or organisations, for example the Gestapo, who could claim to be operating within the sphere of 'Führer-power'.

In 1941, at the height of Germany's military success, Goebbels informed his officials in the Propaganda Ministry that his two notable propaganda achievements were, first: 'the style and technique of the Party's public ceremonies; the ceremonial of the mass demonstrations, the ritual of the great Party occasion', and, second, that through his 'creation of the Führer-myth, Hitler had been given the halo of infallibility, with the result that many people who looked askance at the Party after 1933 had now complete confidence in Hitler'. Ian Kershaw, who has subjected this relationship between Hitler and the German people to a systematic analysis, has demonstrated that Hitler was indeed the most vital legitimizing force within the regime.

By appearing to stand above the day-to-day realities of the regime, Hitler acted as a kind of medieval monarch, as a positive symbol, a focus of loyalty and of national unity. Hitler was presented as not just another party leader but as the Leader for whom Germany had been waiting – a leader who would place the nation before any particularist cause. The nature of Hitler's position as charismatic leader, as the Führer of the German people, rested on his continuing ability to detach himself from day-to-day politics, with the result that he was never personally associated with the worst extremes of the regime. Different social groupings, ranging from the industrial working class to church leaders continued to misperceive Hitler as a 'moderate', opposed to the radical and extreme elements within the Nazi movement. One of the most significant achievements of the propaganda construction of the 'Führer-myth' was success in separating Hitler from the growing unpopularity of the Nazi party itself.

The ritual of the mass meeting was an important element in the projection of the Führer cult. Uniforms, bands, flags and symbols were all part of Goebbels' propaganda machine to increase the impact of Hitler's strong words with strong deeds. This is the fundamental rationale behind the constant display of Nazi symbols in posters and in films like 'Triumph of the Will' (*Triumph des Willens*, 1935) and the weekly German newsreels (*Deutsche Wochenschauen*).

6.10 *Triumph des Willens* ('Triumph of the Will'), Nazi documentary film, 1935

[Leni Riefenstahl's 'Triumph of the Will', the documentary film, commissioned by Hitler, of the 1934 party rally in Nuremberg, opens with a slow fade-up of the German eagle and the title *Triumph des Willens*, with the caption:]

> Twenty years after the outbreak of the First World War,
> Sixteen years after the beginning of Germany's time of trial,
> Nineteen months after the beginning of the rebirth of Germany,

Adolf Hitler flew to Nuremberg to muster his faithful followers …

[The sixth Nazi Party Congress was opened by a speech from the Deputy Leader, Rudolf Hess:]

'My Führer, around are arrayed the flags and standards of our National Socialist movement. Only on the day when their very fabric has turned to dust, only then looking back, will men be able to understand fully the greatness of our time and what you, my Führer, mean to Germany. You are Germany! When you act, the Nation acts; when you judge, the people judge. Our gratitude is expressed in our promise to stand by you in good times and bad – come what may. Thanks to your leadership, Germany will achieve its ultimate aim, to be a true homeland, … a homeland for all Germans.

'You have been our guarantor of victory – you are our guarantor of peace.

'Adolf Hilter. Sieg Heil! Sieg Heil! Sieg Heil!'

Source: D. Welch, *Propaganda and the German Cinema, 1933–45* (Oxford, 1983), pp. 151,157)

Hess's speech is particularly significant for the fact that the rally was taking place very shortly after the death of Hindenburg, the purge of the SA, the emergence of Hitler as Führer and the new personal oath of allegiance that the armed forces were now obliged to swear. This proved to be a crucial period of consolidation for both Hitler and the Nazi party. In projecting the image of the strong leader to an audience that had come to associate the Weimar Republic and the Treaty of Versailles with national ignominy, *Triumph des Willens* portrayed Hitler as a statesman of genius who had single-handedly rebuilt the nation and staunchly defended Germany's territorial rights over the hegemony imposed by foreigners.

Nazi party rallies were carefully staged theatrical events devised to create the impression of national unity. This also explains why the Nazis repeatedly staged 'national moments' (*Stunden der Nation*) when Hitler's speeches would be broadcast simultaneously throughout the Reich. On such occasions life would come to a standstill, demonstrating the sense of national community where the individual participant in the ritual, moved by Hitler's rhetoric and swayed by the crowd, underwent a metamorphosis in Goebbels' famous phrase 'from a little worm into part of a large dragon'.

None the less, Goebbels manipulatory skill alone could not have created the quasi-religious faith in Hitler demonstrated by large sections of the German population. Without concrete achievements Hitler could not have sustained his positive image as Führer. By the spring of 1939 secret reports from both within and outside Germany identified the reduction in unemployment and a series of foreign policy successes as the two major achievements consolidating Hitler's position. In domestic politics, Hitler was recognised for having won the 'battle for work', building the autobahns, and generally revamping the economy. Although industrial workers continued to view the 'economic miracle' in terms of longer hours and low wages, nevertheless they welcomed the restoration of full employment and the social welfare schemes for the poorer sections of the community. The middle class, who had benefited from the rearmament boom of the mid-1930s, remained devoted to Hitler whom they saw as the father-figure of the regime.

Like Mussolini and Italian fascism, National Socialism demanded authority from above and obedience from below. A famous poster of the period showed Hitler above the slogan '*Ein Volk, ein Reich, ein Führer*' ('One People, One Nation, One Leader'). The slogan reinforced the message of Hess's speech at Nuremberg: leadership, loyalty and unity.

6.11 'One People, One Nation, One Leader!', a poster of Hitler, 1938 (see p. 150)

Much of Hitler's popularity after coming to power rested on his achievements in foreign policy. A recurring theme in Nazi propaganda before 1939 was that Hitler was a man of peace but one who was determined to recover German territories 'lost' as a result of the Versailles Treaty (see Hess's speech in the film 'Triumph of the Will', Document 6.10). Document 6.12 is a cartoon from the right-wing magazine *Kladderadatsch*. It appeared after Germany's illegal occupation of the Rhineland, but presents Hitler as the sower of peace.

6.12 'The seed of peace, not dragon's teeth', cartoon of Hitler, 1936 (see p. 151)

When the Second World War came, Hitler's astonishing run of *blitzkrieg* victories, culminating in the fall of France, appeared to confirm Goebbels' propaganda that presented him as a military strategist of genius who even confounded his own generals. However, following the catastrophe of the German defeat at Stalingrad, a defeat for which Hitler was held responsible, his popularity began to decline. With no new military victories to talk of, Hitler retreated into his bunker and refused to address the German people. In the final year of the war Goebbels attempted to resurrect the Führer-cult by depicting Hitler as latter-day Frederick the Great, ultimately triumphing over adversity. This absurd image in the face of the gathering Russian occupation of Germany represented an alarming flight from reality that no amount of propaganda could sustain. The 'Hitler myth' and 'charismatic leadership' could not survive such lack of success, and were on the verge of extinction, as indeed was fascism in its original historical manifestations.

Source: Archiv für Kunst und Geschichte, Berlin

Source: *Kladderadatsch*, 22 March 1936

CHRONOLOGY: NAZI GERMANY, 1933–45

1931	July	Worsening economic crisis in Germany. Unemployment tops 4¼ million. Closure of all banks until 5 August.
1932	24 April	Nazis gain ground in local elections.
1933	28 January	Schleicher's government resigns.
	30 January	Hindenburg accepts a Cabinet made up of Hitler as Chancellor, von Papen as Vice-Chancellor and Nationalists.
	27 February	Communists blamed for Reichstag fire and as a result civil liberties and freedom of press suspended.
	5 March	In elections the Nazis win 288 seats, but fail to secure overall majority.
	13 March	Ministry for Popular Enlightenment and Propaganda set up with Goebbels as Propaganda Minister.
	23 March	Hitler obtains Enabling Law with the support of the Centre party, granting him dictatorial powers for four years.
	6 May	German Labour Front (DAF) founded, a Nazi organisation to replace the trade unions.
	14 July	All parties, other than the NSDAP suppressed. The Nazi party is formally declared the only political party in Germany.
	20 July	Concordat signed between Nazi Germany and the Vatican.
1934	21 March	'Battle for Work' begins.
	24 October	Decree setting out 'Nature and Goals' of the German Labour Front.
1935	13 January	Saar plebiscite votes overwhelmingly to 'return' to Germany.
	15 September	Nuremberg laws deprive Jews of their civil rights, prohibit marriage and sexual intercourse between Jews and German nationals.
1936	7 March	German troops reoccupy the demilitarised Rhineland in violation of the Treaty of Versailles.
	19 October	Four-year plan announced under Goering's supervision.
	1 November	Rome–Berlin Axis.
1938	11 March	German troops enter Austria, which is declared part of the Reich on 13 March.
	30 September	Munich Agreement gives Sudetenland to Germany.
	9–10 November	The *Kristallnacht* (Crystal Night): Jewish synagogues destroyed.
1939	23 August	Nazi–Soviet Non-Aggression Pact signed.
	1 September	Germany invades Poland.
1940	7 April	Germany invades Norway and Denmark.
	22 June	France concludes armistice with Germany.
	23 August	Beginning of 'Blitz' on Britain by *Luftwaffe*. Postponement of 'Operation Sealion', the invasion of Britain.
	18 December	Hitler issues secret plan for invasion of Russia – Operation Barbarossa.
1941	31 July	Göring gives Heydrich a written order to achieve a 'general solution to the Jewish problem in areas of Jewish influence in Europe'.
	11 December	Hitler declares war on America.
1942	20 January	'Wannsee Conference' in Berlin to co-ordinate measures for the 'Final Solution of the Jewish Question'.
1943	18 February	Goebbels announces 'Total War' and calls for greater civilian mobilisation.

1944	20 July	'July Officer's Plot'. Hitler wounded in bomb attack at headquarters in East Prussia. Attempted coup d'état is put down by loyal troops and leading conspirators and suspects are arrested and executed.
1945	12 January	Red Army begins final campaign against Germany.
	30 April	Hitler commits suicide in the Berlin bunker, along with Goebbels. Admiral Dönitz is named Hitler's successor.
	7 May	General Jodl makes final capitulation of Germany to General Eisenhower.
	8 May	Von Keitel surrenders to Zhukov near Berlin. Formal end of the war in Europe.
	5 June	Admiral Dönitz surrenders his powers to the allied occupation forces.

BIBLIOGRAPHY

Sources and documents

J. Noakes and G. Pridham (eds), *Nazism, 1919–1945*, vols 1–4 (1984) consists of a comprehensive range of documents covering the entire Nazi period. See in particular Jeremy Noakes's volume 4 on the *Homefront* (1998). An excellent collection of documentary material can be found in M. Housden, *Resistance and Conformity in the Third Reich* (1996). Hitler's *Mein Kampf* (ed. D.C. Watt, 1969) and Goebbels' *Diaries* (1948, 1978, 1982) provide a valuable insight into the Nazi mentality – both should be read with care. Hitler's speeches have recently been edited by M. Domarus (ed.), *Hitler: Proclamations and Speeches* (1990). Two interesting personal accounts are A. Speer, *Inside the Third Reich* (1970) and R. Semmler, *Goebbels: The Man Next to Hitler* (1947). On the role of propaganda see D. Welch, *The Third Reich: Politics and Propaganda* (1997 edn), which contains a documentary section. D.G. Williamson, *The Third Reich* (1982) consists of a small selection of documents with commentary, as does J.C.G. Rohl (ed.), *From Bismarck to Hitler. The Problem of Continuity in German History* (1970).

Secondary works

An indispensable synthesis to the historiography and interpretation of the Third Reich is I. Kershaw, *The Nazi Dictatorship: Problems and Perspectives of Interpretation* (1993 edn). Further historiographical surveys can be found in P. Ayçoberry, *The Nazi Question* (1981); K. Hilderbrand, *The Third Reich* (1989 edn); J. Hiden and J. Farquharson, *Explaining Hitler's Germany* (1989). The most recent introductory survey is N. Frei, *National Socialist Rule in Germany. The Führer State 1933–45* (1993). General surveys of the period include, H.W. Koch (ed.), *Aspects of the Third Reich* (1985); D. Orlow, *A History of the Nazi Party, 1933–45* (1973). R. Gruenberger, *A Social History of the Third Reich* (1974) and J.P. Stern, *The Führer and the People* (1975) cover various aspects of the Third Reich. A generally sound synthesis and summary of the so-called 'intentionalist' point of view is K. Bracher, *The German Dictatorship* (1971).

There is an enormous amount of work on Hitler and the Nazis. H.R. Trevor-Roper's introduction, *The Last Days of Hitler* (1978 edn) remains a thoughtful analysis. For a perceptive explanation of the Nazi voter, see T. Childers, *Who Voted For Hitler?* (1983). A more recent version of the continuity thesis linked to the broader theories of fascism is F. Fischer, *From Kaiserreich to Third Reich: Elements of Continuity in German History 1871–1945* (1985). For the historiographical background to the debates on the long-term origins of Nazism, see G.G. Iggers, *The Social History of Politics: Critical Perspectives in West German Historical Writing since 1945* (1985). Of the biographies of Hitler, A. Bullock, *Hitler* (1962) remains a readable source. More perceptive is J.C. Fest, *Hitler* (1974). J. Toland, *Adolf Hitler* (1976) is detailed; short accounts can be found in N. Stone, *Hitler* (1980); I. Kershaw, *Hitler* (1991); and a pamphlet by D. Geary, *Hitler* (1993). See also Kershaw's, *The 'Hitler Myth'* (1987). For readers prepared to wade through a myriad of detail, Kershaw has now written a definitive two-volume biography: *Hitler 1889–1936: Hubris* (1998), *Hitler 1937–1945: Nemesis* (1999). For a synthesis of recent scholarship and an attempt to locate Hitler's role and position in the decision-making process see D. Welch *Hitler* (1998). J.C. Fest, *The Face of the Third Reich* (1970) looks at Hitler's henchmen. Detailed accounts of Goebbels can be found in E.K. Bramsted, *Goebbels and National Socialist Propaganda* (1965) and D. Welch, *Propaganda and the German Cinema 1933–45* (1985 edn). See also the individual contributions in D. Welch (ed.), *Nazi Propaganda. The Power and the Limitations* (1983). For an excellent biography of Göring, see R. Overy, *Göring: The Iron Man* (1984). On Ley, see R. Smelser, *Robert Ley. Hitler's Labour Front Leader* (1988).

R. Bessel (ed.), *Life in the Third Reich* (1987) and J. Noakes (ed.), *Government, Party and People in Nazi Germany* (Exeter, 1980) both contain perceptive essays. On the Nazi economy, see H. James, *The German Slump: Politics and Economics 1924–1936* (1986); R. Overy, *The Nazi Economic Recovery 1932–38* (1982). A fascinating analysis is provided by A. Sohn-Rethel, *The Economy and Class Structure of German Fascism* (1987). See also, A. Barhai, *Nazi Economics* (1990), H.A. Turner, *German Big Business and the Rise of Hitler* (1985) and J. Gillingham, *Industry and Politics in the Third Reich* (1985). Still readable is A. Schweitzer, *Big Business in the Third Reich* (1964). This has been superseded by D. Guerin, *Fascism and Big Business* (1979) and P. Hayes, *Industry and Ideology. IG Farben in the Nazi Era* (1987).

For the German economy at war, see A. Milward, *The Germany Economy at War* (1965) and his later work, *War, Economy and Society, 1939–1945* (1977). On Hitler's economic policies, see B.A. Carroll, *Design for Total War: Arms and Economics in the Third Reich* (1968); B.H. Klein, *Germany's Economic Preparations for War* (1959) and R. Overy, *War and Economy in the Third Reich* (1994). T. Mason, 'The primacy of politics: politics and economics in National Socialist Germany', in S.J. Woolf (ed.), *The Nature of Fascism* (1968) discusses the Nazi attitude to economics.

Other aspects are tackled in, R.J. O'Neill, *The German Army and the Nazi Party, 1933–1939* (1966); J.S. Conway, *The Nazi Persecution of the Churches* (1968); G. Lewy, *The Catholic Church and Nazi Germany* (1964). On the role of women, see C. Koonz, *Mothers in the Fatherland* (1987) and J. Stephenson, *The Nazi Organisation of*

Women (1981). For a wider analysis of the attitudes and policies of the Nazi leadership towards the working class, see T. Mason, *Social Policy in the Third Reich: The Working Class and the 'National Community', 1918–39* (1992). See also D. Schoenbaum, *Hitler's Social Revolution* (1966) which retains an enduring interest.

Hitler's opponents are considered in H. Graml *et al.*, *The German Resistance to Hitler* (1970); R. Francis and L.D. Stokes (ed.), *Germans against Nazism: Nonconformity, Opposition and Resistance in the Third Reich* (1990), and I. Kershaw, *Popular Opinion and Political Dissent in the Third Reich: Bavaria, 1933–1945* (1986). For a widening of this debate to include conformity, see D. Peukert, *Inside Nazi Germany: Conformity and Opposition in Everyday Life* (1987). For a discussion of Nazi racial and eugenic policies, see M. Burleigh and W. Wippermann, *The Racial State: Germany 1933–45* (1991). For the means of coercion see H. Krausnick *et al.*, *Anatomy of the SS State* (1968). The origins of the 'Final Solution' are discussed in G. Hirschfeld (ed.), *The Policies of Genocide* (1986); L. Dawidowicz, *The War against the Jews, 1933–45* (1975); G. Fleming, *Hitler and the Final Solution* (1988), C. Browning, *The Path to Genocide* (1992); P. Burrin, *Hitler and the Jews: The Genesis of the Holocaust* (1993); H. Hohne, *The Order of the Death's Head* (1970); K. Schleunes, *The Twisted Road to Auschwitz* (1970). An overall perspective is provided in Y. Bauer, *The Holocaust in Historical Perspective* (1978) and M. Marrus, *The Holocaust in History* (1988). For a perceptive analysis of German reactions to the implementation of the Final Solution, see D. Bankier, *The German and the Final Solution: Public Opinion under Nazism* (1992). One of the most controversial works is Daniel Goldhagen's flawed best-seller, *Hitler's Willing Executioners: Ordinary Germans and the Holocaust* (1996).

Foreign policy is considered in G.I. Weinberg, *The Foreign Policy of Hitler's Germany: Diplomatic Revolution in Europe, 1933–1936* (1970), *The Foreign Policy of Hitler's Germany: Starting World War II* (1980) and *Germany, Hitler and World War II* (1995). K. Hildebrand, *The Foreign Policy of the Third Reich* (1973) stresses Hitler's pragmatism, while W. Carr, *Arms, Autarky and Aggression: A Study in German Foreign Policy, 1933–1939* (1972) links economic policy to foreign policy.

Articles

For a discussion on 'Who voted for Hitler?', see contributions in *C.E.H.* (1984). R. Bressel, 'Living with the Nazis: Some Recent Writing on the Social History of the Third Reich', *E.H.Q.* (1984) is self-explanatory. For a reappraisal of the effectiveness of Nazi propaganda see D. Welch, 'Propaganda and Indoctrination in the Third Reich: Success or Failure?', *E.H.Q.* (1987). On social aspects, see T. Mason, 'Labour in the Third Reich', *P.P.* (1966) and 'Women in Germany, 1925–40: Family, Welfare and Work', *H.W.J.* (1974). On the economy and the war, see R. Overy, 'Germany, "Domestic Crisis", and the War in 1939', *P.P.* (1987). L.D. Stokes, 'The German people and the destruction of the European Jews', *C.E.H.* (1973) analyses the implementation of the Final Solution. For an interesting general analysis, see S. Salter, 'National Socialism, the Nazi Regime, and German Society', *H.J.* (1992). A synthesis of recent work is provided by P.

Baldwin, 'Social Interpretations of Nazism: Renewing a Tradition', *J.C.H.* (1990). For a synthesis of recent research on Hitler's role in the Holocaust, see P. Monteath, 'The Führer's Decision', *H.T.* (September, 1998).

7

Russia under Stalin

The three years following the October Revolution of 1917 in Russia are generally referred to as the period of 'war communism', when Lenin and the Communist party were faced with the formidable task of rebuilding – along socialist lines – an economy shattered by the First World War and then by civil war. The subsequent economic disasters and a serious workers' and sailors' mutiny at Kronstadt in 1921 persuaded Lenin to abandon war communism and introduce a New Economic Policy (NEP), which incorporated a modified market economy in the field of agriculture, light industry and commerce. Document 7.1 is part of Lenin's speech at the Tenth Party Congress announcing the new economic policy.

7.1 The New Economic Policy (NEP), 23 March 1921

1. In order to assure an efficient and untroubled economic life on the basis of a freer use by the farmer of the products of his labour and of his economic resources, in order to strengthen the peasant economy and raise its productivity and also in order to calculate precisely the obligation to the State which falls on the peasants, requisitioning, as a means of state collection of food supplies, raw material and fodder, is to be replaced by a tax in kind.

2. This tax must be less than what the peasant has given up to this time through requisitions …

3. The tax is to be taken in the form of a percentage or partial deduction from the products raised in the peasant holding, taking into account the harvest, the number of eaters in the holding and the number of cattle.

4. The tax must be progressive; the percentage must be lower for the holdings of middleclass and poorer peasants and town workers …

The industrious peasants who increase the amount of land planted and the number of cattle in their holdings and those who increase the general productivity of their holdings receive privileges in paying the tax in kind …

7. The responsibility for paying the tax rests with each individual household …

8. All the reserves of food, raw material and fodder which remain with the peasants after the tax has been paid are at their full disposition and may be used by them for improving and strengthening their holdings, for increasing personal consumption and for exchange for products of factory and hand industry and of agriculture.

Exchange is permitted within the limits of local economic turnover, both through co-operative organizations and through markets.

9. Those farmers who wish to deliver to the state the surplus in their possession after the tax has been paid must receive, in exchange for the voluntary delivery of this surplus, objects of general consumption and agricultural machinery …

Source: Quoted in W.H. Chamberlin, *The Russian Revolution 1917–1921*
(New York, 1935), vol. 2, pp. 499–501

The first measure of the New Economic Policy involved a major policy switch from government requisitioning to a tax in kind on foodstuffs (Article 1). Although the State retained control of heavy industry, banking and foreign trade, under the NEP peasants and private traders were allowed to keep surplus produce, which could be sold on the open market after payment of a tax representing a certain proportion of the surplus (Article 3). The NEP therefore represented a mixed economy of state control and private enterprise and as such constituted an ideological shift from Marxist and Bolshevik principles.

The NEP measures did lead to a rapid increase in agricultural output, but they also aroused unease on the part of opponents within the Communist party, who pointed to the rise of the *kulaks* (rich peasants) into a class of 'bourgeois capitalists'. Equally significantly, March 1921 witnessed the failure of the German communists to gain power in the 'March of Action'. This left the Soviet Union isolated internationally as the first and only communist state. Interestingly enough, the economic concessions associated with the NEP were not matched by a relaxation in the political sphere. In March 1921 Lenin banned criticism of his policies within the Communist party, and almost one-third of party members were either purged or expelled.

Stalin and the Five-Year Plans

When Lenin died in January 1924 it was widely expected that Leon Trotsky (Lev Bronstein) would take over as leader, but a complex power struggle developed from which Joseph Stalin (Joseph Djugashvili) finally emerged as undisputed leader by 1929. The problem of the succession had troubled Lenin increasingly during the last two years of his life, following his first stroke in 1922. In Lenin's so-called Testament he called for the removal of Stalin from his post as General Secretary of the Party.

7.2 Lenin's Testament, 24 December 1922 and his Postscript of 4 January 1923

... Our Party rests upon two classes, and for that reason its instability is possible, and if there cannot exist an agreement between those classes its fall is inevitable. In such an event it would be useless to take any measures or in general to discuss the stability of our Central Committee. In such an event no measures would prove capable of preventing a split. But I trust that this is too remote a future, and too improbable an event to talk about.

I have in mind stability as a guarantee against a split in the near future ...

I think that the fundamental factor in the matter of stability ... is such members of the central committee as Stalin and Trotsky. The relation between them constitutes, in my opinion, a big half of the danger of that split, which might be avoided, and the avoidance of which might be promoted, in my opinion, by raising the number of members of the central committee to fifty or one hundred.

Comrade Stalin, having become general secretary, has concentrated an enormous power in his hands; and I am not sure that he always knows how to use that power with sufficient caution. On the other hand, comrade Trotsky ... is distinguished not only by his exceptional abilities – personally he is, to be sure, the most able man in the present Central Committee – but also by his too far-reaching self-confidence and a disposition to be too much attracted by the purely administrative side of affairs.

These two qualities of the two most able leaders of the present central committee might, quite innocently, lead to a split; if our party does not take measures to prevent it, a split might arise unexpectedly. ... I will not characterise the other members of the Central Committee as to their personal qualities. I will only remind you that the October episode of Zinoviev and Kamenev was not, of course, accidental but that it ought as little to be used against them personally as the non-Bolshevism of Trotsky ...

Bukharin is not only the most valuable and biggest theoretician of the Party, but may legitimately be considered the favourite of the whole Party; but his theoretical views can only with the very greatest doubt be regarded as fully Marxist ...

POSTSCRIPT, 4 JANUARY 1923

Stalin is too rude, and his fault entirely supportable in relations among us Communists, becomes insupportable in the office of General Secretary. Therefore, I propose to the comrades to find a way to remove Stalin from the position and appoint to it another man who in all respects differs from Stalin only in superiority – namely, more patient, more loyal, more polite and more attentive to comrades. ...

Source: E.H. Carr, *The Interregnum 1923–24* (London, 1954), copyright E.H. Carr, reproduced by permission of the Curtis Brown Group, Ltd, London

Lenin had originally dictated his 'Letter to the Congress', part of the Testament, in December 1922, when he referred to the growth of bureaucracy and the danger of polarisation within the Communist party. In January 1923 he added a codicil warning of Stalin's ambitions. The Testament criticised both Stalin and Trotsky as possible party leaders and as the catalysts for future splits within the party. By 1922 Joseph Djugashvili (he took the name 'Stalin' – man of steel – some time after joining the Bolsheviks in 1904) was General Secretary of the party and also a member of the Politburo, which decided government policy.

Lenin had become increasingly distrustful of Stalin's ruthless ambition and in his Testament expressed fears about Stalin's concentration of 'enormous power', suggesting that he be replaced as General Secretary ('I am not sure that he always knows how to use that power with sufficient caution'). Trotsky, on the other hand, while praised for his 'exceptional abilities', was also condemned by Lenin for his 'too far-reaching self-confidence and a disposition to be too much attracted by the purely administrative side of affairs'. Lenin was, in effect, anticipating a confrontation between Trotsky and Stalin brought about by a struggle for leadership; and he warned that, unless these personalities were checked, the party would split. Conspicuous by its absence in the Testament is any positive alternative; Zinoviev, Kamenev and Bukharin are mentioned but are dismissed as unsuitable. Although Lenin suggested increasing the size of the Central Committee, he failed to suggest who his successor should be.

Lenin's attack on Stalin was made known to the Central Committee, but Stalin was saved by the intervention of Zinoviev, backed by Kamenev, who argued that Lenin's fears had proved groundless. As a result, the Testament was not published, although Lenin's prediction proved correct. The 'triumvirate' of Stalin, Zinoviev and Kamenev embarked upon a vigorous campaign to discredit Trotsky and oust him from the left wing of the party. In fact, Stalin cleverly began to manipulate both allies and opponents alike.

Debate over economic policy centred on the role of the peasantry and the best method of industrialisation. The 'left opposition', led by Trotsky, wanted to abandon NEP and concentrate on rapid industrial development at the expense of the peasantry. In addition, Trotsky called for the active promotion of permanent (world) revolution, arguing that this would help Russia with its industrialisation. The 'right opposition', led by Bukharin, Rykov and Tomsky, called for the consolidation of Soviet power based on a prosperous peasantry and for very gradual industrialisation – what became known as 'socialism in one country'. So what began as an attack on Trotsky's theory of permanent revolution later formed the basis for Stalin's own policies.

When in 1926, Zinoviev, Kamenev and Trotsky formed the 'united opposition' to challenge NEP, Stalin, who skilfully played the role of moderate, backed the Bukharin line and, by astute political management, expelled Trotsky and his allies from the party (1927). With Trotsky out of the way, Stalin then turned against his former 'rightist' allies and declared that the NEP must go, as the *kulaks* were holding up agricultural progress. As a result, the December 1927 Party Congress (which expelled Trotsky) adopted resolutions to raise taxation of the *kulaks* and establish a Five-Year Plan for industrial development. When Bukharin protested, he too was expelled (1929).

The First Five-Year Plan, which began in 1928, marked a break with the NEP. Stalin reversed the process and embraced intensive industrialisation. The key to the Five-Year Plan was the reorganisation of agriculture to eliminate capitalist elements existing under NEP, in order to provide resources and labour for industry. Once Stalin had undermined the power of Bukharin and the 'right opposition', he embarked upon the policy of collectivisation of peasant holdings and the elimination of the *kulaks* as a class. Having committed himself to collectivisation, Stalin was determined to achieve it at whatever cost in human suffering.

7.3 Stalin's speech on agrarian policy, 27 December 1929

... The characteristic feature in the work of our Party during the past year is that we, as a party, as the Soviet Power:

(a) have developed an offensive along the whole front against capitalist elements in the countryside;
(b) that this offensive, as you know, has yielded and continues to yield very appreciable, *positive* results.

What does this mean? It means that we have passed from the policy of *restricting* the exploiting tendencies of the kulaks to the policy of *eliminating* the kulaks as a class. It means that we have carried out, and are continuing to carry out, one of the decisive turns in our whole policy.

Until recently the Party adhered to the policy of *restricting* the exploiting tendencies of the kulaks. ... Was this policy correct? Yes, it was absolutely correct at the time. Could we have undertaken such an offensive against the kulaks some five years or three years ago? Could we then have counted on success in such an offensive? No, we could not. That would have been the most dangerous adventurism. It would have been very dangerous playing at an offensive. For we should certainly have failed, and our failure would have strengthened the position of the kulaks. Why? Because we did not yet have in the countryside strong points in the form of a wide network of state farms and collective farms which could be the basis for a determined offensive against the kulaks. Because at that time we were not yet able to *replace* the capitalist production of the kulaks by the socialist production of the collective farms and state farms ...

An offensive against the kulaks is a serious matter. It should not be confused with declamations against the kulaks. Nor should it be confused with a policy of pin-pricks against the kulaks, which the Zinoviev-Trotsky opposition did its utmost to impose upon the Party. To launch an offensive against the kulaks means that we must smash the kulaks, eliminate them as a class. Unless we set ourselves these aims, an offensive would be mere declamation, pin-pricks, phrase-mongering, anything but a real Bolshevik offensive. To launch an offensive against the kulaks means that we must prepare for it and then strike at the kulaks, strike so hard as to prevent them from rising to their feet again …

Today, we have an adequate material base for us to strike at the kulaks, to break their resistance, to eliminate them as a class, and to *replace* their output by the output of the collective farms and state farms …

Source: J.V. Stalin, *Works* (London, 1955), vol. 12, pp. 172–5

The rationale behind forced collectivisation was that peasant small-holdings should merge to form large collective farms (*kolkhoz*). To achieve this, Stalin believed that he had to obliterate the *kulak* class, some of whom responded to the changes by destroying crops, lifestock and property rather than allow the state to take them. In order to liquidate the *kulaks* Stalin sought the support of the poorer peasants. His speech of 27 December 1929 to party activists set out his agrarian policy and contained his justification for the treatment of the *kulaks*, who were viewed as a political rather than a genuine social category, and as such were presented as the enemy of communism. Since the *kulaks* had persisted in being uncooperative, Stalin was able to insist that 'we have passed from the policy of *restricting* the exploiting tendencies of the kulaks to the policy of *eliminating* the kulaks as a class'. According to Stalin the 'capitalist production of the kulaks' was necessary in the past (under NEP), but the countryside network of socialist farm collectives formed the basis for 'a determined offensive against the kulaks'. Stalin rounded off his speech in strikingly uncompromising terms; the forth-coming offensive would strike at the *kulaks* so hard that it would 'prevent them from rising to their feet again … '

There is considerable controversy over the results of collectivisation; estimates and available statistics vary widely according to the sources used. By 1940 well over 90 per cent of peasant holdings had been collectivised into *kolkhozy*, and this facilitated greater mechanisation, which gradually increased grain output (although not livestock production). Moreover, the Communist party now controlled the countryside. On the other hand, collectivisation led to large-scale famine during 1932–3, along with the deportation to labour camps and the execution of up to 10 million (so-called) *kulaks*.

The overriding aim of the series of five-year plans was to transform Russia into a modern industrial state by means of rapid industrialisation. This was to be achieved by combining maximum production with minimum consumption, hence the need to destroy the *kulaks*. The First Five-Year Plan (1928–32) concen-trated on heavy industry and was declared to have been completed nine months ahead of schedule, although many of the targets set were hopelessly unrealistic. The Second Five-Year Plan (1933–7) again concentrated on heavy industry but also provided for increases in consumer goods. Document 7.4 is another speech by Stalin, this time addressing industrialists charged with the task of realising the production targets set in 1928.

7.4 Stalin's speech at the First All-Union Conference of Leading Personnel of Socialist Industry, 4 February 1931

What else is needed in order to fulfil and overfulfil the control figures for 1931?

That this government should enjoy the *support* of the vast masses of workers and peasants. Does our government enjoy such support? Yes, it does. You will find no other government in the world that enjoys such support from the workers and peasants as does the Soviet Government. ...

What else is needed ... ?

A *system* that is free from the incurable diseases of capitalism and has great advantages over capitalism. Crises, unemployment, waste, destitution among the masses – such are the incurable diseases of capitalism. Our system does not suffer from these diseases because power is in our hands, in the hands of the working class; because we are conducting a planned economy, systematically accumulating resources and properly distributing them among the different branches of the national economy. ...

Our superiority lies in the fact that we have no crises of over-production, we have not and never will have millions of unemployed, we have no anarchy in production, for we are conducting a planned economy. ...

What else is needed in order to advance with giant strides?

A *party* sufficiently solid and united to direct the efforts of all the best members of the working class to *one point*, and sufficiently experienced to be unafraid of difficulties and to pursue systematically a correct, revolutionary Bolshevik policy. Have we such a party? Yes, we have. Is its policy correct? Yes, it is, for it is yielding important successes. ...

There, comrades, you have all those objective possibilities which assist us in realizing the control figures for 1931, which help us to fulfil the five-year plan in four years, and in key industries even in three years. ...

It is sometimes asked whether it is not possible to slow down the tempo somewhat, to put a check on the movement. No, comrades, it is not possible! The tempo must not be reduced! On the contrary, we must increase it as much as is within our powers and possibilities. This is dictated to us by our obligations to the workers and peasants of the USSR. This is dictated to us by our obligations to the working class of the whole world.

To slacken the tempo would mean falling behind. And those who fall behind get beaten. But we do not want to be beaten. No, we refuse to be beaten! One feature of the history of old Russia was the continual beatings she suffered because of her backwardness. She was beaten by the Mongol khans. She was beaten by the Turkish beys. She was beaten by the Swedish feudal lords. She was beaten by the Polish and Lithuanian gentry. She was beaten by the British and French capitalists. She was beaten by the Japanese barons. All beat her – because of her backwardness, because of her military backwardness, cultural backwardness, political backwardness, industrial backwardness, agricultural backwardness. They beat her because to do so was profitable and could be done with impunity. You remember the words of the pre-revolutionary poet: 'You are poor and abundant, mighty and impotent, Mother

Russia.' Those gentlemen were quite familiar with the verses of the old poet. They beat her, saying: 'You are abundant', so one can enrich oneself at your expense. They beat her, saying: 'You are poor and impotent', so you can be beaten and plundered with impunity. Such is the law of the exploiters – to beat the backward and the weak. It is the jungle law of capitalism. You are backward, you are weak – therefore you are wrong; hence you can be beaten and enslaved. You are mighty – therefore you are right; hence we must be wary of you.

That is why we must no longer lag behind.

In the past we had no fatherland, nor could we have had one. But now that we have overthrown capitalism and power is in our hands, in the hands of the people, we have a fatherland, and we will uphold its independence. Do you want our socialist fatherland to be beaten and to lose its independence? If you do not want this, you must put an end to its backwardness in the shortest possible time and develop a genuine Bolshevik tempo in building up its socialist economy. There is no other way. That is why Lenin said on the eve of the October Revolution: 'Either perish, or overtake and outstrip the advanced capitalist countries'.

We are fifty or a hundred years behind the advanced countries. We must make good this distance in ten years. Either we do it, or we shall go under.

That is what our obligations to the workers and peasants of the USSR dictate to us. . . .

J.V. Stalin, *Works* (London, 1955), vol. 13, pp. 33–44

The speech was reported in *Pravda* and so it would have been an officially approved account. The imperative need to meet production targets underpinned the speech. Stalin began by claiming that his government enjoyed the support of workers and peasants; not surprisingly, there is no mention of those who have perished or who have been exiled. The *system* of state-sponsored socialism is contrasted favourably with 'the incurable disease of capitalism'. According to Stalin the superiority of the planned economy lay in 'the fact that we have no crises of over-production, no unemployment and no anarchy in production' (important considerations in the light of the Wall Street Crash and the ensuing economic Depression). As a consequence of targets being realised, real signs of economic growth could now be seen. Consequently it was crucial not to reduce the tempo; 'On the contrary, we must increase it as much as is within our powers and possibilities'. Note that Stalin was happy to quote from Lenin.

Stalin was clearly determined to implement dramatic changes designed to modernise the country in the shortest possible time. He referred to Russia being 'fifty to a hundred years behind the advanced countries', but demanded that 'We must make good this distance in ten years'. It was a speech reaffirming Stalin's commitment to the Five-Year Plans and the forced pace of his revolution; but equally, it is a speech by a leader who had emerged from a power struggle, confident that he has out-manoeuvred his opponents.

Although, under the Second Five-Year Plan, the production of consumption goods did rise slowly, workers were urged not to slacken. Realising (and surpassing) production targets became as much a psychological stimulus, a promise of better things to come, as an opportunity to show solidarity with the party. Propaganda eulogising the achievements of the regime had an important function in mobilising enthusiasm and pride in the modernisation of Russia. Posters in particular had an important role to play. Posters would urge workers to 'Work, build, and no complaining', or 'Let's storm the production targets!'. Document 7.5 is one of a poster series designed to illustrate the achievements of the First Five-Year Plan.

7.5 'Fulfil the Five-Year Plan in Four Years!', a Soviet propaganda poster of 1930

Source: Stephen White, University of Glasgow

This poster is a colour lithograph published by the Communist party in Moscow in 1930 and designed by Yuri Pimenov. The full message read: 'Long live industrial and financial development! Fulfil the Five-Year Plan in four years! No religion!'. Posters were employed during this period to convey the extraordinary power and enthusiasm of those who were building the new society. The main features and themes of poster design were pictures of blast furnaces, power stations, technological advance and the people at work. Many of the finest Soviet artists turned to poster design at this time. As a source, posters of the 1930s provide a panoramic view of Soviet life and record the Soviet obsession with mechanisation and technology.

This particular poster by Yuri Pimenov contained many familiar features of the period. In the top left-hand corner can be seen the factories and blast furnaces from which emerges the thrusting locomotive (red in colour in the original) – a powerful symbol of the new Russia. Spread across the tracks in a doomed attempt to prevent the speeding train from passing are pieces of string (!) held together by six individuals (including a priest) associated with the old, discredited, capitalist order. The string, which is about to be broken, symbolises religious prejudice; wrecking tactics; drunkenness; absenteeism and poor-quality production. 'Soviet Realism', in which art was supposed to serve politics, became the order of the day. Heroic, optimistic images that were intended to mirror everyday life were a feature of Soviet art in the 1930s and part of the wider 'cultural revolution' that was being forced through as an important corollary of the economic changes.

Stalin as dictator

Having emerged from a complex and bitter power struggle to assume a dominant position in the party and state, Stalin remained for the rest of his life conscious of potential opponents and rivals, and he became increasingly intolerant of criticism. He was not, however, the first Russian leader to employ large-scale terror and coercion. The *Cheka* (secret police) had been formed in 1917 to deal with counter-revolution, changing its name (but not its methods) to GPU in 1922 and, in July 1934, being reorganised as NKVD. Some months later, the murder of Sergei Kirov, a member of the Central Committee, was used by Stalin as an excuse for the summary trial and execution of a large number of potential or suspected opponents. Although there is some evidence that Stalin was responsible for Kirov's murder, it none the less provided the pretext for a series of trials in which old Bolshevik contemporaries of Stalin – including Zinoviev, Kamenev, Bukharin and Rykov – were found guilty of 'terrorist activities' and executed.

In order that his enemies should die as traitors and not martyrs, grossly inflated charges of 'Trotskyite conspiracies' were levelled at former heroes of the Revolution on a scale and intensity that had not been seen in Europe since the Jacobin reign of terror in the 1790s. Then, in 1937, having purged the party, Stalin eliminated a number of military leaders, including Commanding Chief Marshal Tukhachevsky – either by execution, or by imprisonment in forced labour camps. It has been estimated that half the total officer corps was purged, including 90 per cent of the generals. Such wholesale removal of the 'old Bolsheviks' not only eliminated the potential for an alternative government to form, it also facilitated the creation within the party of a younger generation of Stalinist acolytes.

In the midst of the so-called 'great terror', a new constitution (see Document

7.6) was introduced that gave the illusion of being more democratic than the former one.

7.6 The Soviet Constitution, 5 December 1936

1. The Union of Soviet Socialist Republics (USSR) is a socialist state of workers and peasants.

2. The political foundation of the USSR is formed by the Soviets of toilers' deputies which have grown and become strong as a result of the overthrow of the power of the landlords and capitalists and the conquests of the dictatorship of the proletariat.

3. All power in the USSR belongs to the toilers of the town and village in the form of Soviets of toilers' deputies.

4. The economic foundation of the USSR consists in the socialist system of economy and socialist ownership of the implements and means of production, firmly established as a result of the liquidation of the capitalist system of economy, the abolition of private ownership of the implements and means of production and the abolition of exploitation of man by man.

5. Socialist ownership in the USSR has either the form of state ownership (public property) or the form of co-operative and collective-farm ownership (property of individual collective farms, property of co-operative association) ...

9. Alongside the socialist system of economy, which is the dominant form of economy in the USSR, the law allows small private economy of individual peasants and handicraftsmen based on individual labour and excluding the exploitation of the labour of others ...

12. Work in the USSR is the obligation and matter of honour of each citizen capable of working, according to the principle: 'He who does not work shall not eat'. In the USSR the principle of socialism is being realized: 'From each according to his ability, to each according to his work' ...

13. The USSR is a federal state, formed on the basis of the voluntary association of the Soviet Socialist Republics with equal rights ...

30. The supreme organ of state power of the USSR is the Supreme Council [Soviet] of the USSR ...

32. The legislative power of the USSR is exercised exclusively by the Supreme Council of the USSR.

33. The Supreme Council of the USSR consists of two Chambers: the Council of the Union and the Council of Nationalities.

34. The Council of the Union is elected by election districts by the citizens of the USSR on the basis of one deputy per 300,000 of population.

35. The Council of Nationalities is elected by the citizens of the USSR, by Union republics and autonomous republics, by autonomous regions and national districts, on the basis of 25 deputies from each Union republic, 11 deputies from each autonomous republic, 5 deputies from each autonomous region and one deputy from each national district ...

48. The Supreme Council of the USSR elects, at a joint session of both chambers, the Presidium of the Supreme Council of the USSR ...

56. The Supreme Council of the USSR at a joint session of both chambers forms the Government of the USSR – the Council of People's Commissars of the USSR ...

64. The supreme executive and administrative organ of state power in the USSR is the Council of People's Commissars of the USSR ...

94. The organs of state power in territories, provinces, autonomous provinces, regions, districts, cities and villages ... are Soviets of toilers' deputies ...

95. The Soviets of toilers' deputies of territories [etc.] are elected by the toilers of the respective territory [etc.] ...

126. In accordance with the interests of the toilers and for the purpose of developing the organizational self-expression and political activity of the masses of the people, citizens of the USSR are ensured the right of combining in public organizations: trade unions, co-operative associations, youth organizations, sport and defence organizations, cultural, technical and scientific societies, and for the most active and conscientious citizens from the ranks of the working class and other strata of the toilers, of uniting in the All-Union Communist Party (of Bolsheviks), which is the vanguard of the toilers in their struggle for strengthening and developing the socialist system and which represents the leading nucleus of all organizations of the toilers, both public and state ...

134. Deputies to all Soviets of toilers' deputies, the Supreme Council of the USSR [etc.] are elected by the electors on the basis of universal, equal and direct suffrage by secret ballot.

135. Elections of the deputies are universal: all citizens of the USSR who have reached the age of 18, irrespective of race or nationality, religion, educational qualifications, residential qualifications, social origin, property status and past activity, have the right to participate in elections of deputies and to be elected, with the exception of the mentally deficient and persons deprived of electoral rights by the courts ...

141. Candidates are put forward for election according to electoral districts. The right to put forward candidates is granted to social organizations and societies of the toilers: Communist Party organizations, trade unions, co-operatives, youth organizations and cultural societies ...

Source: G.A. Kertesz (ed.), *Documents in the Political History of the European Continent 1815–1939* (Oxford, 1968), pp. 446–9; taken from *Rappard's Source Book on European Government* (New York, 1937), pp. V 107–29

These brief excerpts from the 1936 constitution illustrate the changes in the structure of the Soviet Union. At first glance the constitution appeared to guarantee democratic rights and individual liberties to all citizens over the age of eighteen, who were allowed to vote by secret ballot (Article 134) for members of the 'supreme organ of state power', the Supreme Council (Article 30). However, as you will see from Article 141, only the Communist party and its subordinate organisations could actually nominate candidates for election. Moreover the Supreme Council would rarely meet, delegating responsibilities to a smaller body, the Presidium (Article 48), which in turn chose the real seat of power, the Council of Commissars, a small group of ministers under Stalin's control. Although regional rights were apparently guaranteed under Articles 33 and 35, in fact Communist rule grew in strength in the regions, so Lenin's promise of self-determination for non-Russians was never realised.

At a time when the NKVD was eliminating anybody considered to pose a threat to Stalin's position by extracting confessions to trumped-up charges of 'Trotskysim' or 'terrorism', the notion that the constitution represented the dawn of a new democratic era was patently absurd. While Marx's 'dictatorship of the proletariat' remained enshrined in the constitution (Article 2), in practice, Stalin now retained more power than Lenin ever had. The 'cult of personality', or the dictatorship of Stalin, had strayed from strict Marxist-Leninist principles, and the new constitution was a clever ploy to disguise the enormous amount of power that Stalin and the party now retained. Thus, although he still needed the memory of Lenin to provide ideological legitimacy for his actions, the cult of personality was such that Stalin could now re-write Soviet history in his own image.

7.7 The removal of Trotsky from history, photographic evidence

Source: David King Collection

The first photograph shows Lenin addressing a workers' meeting shortly after the 1917 Revolution. Trotsky is clearly seen standing to Lenin's side. In the 1930s, after Stalin had defeated and humiliated Trotsky in the power struggle that followed Lenin's death, Stalin insisted that the second 'doctored' official photograph be incorporated in history textbooks. Trotsky has been 'removed' from Russian history. Trotsky continued his accusations against the betrayal of the Revolution in a steady torrent of hostile literature while in exile. Stalin resented these attacks, and in 1940 Trotsky was hacked to death with an ice pick by Stalin's agents in Mexico, where he then lived. Thus ended one of the bloodiest personal feuds in modern history. Only when the entire 'old guard' of Bolsheviks had been destroyed could Stalin feel secure enough to call a halt to the purges.

The example of the expunging of Trotsky from history in this way raises wider questions about the nature of photographic or visual evidence. The second photograph of Lenin without Trotsky was the 'official' photographic record in the Soviet Union for many years. And yet it is not an original or accurate record at all, but rather an example of state propaganda. The two photographs thus provide a valuable insight into the nature of the regime and the *attitudes* of Soviet authorities. But they also illustrate that visual evidence, perhaps even more than written evidence, should not be taken at face value, but needs to be handled with care and approached critically.

By 1945 the Soviet Union had lost 20 million citizens, the majority of them civilians, as a result of Hitler's invasion of Russia. Stalin continued to rule the Soviet Union after 1945; indeed, as a result of the 'Great Patriotic War', his prestige was at its highest. The Fourth Five-Year Plan was inaugurated in 1946 and miraculously, as it seemed, restored industrial production to pre-war levels. Document 7.8 is an example of the manner in which Stalin was portrayed on his seventieth birthday.

7.8 Stalin's seventieth birthday celebration, photographed in December 1949 (see p. 171)

In the 1930s Stalin emerged from the power struggle within the party to become an authentic totalitarian dictator, but the 'cult of the personality' was still largely confined to idealised images of Lenin as the Father of the Revolution. By continuing to claim that he was Lenin's chosen successor and by constantly keeping Lenin's memory before the people, Stalin provided ideological 'legitimacy' for his ruthless policies. Only during and after the 'Great Patriotic War' did Stalin's image displace that of Lenin. Stalin was able to take credit for the defeat of Nazism and the emergence of the Soviet Union as a 'superpower' with an unprecedented empire in eastern Europe (see Chapter 9). Stalin's seventieth birthday celebrations in December 1949 were the high point of the 'cult of Stalin'. In Document 7.8 Stalin's picture can be seen hanging from an invisibly

Source: Centre for the Study of Propaganda, University of Kent at Canterbury

tethered balloon shimmering in the spotlights. This god-like icon, high above the mortals below, represented the culmination of dictatorial infallibility.

By the beginning of 1953 it looked as though a renewed purge on the lines of that of the late 1930s might be under way. However, on 5 March 1953, Stalin died suddenly of a stroke, aged seventy-three. Immediately his successors asserted the principle of collective leadership, with Georgi Malenkov, Chairman of the Council of Ministers, and Nikita Khrushchev, Party Secretary, the key figures. Within four years Malenkov was dismissed, and Khrushchev had consolidated his position as the dominant personality. At the Twentieth Party Congress, in February 1956, Khrushchev denounced various aspects of Stalin's policies and proclaimed the new doctrine of 'different roads to socialism'.

7.9 Khrushchev's 'secret' speech at the Twentieth Party Congress, February 1956

Comrades: We must abolish the cult of the individual decisively, once and for all; we must draw the proper conclusions concerning both ideological-theoretical and practical work.

It is necessary for this purpose:

First, in a Bolshevik manner to condemn and to eradicate the cult of the individual as alien to Marxism-Leninism and not consonant with the principles of Party leadership and the norms of Party life, and to fight inexorably all attempts at bringing back this practice in one form or another.

To return to and actually practice in all our ideological work the most important theses of Marxist-Leninist science about the people as the creator of history and as the creator of all material and spiritual good of humanity, about the decisive role of the Marxist Party in the revolutionary fight for the transformation of society, about the victory of Communism.

In this connection we will be forced to do much work in order to examine critically from the Marxist-Leninist viewpoint and to correct the widely spread erroneous views connected with the cult of the individual in the sphere of history, philosophy, economy and of other sciences, as well as in literature and the fine arts. It is especially necessary that in the immediate future we compile a serious textbook of the history of our Party which will be edited in accordance with scientific Marxist objectivism, a textbook of the history of Soviet society, a book pertaining to the events of the Civil War and the Great Patriotic War.

Secondly, to continue systematically and consistently the work done by the Party's Central Committee during the last years, a work characterized by minute observation in all Party organizations, from the bottom to the top, of the Leninist principles of Party leadership, characterized, above all, by the main principle of collective leadership, characterized by the observation of the norms of Party life described in the Statutes of our Party, and finally, characterized by the wide practice of criticism and self-criticism.

Thirdly, to restore completely the Leninist principles of Soviet socialist democracy, expressed in the Constitution of the Soviet Union, to fight wilfulness of individuals abusing their power. The evil caused by acts violating revolutionary socialist legality which have accumulated during a long time as a result of the negative influence of the cult of the individual has to be completely corrected. Comrades! The XXth Congress of the Communist Party of the Soviet Union has manifested with a new strength the unshakeable unity of our Party, its cohesiveness around the Central Committee, its resolute will to accomplish the great task of building Communism. [*Tumultuous applause.*] And the fact that we present in all their ramifications the basic problems of overcoming the cult of the individual which is alien to Marxism-Leninism, as well as the problem of liquidating its burdensome consequences, is an evidence of the great moral and political strength of our Party. [*Prolonged applause.*]

We are absolutely certain that our Party, armed with the historical resolutions of the XXth Congress, will lead the Soviet people along the Leninist path to new successes, to new victories. [*Tumultuous, prolonged applause.*]

Long live the victorious banner of our Party – Leninism! [*Tumultuous, prolonged applause ending in ovation. All rise.*]

Source: *Khrushchev Remembers* (London, 1971), vol. I, pp. 642–3

Document 7.9 comprises Khrushchev's concluding remarks to a very long speech. Although he now denounced Stalin after his death, remember that Khrushchev's political career had depended on Stalin's patronage; and as party boss in the Ukraine, Khrushchev had been responsible for carrying out the purges there. The speech listed a gamut of charges against Stalin, including cultivating his own personality, the atrocities of the purges, his misconduct in the war and his inability to consider other routes to socialism. The speech was supposed to be secret, but news of it leaked out and caused a sensation. Khrushchev's own position when he made the speech was not entirely secure, and he was challenged by Malenkov and Molotov. Nevertheless, 'de-Stalinisation' did take place, and Khrushchev remained in power until 1964, when he was voted out of office and forced to retire. Unlike many of Stalin's victims, Khrushchev was at least allowed to retire without being impeached, imprisoned or executed.

CHRONOLOGY: RUSSIA UNDER STALIN

1924	21 January	Death of Lenin.
1925	14 April	Party Conference adopts 'socialism in one country'.
1926	19 October	Trotsky and Kamenev expelled from Politburo.
1927	November	Trotsky expelled from Communist party.
	December	Fifteenth Party Conference condemns all deviations from party line. Attack upon the *kulaks* and agreement on the collectivisation of agriculture. Stalin emerges from power struggle as dominant figure.

1928	January	Trotsky banished to provinces.
	1 October	Beginning of First Five-Year Plan aiming to develop heavy industries.
	November	Bukharin and Tomsky exiled to Turkey.
1929	January	Trotsky exiled to Turkey.
	Autumn	Start of forced collectivisation and the removal of the *kulaks*.
	17 November	Bukharin and other 'rightists' expelled from party.
1930	January	Tempo of collectivisation increased; widespread coercion and deportation for those who resisted.
	March	Stalin publishes *Dizzy with Success*, which calls for slowing down of collectivisation.
1933	November	Second Five-Year Plan introduced.
1934	January	Seventeenth Party Conference.
	July	NKVD replaces GPU (former *Cheka*).
	September	USSR joins League of Nations.
	December	Assassination of Kirov. Central Executive Committee issue directive ordering summary trial and execution of 'terrorists' without appeal.
1935	January	Zinoviev, Kamenev and others tried in secret for 'moral responsibility' for Kirov's assassination and sentenced to imprisonment. Widespread arrests.
	December	Purge of 'oppositionists' declared over by Central Committee.
1936	January	Renewed purge of party members.
	19–24 August	Trial and execution of Zinoviev, Kamenev and other members of the 'Trotskyite–Zinovievite Counter-Revolutionary Bloc' for allegedly plotting against the leadership. Tomsky commits suicide following accusations made at the trial.
	25 September	Yagoda replaced by Yezhov as head of NKVD. Purges now referred to as 'Yezhovshchina'.
	5 December	Eighth Congress of Soviets approves the new Constitution.
1937	March	Bukharin, Rykov and Yagoda expelled from the party.
	June	Marshal Tukhachevsky, Chief of the General Staff, and other senior officers tried in secret for plotting with Germany and executed. Widespread purge of the armed forces begins, removing over 400 senior officers.
1938	2–13 March	Third Five-Year Plan inaugurated. Trial of Bukharin, Rykov, Krestinsky, Rakovsky, Yagoda, and other leading party and NKVD members for terrorism, sabotage, treason and espionage.
	December	Beria succeeds Yezhov as head of NKVD.
1939	March	Eighteenth Party Congress.
	23 August	Nazi–Soviet Non-Aggression Pact signed, which secretly agrees on the partition of Poland and allocation of Finland, Latvia, Estonia and Bessarabia to Soviet sphere of influence.
	17 September	Red Army invades eastern Poland.
	29 November	USSR breaks off diplomatic relations with Finland.
1940	18 December	Hitler issues directive for Operation Barbarossa, the invasion of Russia.
1941	22 June	Germany invades USSR.
	3 July	Stalin broadcasts to the people.
	2 October	German offensive against Moscow opens.
	27 November	German forces come within 20 miles of Moscow.
1942	March	Soviet winter offensive ends.
1943	2 February	Last German forces surrender at Stalingrad.
1946		Fourth Five-Year Plan introduced.

1947	September	Cominform established.
1951		Fifth Five-Year Plan inaugurated.
1953	5 March	Death of Stalin. Malenkov becomes Prime Minister.
	September	Khrushchev becomes First Secretary.
1956	February	Twentieth Party Congress, Khrushchev denounces Stalin and the 'Cult of the Personality'.
1957		Khrushchev becomes Prime Minister.
1964		Khrushchev is deposed following economic failures.

BIBLIOGRAPHY

Sources and documents

The most comprehensive documentary analyses can be found in P. Boobbyer, *The Stalin Era* (2000) and R. Sakwa, *The Rise and Fall of the Soviet Union* (1999). M. McCauley, *Stalin and Stalinism* (1983) is hardly exhaustive but contains some useful documents, as indeed does A. Wood, *The Russian Revolution* (1986) ending with the NEP. J. Degras (ed.), *Soviet Documents on Foreign Policy* (1953), concentrates on foreign policy. L. Trotsky, *Problems of Life* (1924), provides an absorbing account of the lessons of the Revolution that were intended to be incorporated into the new Soviet society. A vivid contemporary account leading up to the purges can be found in V. Serge, *From Lenin to Stalin* (1937). See also Stalin's revealing letters written over a ten-year period in, L.T. Lih *et al.* (ed.), *Stalin's Letters to Molotov 1925–1936* (1995). On the purges themselves, see the experiences of V. Serge, *Memoirs of a Revolutionary* (1963) and E. Ginsberg, *Into the Whirlwind* (1968). M. Djilas, *Conversations with Stalin* (1962) reveals the later Stalin. For Stalin's own account of his policies see his *Works* (1955). For a different perspective by his successor, see N. Khrushchev, *Khrushchev Remembers* (1971), now considered to be authentic by historians. Finally, two revealing accounts can be found in S. Allilyeva (Stalin's daughter), *Twenty Letters to a Friend* (1967) and one of Stalin's most vehement critics, A. Solzhenitsyn, *The Gulag Archipelago 1918–56* (1974). A moving novel of the 1930s that was suppressed for many years is A. Rybakov, *Children of the Arbat* (1989).

Secondary works

A readable introduction to some of the main issues and events is M. McCauley, *The Soviet Union 1917–91* (1993). Equally recommended as general textbooks are: C. Ward, *Stalin's Russia* (1993); G. Hosking, *A History of the Soviet Union* (1985); E. Acton, *Russia* (1986). A. Nove, *An Economic History of the USSR* (1969) remains an authoritative survey of the theory and practice of the Soviet economy. This has now, however, been superseded by R.W. Davies, *Soviet Economic Development from Lenin to Khrushchev* (1998).

On Stalin himself there are excellent biographies: I. Deutscher, *Stalin* (1966); A.B. Ulam, *Stalin: the Man and his Era* (1973); D. Volkogonov, *Stalin* (1991). An excellent essay can be found in R. Service, 'Joseph Stalin: The Making of a

Stalinist', in J. Channon (ed.), *Politics, Society and Stalinism in the USSR* (1998). For a limited 'dual' biography, see M. Lynch, *Stalin and Khrushchev: The USSR 1924–64* (1990). The transitional period after Lenin's death is discussed in E.H. Carr, *The Interregnum, 1923–4* (1974), *Socialism in One Country, 1924–6* (1978) and his *The Russian Revolution from Lenin to Stalin, 1917–29* (1970). The political demise of Trotsky is dealt with in I. Deutscher, *The Prophet Outcast* (1963) and R. Segal, *The Tragedy of Leon Trotsky* (1983). For the debates after Lenin's death, see A. Erlich, *The Soviet Industrialization Debate, 1924–1928* (1960). On the decision-making process, see E.A. Rees, *Decision-Making in the Stalinist Command System* (1997). Also of interest is M. Lewin, 'Bureaucracy and the Stalinist State', in I. Kershaw and M. Lewin (eds), *Stalinism and Nazism* (1997); this edited collection is an excellent comparative volume. See also S. Fitzpatrik's (ed.) controversial new addition to the current debates, *Stalinism* (1999).

P. Kenez, *The Birth of the Propaganda State* (1985) is a readable and informative account of the role of propaganda in the 1920s. An excellent analysis of Soviet films in the years immediately following the 1917 Revolution can be found in R. Taylor, *The Politics of the Soviet Cinema, 1917–29* (1979) and R. Taylor (ed.), *Stalinism and the Soviet Cinema* (1993). See also Taylor's comparative analysis, *Film Propaganda. Soviet Russia and Nazi Germany* (1998). For a wider analysis, see P. Kenez, *Cinema and Soviet Society 1917–1953* (1992).

The role of women is discussed in W. Goldman, *Women, the State and Revolution* (1993).

On the collectivisation of agriculture, see R.W. Davies, *The Socialist Offensive* (1980) and S. Fitzpatrick, *Stalin's Peasants* (1994). See also, L. Viola, *Peasant Rebels under Stalin* (1996). R. Conquest, *The Great Terror* (1971) provides a thorough account of all aspects of the purges, as does, J.A. Getty and R.T. Manning (eds), *Stalinist Terror* (1993) and R. Thurston, *Life and Terror in Stalin's Russia, 1934–1941* (1996). L.L. Schapiro, *The Communist Party of the Soviet Union* (1970) has still not been surpassed as a broad interpretation.

For the war period see J. Barber and M. Harrison, *The Soviet Home Front 1941–45* (1991); A. Werth, *Russia at War* (1965); A. Dallin, *German Rule in Russia, 1941–5* (1957); S.J. Linz (ed.), *The Impact of World War II on the Soviet Union* (1985); R. Stites (ed.) *Culture and Entertainment in Wartime Russia* (1995). On the post-war years, see A. Wath, *Russia: 1945–53* (1984). Stalin's foreign policy is discussed in G.F. Kennan, *Russia and the West under Lenin and Stalin* (1961); A.B. Ulam, *Expansion and Co-existence* (1967); and J. Haslam, *Soviet Foreign Policy, 1930–3* (1983) and *The Soviet Union and the Struggle for Collective Security* (1984). The experiences of the Second World War are recounted by Stalin in *On the Great Patriotic War* (1945).

Articles

For an interesting analysis of the early intellectual debate in Stalinist Russia, see J. Barker, 'The Establishment of Intellectual Orthodoxy in the USSR 1928–34', *P.P.* (1979). Cultural changes are discussed in S. Fitzpatrik, 'Cultural Revolution in Russia, 1928–32', *J.C.H.* (1974). A regional account of the effects of collectivisation is tackled in D.R. Brower, 'Collectivised Agriculture in Smolensk: The Party, the Peasantry and the Crisis of 1932', *The Russian Review* (1977); S. Cohen, 'Stalin's revolution reconsidered', *S.R.* (1973). For an account of Russian foreign policy on the eve of the Second World War, see J. Haslam, 'The Soviet Union and the Czechoslovakian Crisis of 1938', *J.C.H.* (1979). M Shkarrovskii, 'The Russian Orthodox Church versus the State: The Josephite Movement, 1927–1940', *S.R.* (1995) is an interesting analysis; see also, R. Thurston, 'The Soviet Family during the Great Terror, 1935–41', *Soviet Studies* (1991).

8

The approach to the Second World War

With the benefit of hindsight, we can see that international security established in the 1920s was something of a facade. The fragile safeguards that the League of Nations had implemented to secure peace were increasingly undermined by a series of challenges to its authority. In 1931 Japan seized Manchuria, an important economic region in north-east China. Italy invaded Abyssinia (Ethiopia) in October 1935 and in the same year Hitler announced the introduction of conscription and embarked on a heavy rearmament programme. The failure of the League to respond to these acts of international aggression persuaded Hitler to take a calculated risk and, in March 1936, he ordered his troops to reoccupy the Rhineland, which had been demilitarised since 1919. Despite the fact that his earlier actions had repudiated both the Treaty of Versailles and the Locarno Pact (1925), Hitler justified the reoccupation of the Rhineland by arguing that the Franco-Soviet Pact (1935), in which each side pledged to aid the other in case of attack, was a direct threat to Germany's security. The failure of the League to check unprovoked aggression and the repudiation of its Covenant, irrevocably undermined its authority.

The Spanish Civil War

As we have seen, in the 1930s Europe became increasingly polarised ideologically and politically between the Left and the Right. International relations were intended to be governed through the League by means of collective security (see Chapter 4), but the already questionable standing of the League was damaged further by the outbreak of the Spanish Civil War in July 1936. Since the foundation of the Spanish Republic in 1931, the political situation in Spain had become increasingly unstable and tense. In July 1936 Spanish generals led by Francisco Franco rose against the Republican government and plunged Spain into civil war. Document 8.1 is General Franco's manifesto, which challenged the authority of the democratically elected Republican government and thus precipitated the Civil War.

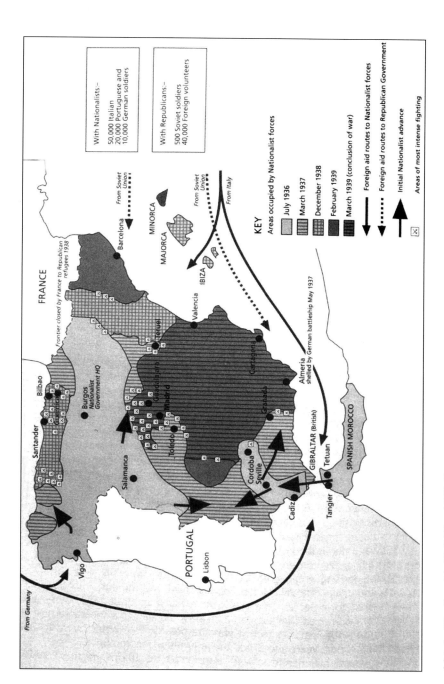

Map 4 The Spanish Civil War, 1936–9

8.1 General Franco's manifesto, 18 July 1936

Spaniards!

The Nation calls to her defence all of you who feel a holy love for Spain, you who, in the ranks of the Army and the Navy, have made a profession of faith in the service of our Country, you who have sworn to defend her with your lives against her enemies.

The situation in Spain is becoming more critical every day; anarchy reigns over most of the countryside and in the towns; authorities appointed by the Government preside over, if they do not foment, the revolts …

Revolutionary strikes of all kinds paralyse the life of the Nation; they destroy her sources of wealth and produce a famine which reduces the workers to despair.

In obedience to orders from foreign leaders, who count on the complicity or negligence of governors and officials, most violent attacks on monuments and artistic treasures are carried out by revolutionary bands.

Gravest offences are committed in the cities and the countryside while the forces of public order remain in their quarters, corroded by the desperation caused by [the necessity] of blindly obeying leaders who intend to dishonour them. The Army, the Navy, and other armed organizations are the target of the vilest and most slanderous attacks precisely on the part of those who ought to protect their good name.

States of emergency and alert are only imposed to gag the people, to keep Spain ignorant of what goes on outside everybody's own city or town, and to imprison pretended political enemies.

The Constitution is gravely violated by all and is suffering total eclipse …

The Magistracy, whose independence is guaranteed by the Constitution, is weakened and undermined by persecution …

Electoral pacts made at the expense of the integrity of the Country, combined with attacks on government offices and strongrooms to falsify election returns, constitute the masquerade of legality which now rules us. There is no restraint on the thirst for power, on the illegal dismissal of moderate elements, on the glorification of the revolutions in Asturias and Catalonia – all violations of the Constitution. …

To the blind revolutionary spirit of the masses (deceived and exploited by Soviet agents who conceal the bloody reality of that [Soviet] régime which has sacrificed twenty-five million people to its survival) is allied the malice and negligence of the authorities at every level who, sheltered behind the bungling of the [Central] Power, lack the authority and prestige to impose order and the rule of liberty and justice.

Can we tolerate for another day the disgraceful spectacle we are giving to the world?

Can we abandon Spain to her enemies by cowardly and traitorous behaviour, surrender her without struggle, without resistance?

No! Traitors may do so, but not we who have sworn to defend her.

We offer you justice and equality before the law; peace and love between Spaniards; liberty and fraternity, freed from licence and tyranny; work for all; social justice achieved without rancour or violence; and an equitable distribution of wealth without destroying or endangering the Spanish economy.

But, before this, war without quarter to the political exploiters, to the deceivers of the honest worker, to the foreigners and their would-be imitators, who intend, directly or indirectly, to destroy Spain ...

Since the purity of our intentions prevents us stifling such achievements [of the recent past] as represent progress in social and political betterment, and since the spirit of hatred and revenge has no place in our heart, we shall know how to salvage from the inevitable wreck of certain legislative projects all that is compatible with the internal peace of Spain and the greatness we desire for her, making real in our Country, for the first time, and in this order, the threefold watchword of FRATERNITY, LIBERTY AND EQUALITY.

Spaniards: long live Spain!!!

Long live the honourable Spanish People!!!

> The Commandant General of the Canary Islands

Source: G.A. Kertesz (ed.), *Documents in the Political History of the European Continent 1815–1939* (Oxford, 1968), pp. 489–90

As with so many conflicts in the inter-war years, the Civil War in Spain was a direct clash between political forces of the Left and the Right. In the elections of February 1936 a Popular Front coalition of the republican Left, socialists and communists had triumphed over a right-wing combination of fascists (Falange), monarchists and conservatives who had demanded that the parliamentary republic be replaced by a more authoritarian regime. The Nationalist challenge had begun as a revolt by disillusioned army officers in Spanish Morocco, led by General Franco. Alarmed by what they claimed was the increasingly socialist and anti-clerical policies of the Republican government of Manuel Azaña, a carefully planned *coup* of the army rebels had succeeded, by the summer of 1936, in gaining control over much of the country.

From his position as Commandant General of the Canary Islands (he had been demoted the previous March), Franco issued his manifesto of 18 July 1936. It was a declaration of intent, a patriotic appeal for all Spaniards to unite behind traditionally conservative values and forestall what he claimed was a communist uprising engineered by 'Soviet agents'. Ironically, given that he opposed the democratically elected Popular Front government, Franco's manifesto referred to impeccably 'liberal' notions such as 'fraternity, liberty and equality'. Franco hoped that such an appeal would lead to a speedy seizure of power throughout Spain. In fact, it was the prelude to a bitter civil war that would last for three years and divide the international community.

Having issued his manifesto, and transferred his troops to the Spanish mainland, Franco immediately appealed to Germany and Italy for military aid. The League of Nation's adopted a position of non-intervention, but Germany and Italy, while paying lip-service to the principle, disregarded it in practice and continued to send economic and military support to the Nationalist forces under Franco. The Republicans, on the other hand, received support from Russia and from the International Brigades, formed by volunteers from many countries. In September 1936, the Non-intervention Committee established in London by interested foreign governments, tried ineffectually to prevent the flow of arms and volunteers to Spain. Although it purported to treat both sides equally, the policy of 'non-intervention' favoured, in practice, the Nationalists at the expense of the legitimate Spanish government. The Soviet Union viewed these developments with considerable alarm and made their feelings clear in an address to the Non-Intervention Committee.

8.2 The Soviet view of non-intervention. A statement by Maisky, the Soviet Ambassador to Britain, at the Non-intervention Committee, 30 October 1936

There is a marked tendency in many quarters to represent the USSR as intending to try to turn Spain into a Communist Republic. These suspicions have no basis in fact. Of course the sympathy of the people of Soviet Russia is on the side of the forces of the Popular Front now conducting a heroic struggle in Spain and we have no reason to apologise for this. ...

If the Spanish Government eventually succeeds in suppressing the rebellion it will not only keep one more country in the camp of peace, but it will also profoundly influence the whole situation in Europe by inspiring new confidence in the strength of democracy and in the possibility of the peaceful settlement of international questions. In this event the danger of war which today looms so dark on the horizon would be greatly lessened and the political sky of Europe be cleared of its present clouds.

But if, on the contrary, success goes to the rebel generals, supported in contravention of the Non-intervention Agreement by certain powers, then not only will Spain suffer internal disaster, but the whole outlook in Europe will be blackened in the last degree, because the victory of the rebels would mean such a tremendous encouragement to all the forces of aggression, hatred and destruction in Europe that war would advance to the very threshold of our homes and engulf our part of the world in the very near future. This and this alone is the real reason why the Soviet Government and peoples take the present events in Spain so closely to heart, their attitude is determined by their policy of peace.

Source: Statement by Maisky (the Soviet Ambassador to Britain) at the Non-Intervention Committee, 30 October 1936, quoted in J. Degras (ed.), *Soviet Documents of Foreign Policy, vol. 3, 1933–41* (London, 1953), pp. 214–15

The speech was made by Maisky, the Soviet Ambassador to Britain. On 24 October 1936 he had informed the Committee that violations by fascist governments had rendered the non-intervention agreement 'an empty, torn scrap of paper ... that ceased to exist'. In his speech of 30 October, Maisky outlined what the Soviets viewed as the wider ramifications of the Spanish conflict. He started by refuting the Nationalist claim that the USSR was trying 'to turn Spain into a Communist Republic'. According to Maisky, it was essential to crush the 'rebel generals'; a victory for Republican government, would 'profoundly influence the whole situation in Europe'. In this period, Stalin was attempting to establish closer economic ties with western Europe and divert attention away from the purges in the Soviet Union (see Chapter 7). Maisky's speech is, nevertheless, couched in the ideological language of the Comintern, which viewed the Spanish Civil War as a dialectical conflict that required a united stand against fascism. The Soviets, for their part, supplied the Spanish government with arms, obtaining in return the entire Spanish gold reserves.

The desperate state of the Spanish government was highlighted when they made a formal appeal to the League of Nations for assistance in November 1936.

8.3 The Spanish government's appeal to the League of Nations, 27 November 1936

In notes addressed to the Powers parties to the Non-Intervention Agreement, in a letter to the Secretary-General of the League of Nations and in my speech to the Assembly of the League, the Spanish Government has denounced the armed intervention of Germany and Italy in favour of the rebels in the Spanish civil war – such intervention constituting the most flagrant violation of international law. This intervention has culminated in the recognition of the chief of the rebels set up as a Government by the 'wire-pullers' of the same Powers. Such a proceeding is virtually an act of aggression against the Spanish Republic. The declared intention of the rebels of forcibly preventing free commerce with the ports controlled by the Government claims attention as a factor likely to create international difficulties – difficulties which, as is well known, Franco declared his intention of provoking from the outset of the rebellion. These difficulties are increased by the fact that the rebels have been recognized by Germany and Italy, which, and particularly one of them, as is proved by information in the possession of the Government of the Republic, are preparing to co-operate with them in the naval sphere as they have done in the air and on land. These facts, through their very simultaneity, constitute for the Spanish Government a circumstance affecting international relations which threatens to disturb international peace or the good understanding between nations upon which peace depends. On behalf of the Spanish Government, I therefore request Your Excellency in the supreme interests of peace and in virtue of Article 11 of the Covenant, to take the necessary steps to enable the Council to proceed, at the earliest possible moment, to an examination of the situation outlined above.

Julio Alvarez del Vayo, Minister for Foreign Affairs of the Spanish Republic

Source: *League of Nations Official Journal, 1937*, pp. 18–19

On 18 November 1936, Germany and Italy officially recognised Franco's government, whose troops were advancing on Madrid, forcing the Republican government to flee to Valencia. Prolonged resistance was not anticipated. The appeal made by Julio Alvarez was a staunch defence of international law and an attack on Germany and Italy for their intervention in the conflict. The reference to a 'Government by the "wire-pullers" of the same Powers' was an attempt to depict Franco as the 'puppet' of the recently formed Rome–Berlin Axis. By invoking Article 11 of the League of Nations Covenant (see Document 4.8), the Spanish government was appealing to the League to implement its declared intention of securing international peace by means of collective security. The League responded sympathetically by reaffirming that all states were under an obligation not to intervene. However, military sanctions that were available under Article 16 of the Covenant were never used.

In sending the Condor Legion of bombers to assist the Spanish rebels, the German High Command saw an opportunity to test the strategy of *blitzkrieg* under military conditions. In April 1937 the Basque city of Guernica was destroyed by German bombers. The destruction of Guernica, which was captured by the realism of the newsreel cameras and later commemorated by the Spanish artist Pablo Picasso, provided a frightening glimpse of the horror of total war and a sobering reminder that European cities like London and Paris were equally vulnerable to squadrons of bombers. For some historians, the real roots of the later appeasement of the Nazis by Britain and France can be found in the brutal images of the Spanish Civil War and the determination on the part of democratic governments to spare their own population such misery and suffering.

By the end of 1938 Franco's Nationalist forces were in control of most of Spain and about to begin the final offensive against Catalonia. Franco was already claiming victory, employing the Falange slogan 'Spain Awake, Spain Forward' to unite the nation. A typical propaganda poster of 1938 celebrating Spanish unity is given as Document 8.4.

8.4 'The Unity of the Spanish Lands', a Nationalist poster of 1938 (see p.185)

The poster was produced by the Department of Applied Art, which served the National Propaganda Service. The official symbol of the eagle can be seen in the bottom left-hand corner. Written across the outline of the map of Spain are the words: 'With the triumph of the armies [comes] the unity of the Spanish lands.' Nationalist propaganda emphasised the role of the military and often employed military icons such as the rifle. The arm embracing the rifle conveniently obscured the Catalan region that was still resisting heroically. Note also, the Falange symbol of the bow and arrows in the centre of the poster. Another Nationalist propaganda slogan that eulogised armed struggle proclaimed: 'For

Source: Centre for the Study of Propaganda, University of Kent at Canterbury

Arms – the Fatherland, Bread and Justice', with a poster showing a hand firmly clenched around the trigger of a rifle.

Most historians would agree that Franco could not have won the Civil War without the unstinting aid of Hitler and Mussolini, which far surpassed the assistance that Republicans received from the Soviet Union. Tanks and air power proved decisive factors in determining the outcome of the war, and the Nationalists held a superiority in both. In fact, Soviet aid began to dry up by 1938. The resolutions that the League of Nations passed showed it to be sympathetic to the plight of the legitimate Spanish government but largely ineffectual. By continuing to support the principle of non-intervention, Britain and France (still the major powers in Europe) revealed the timidity and moral indifference of the parliamentary democracies when challenged from both the Left (communism) and Right (fascism). Moreover the ideological issues of the war undermined national unity in Britain and France and helped shape their policy of appeasement.

Although the level of international aid and intervention in Spain should not be exaggerated, its significance in terms of Europe's immediate future was that it conditioned diplomacy for the next three years. Salutary lessons were learned by all the major protagonists in the conflict. Mussolini and Hitler viewed the inertia of Britain and France as a further sign that parliamentary democracy was in terminal decline. The fascist dictators emerged with their reputation enhanced as the champions of anti-communism and duly signed the Anti-Comintern Pact in November 1937. The Soviet Union's resolve and ability to support a Popular Front government was called into question, as was the League's policy of collective security to resist fascist aggression. Stalin would not forget the unwillingness of Britain and France to unite against fascism. The effete democracies, on the other hand, were disposed to appease the dictators and persuade them to return to the concert of Europe. In all this the major casualty was the Spanish Republic. Franco achieved victory in 1939, establishing a personal dictatorship which was to last until his death in 1975. Moreover, the Spanish Civil War created the sense that an international conflict between fascism and communism was impending.

The Spanish Civil War has often been described as a dress rehearsal for the Second World War. In a military sense that was not the case at all. However, what we do witness during this period is a growing propensity on the part of the great powers to ignore the forum of the League of Nations and resume the type of bilateral diplomacy that characterised international relations in the period leading up to war in 1914. There is no better illustration of this trend than the events that led to the Munich Agreements. Munich came to symbolise 'appeasement' – the policy followed first by Britain and then by France of avoiding war with fascist dictators by giving way to their demands, provided they were not too unreasonable.

The Munich Crisis

The Rome–Berlin Axis signed in November 1936 had changed the balance of power in Europe. Austria, in particular, was left isolated as a result. Previously, Austria had depended on an alliance between Britain, France and Italy to secure its independence in the face of German demands. With Italy now on Germany's side, the balance of power in Central Europe had shifted dramatically.

In February 1938, Hitler summoned the Austrian Chancellor, Kurt von Schuschnigg and increased the pressure on the Austrian government to include a Nazi nominee in the Cabinet. Schuschnigg had been worried by increased Nazi activity in Austria and had come to Germany hoping to secure assistance from Hitler. Austrian Nazis had, in fact, attempted an earlier *coup* in 1934 with the assassination of Chancellor Dollfuss. On that occasion they were thwarted by Mussolini, who opposed German intervention in Austria. As a result of the Rome–Berlin Axis, Hitler was now in a stronger position, and in the meeting with Schuschnigg he made far-reaching demands, which the Austrian Chancellor at first accepted. On 9 March, however, Schuschnigg announced a plebiscite to decide on Austria's fate, confident that the people would vote to remain independent. Schuschnigg's initiative forced Hitler to act; on 12 March 1938, German troops crossed the border and Austria was declared part of the German Reich. Document 8.5 is the text of the final radio broadcast made by Schuschnigg on the evening of 11 March, protesting at the planned German annexation of Austria.

8.5 Radio broadcast by Kurt von Schuschnigg to the Austrian people, 11 March 1938

Men and women of Austria!

Today we have been confronted with a difficult and decisive situation. I am authorized to report to the Austrian people on the events of the day.

The Government of the German Reich presented the Federal President with an ultimatum with a time-limit, according to which he had to appoint as Federal Chancellor a prescribed candidate, and constitute a Government in accordance with the proposals of the Government of the German Reich. Otherwise it was intended that German troops should march into Austria at the hour named.

I declare before the world that the reports which have been spread in Austria that there have been labour troubles, that streams of blood have flowed, and that the Government was not in control of the situation and could not maintain order by its own means, are fabrications from A to Z.

The Federal President authorizes me to inform the Austrian people that we yield to force. Because we are not minded, at any cost and even in this grave hour, to shed German blood, we have ordered our armed forces, in case the invasion is carried out, to withdraw without resistance and to await the events of the next hours ...

So I take my leave in this hour of the Austrian people with a German word and a heartfelt wish – God protect Austria!

Source: *Documents on International Affairs 1938* (Royal Institute of International Affairs), vol. II, p. 66

The radio broadcast represented Schuschnigg's last, defiant stand against Nazi aggression. During the secret negotiations that had been taking place since the announcement of the plebiscite, a furious Hitler, had demanded that Schuschnigg should be replaced as Chancellor by the Austrian Nazi Minister of the Interior, Seyss-Inquart. When it became clear to Schuschnigg that he could expect no help from Britain and France, he resigned. The Austrian President, Miklas, had initially refused to appoint Seyss-Inquart, and on 11 March Hitler ordered the invasion. During the evening Miklas capitulated but it was too late to prevent the invasion.

Schuschnigg had stayed on as a 'caretaker' Chancellor, and in his emotional broadcast to the 'men and women of Austria', he made it clear that both he and Austria were giving way to force. Conscious that the Nazis would present themselves as liberators and claim the *anschluss* (union) as a victory for self-determination, Schuschnigg took great care to deny, 'before the world', that his government 'was not in control of the situation and could not maintain order' and that this had resulted in 'streams of blood'. Nevertheless, the Austrian armed forces had been ordered not to resist. The German invasion of Austria was Hitler's first move outside German territory in defiance of the Treaty of Versailles. Shortly afterwards a plebiscite was arranged so effectively in both Germany and Austria that 99 per cent of those voting supported Hitler's actions. Austria was relegated to a mere province of the Reich.

The *anschluss* with Austria not only revealed the extent of Hitler's ambitions; it also dealt a strategic blow at Czechoslovakia, which could now be attacked from the south as well as from the west and north. The Republic of Czechoslovakia had been created in 1918 and contained a volatile racial mix of Czechs, Slovaks, Hungarians, Ruthenes, and some three million Germans, mostly living in the Sudetenland. Nevertheless, it had shown itself to be more genuinely democratic than many of its neighbours. Hitler, however, decided to use the grievances of the German minority, led by Konrad Henlein, as a pretext for his expansionist ambitions.

When Neville Chamberlain became British Prime Minister in May 1937 he gave a new impetus to appeasement. For Chamberlain, appeasement meant taking the initiative and showing the fascist powers that 'reasonable' claims could be achieved by negotiation and not force. Chamberlain and Edouard Daladier, the new French Prime Minister, feared that the Czech crisis could precipitate a wider conflict and decided that Czechoslovakia was simply not worth a European war. The Czech President, Eduard Beneš, was urged therefore to make concessions to the Sudeten Germans. Chamberlain had three meetings with Hitler: at Berchtesgaden on 15 September, at Bad Godesberg on 22–3 September, and at Munich on 29–30 September. At the first meeting, Hitler stated his intention to annex the Sudetenland on the principle of self-determination. At Bad Godesburg he insisted on immediate German occupation, and finally at Munich was persuaded to accept a phased occupation with an international commission to arbitrate over disputed boundaries.

As President Beneš, urged on by Britain and France, offered the Sudeten Germans wider measures of autonomy, Henlein was instructed to 'demand so much that we can never be satisfied'. On 29 September 1938, an international conference was held at Munich. The participants were Germany, Italy, Britain and France. Conspicuous by its absence was Czechoslovakia, whose fate was to be decided, and the Soviet Union, which was not invited. At Munich a number of deals were struck at the expense of Czech sovereignty. The agreement, signed on 30 September, stipulated that the Germans were to occupy the Sudetenland between 1 and 10 October and the four powers together with Czechoslovakia were to form a commission which was to supervise the take-over and deal with any disputes arising from the agreement. An annex to the agreement stated that, once the Polish and Hungarian claims had been settled, the rump state of Czechoslovakia was to be guaranteed by the four powers. Later that day Chamberlain, without consulting the French, persuaded Hitler to sign a piece of paper declaring Britain and Germany's intention never to go to war with one another again. Hitler scarcely bothered to read it, but duly signed. Chamberlain returned to Britain in triumph, proclaiming that he had brought back 'peace in our time'. Czechoslovakia was now a defenceless rump but was still an independent republic.

The peace had been saved, but the achievements of Munich were soon to prove illusory. The vulnerability of Czechoslovakia was underlined when Slovak separatists, demanding independence, appealed to Hitler for military assistance. On 15 March 1939 Hitler sent his army into Prague, in clear violation of the Munich Agreement, and Czechoslovakia was finally dismembered. Bohemia and Moravia became a 'protectorate' of the Third Reich and placed under direct German rule, Slovakia became an independent state and Hungary occupied the province of Ruthenia. Czechoslovakia had paid the supreme price for the democracies' attempts to preserve peace in Europe. It was now almost inevitable that Hitler's next victim would be Poland.

Munich represented both the apotheosis and the end of appeasement. Far from securing 'peace in our time', it culminated in a triumph for naked aggression. By the end of 1938 Hitler, not Chamberlain, dominated the diplomatic stage of Europe. Nevertheless, the butchering of Czechoslovakia marked a significant turning point in British and French diplomacy towards Germany. The events in Czechoslovakia had persuaded Chamberlain and Daladier that Hitler was bent on the domination of Central and Eastern Europe. Both Britain and France used the year between Munich and the outbreak of war to speed up their rearmament programme.

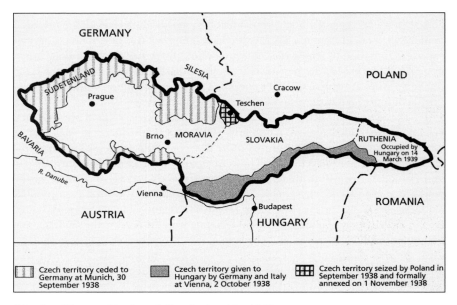

Map 5a The partitioning of Czechoslovakia, 1938

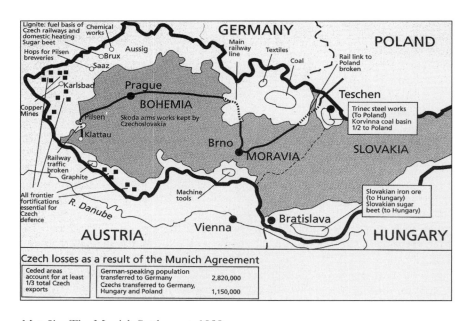

Map 5b The Munich Settlement, 1938

Origins of the Second World War

There has been much discussion about appeasement and what might have happened if Britain and France had decided to go to war with Germany in 1938. As with the First World War, the origins of the Second World War have sparked considerable controversy. In assessing Hitler's responsibility for the outbreak of war in 1939, much attention has been devoted to the so-called Hossbach Memorandum.

8.6 Extract from the Hossbach Memorandum, 5 November 1937

Minutes of the Conference in the Reich Chancellery, Berlin, November 5, 1937, from 4:15 to 8:30 p.m.

Present: The Führer and Chancellor, Field Marshal von Blomberg, War Minister, Colonel General Baron von Fritsch, Commander in Chief, Army. Admiral Dr. H.C. Raeder, Commander in Chief, Navy. Colonel General Göring, Commander in Chief, *Luftwaffe*, Baron von Neurath, Foreign Minister, Colonel Hossbach.

The Führer began by stating that the subject of the present conference was of such importance that its discussion would, in other countries, certainly be a matter for a full Cabinet meeting, but he – the Führer – had rejected the idea of making it a subject of discussion before the wider circle of the Reich Cabinet just because of the importance of the matter. His exposition to follow was the fruit of thorough deliberation and the experiences of his 42 years of power. He wished to explain to the gentlemen present his basic ideas concerning the opportunities for the development of our position in the field of foreign affairs and its requirements, and he asked, in the interests of a long-term German policy, that his exposition be regarded, in the event of his death, as his last will and testament.

The Führer then continued:

The aim of German policy was to make secure and to preserve the racial community and to enlarge it. It was therefore a question of space. ...

German policy had to reckon with two hate-inspired antagonists. Britain and France, to whom a German colossus in the center of Europe was a thorn in the flesh, and both countries were opposed to any further strengthening of Germany's position either in Europe or overseas; in support of this opposition they were able to count on the agreement of all their political parties. Both countries saw in the establishment of German military bases overseas a threat to their own communications, a safeguarding of German commerce, and, as a consequence, a strengthening of Germany's position in Europe. ...

Germany's problem could be solved by means of force and this was never without attendant risk. The campaigns of Frederick the Great for Silesia and

Bismarck's wars against Austria and France had involved unheard-of risk, and the swiftness of the Prussian action in 1870 had kept Austria from entering the war. If one accepts as the basis of the following exposition the resort to force with its attendant risks, then there remain still to be answered the questions 'when' and 'how'. In this matter there were three cases to be dealt with:

CASE 1: PERIOD 1943–1945

After this date only a change for the worse, from our point of view, could be expected.

The equipment of the army, navy, and *Luftwaffe*, as well as the formation of the officer corps, was nearly completed. Equipment and armament were modern; in further delay there lay the danger of their obsolescence. In particular, the secrecy of 'special weapons' could not be preserved forever. The recruiting of reserves was limited to current age groups; further drafts from older untrained age groups were no longer available.

Our relative strength would decrease in relation to the rearmament which would by then have been carried out by the rest of the world. If we did not act by 1943–45, any year could, in consequence of a lack of reserves, produce the food crisis, to cope with which the necessary foreign exchange was not available, and this must be regarded as a 'waning point of the regime.' Besides, the world was expecting our attack and was increasing its counter-measures from year to year. It was while the rest of the world was still preparing its defences that we were obliged to take the offensive.

Nobody knew today what the situation would be in the years 1943–45. One thing only was certain, that we could not wait longer.

On the one hand there was the great *Wehrmacht*, and the necessity of maintaining it at its present level, the aging of the movement and of its leaders; and on the other, the prospect of a lowering of the standard of living and of a limitation of the birth rate, which left no choice but to act. If the Führer was still living, it was his unalterable resolve to solve Germany's problem of space at the latest by 1943–45. The necessity for action before 1943–45 would arise in cases 2 and 3.

CASE 2

If internal strife in France should develop into such a domestic crisis as to absorb the French Army completely and render it incapable of use for war against Germany, then the time for action against the Czechs had come.

CASE 3

If France is so embroiled by a war with another state that she cannot 'proceed' against Germany.

For the improvement of our politico-military position our first objective, in the event of our being embroiled in war, must be to overthrow Czechoslovakia and Austria simultaneously in order to remove the threat to our flank in any possible operation against the West. In a conflict with France it was hardly to be regarded as likely that the Czechs would declare war on us on the very same day as France. The desire to join in the war would, however, increase among the Czechs in proportion to any weakening on our part and then her participation could clearly take the form of an attack toward Silesia, toward the north or toward the west.

If the Czechs were overthrown and a common German-Hungarian frontier achieved, a neutral attitude on the part of Poland could be the more certainly counted on in the event of a Franco-German conflict. Our agreements with Poland only retained their force as long as Germany's strength remained unshaken. In the event of German setbacks a Polish action against East Prussia, and possibly against Pomerania and Silesia as well, had to be reckoned with.

On the assumption of a development of the situation leading to action on our part as planned, in the years 1943–45, the attitude of France, Britain, Italy, Poland, and Russia could probably be estimated as follows:

Actually, the Führer believed that almost certainly Britain, and probably France as well, had already tacitly written off the Czechs and were reconciled to the fact that this question would be cleared up in due course by Germany. Difficulties connected with the Empire, and the prospect of being once more entangled in a protracted European war, were decisive considerations for Britain against participation in a war against Germany. Britain's attitude would certainly not be without influence on that of France. An attack by France without British support, and with the prospect of the offensive being brought to a standstill on our western fortifications, was hardly probable. Nor was a French march through Belgium and Holland without British support to be expected; this also was a course not to be contemplated by us in the event of a conflict with France, because it would certainly entail the hostility of Britain. It would of course be necessary to maintain a strong defence on our western frontier during the prosecution of our attack on the Czechs and Austria. And in this connection it had to be remembered that the defence measures of the Czechs were growing in strength from year to year, and that the actual worth of the Austrian Army also was increasing in the course of time. Even though the populations concerned, especially of Czechoslovakia, were not sparse, the annexation of Czechoslovakia and Austria would mean an acquisition of foodstuffs for 5 to 6 million people, on the assumption that the compulsory emigration of 2 million people from Czechoslovakia and 1 million people from Austria was practicable. The incorporation of these two States with Germany meant, from the politico-military point of view, a substantial advantage because it would mean shorter and better frontiers, the freeing of forces for other purposes, and the possibility of creating new units up to a level of about 12 divisions, that is, 1 new division per million inhabitants.

Italy was not expected to object to the elimination of the Czechs, but it was impossible at the moment to estimate what her attitude on the Austrian question would be; that depended essentially upon whether the Duce were still alive.

The degree of surprise and the swiftness of our action were decisive factors for

Poland's attitude. Poland – with Russia at her rear – will have little inclination to engage in war against a victorious Germany.

Military intervention by Russia must be countered by the swiftness of our operations; however, whether such an intervention was a practical contingency at all was, in view of Japan's attitude, more than doubtful.

Should case 2 arise – the crippling of France by civil war – the situation thus created by the elimination of the most dangerous opponent must be seized upon *whenever it occurs* for the blow against the Czechs.

The Führer saw case 3 coming definitely nearer; it might emerge from the present tensions in the Mediterranean, and he was resolved to take advantage of it whenever it happened, even as early as 1938. ...

If Germany made use of this war to settle the Czech and Austrian questions, it was to be assumed that Britain – herself at war with Italy – would decide not to act against Germany. Without British support, a warlike action by France against Germany was not to be expected ...

In appraising the situation Field Marshal von Blomberg and Colonel General von Fritsch repeatedly emphasized the necessity that Britain and France must not appear in the role of our enemies, and stated that the French Army would not be so committed by the war with Italy that France could not at the same time enter the field with forces superior to ours on our western frontier. General von Fritsch estimated the probable French forces available for use on the Alpine frontier at approximately twenty divisions, so that a strong French superiority would still remain on the western frontier, with the role, according to the German view, of invading the Rhineland. In this matter, moreover, the advanced state of French defence preparations [*Mobilmachung*] must be taken into particular account, and it must be remembered apart from the insignificant value of our present fortifications – on which Field Marshal von Blomberg laid special emphasis – that the four motorized divisions intended for the West were still more or less incapable of movement. In regard to our offensive toward the southeast, Field Marshal von Blomberg drew particular attention to the strength of the Czech fortifications, which had acquired by now a structure like a Maginot Line and which would gravely hamper our attack.

General von Fritsch mentioned that this was the very purpose of a study which he had ordered made this winter, namely, to examine the possibility of conducting operations against the Czechs with special reference to overcoming the Czech fortification system; the General further expressed his opinion that under existing circumstances he must give up his plan to go abroad on his leave, which was due to begin on November 10. The Führer dismissed this idea on the ground that the possibility of a conflict need not yet be regarded as so imminent. To the Foreign Minister's objection that an Anglo-French-Italian conflict was not yet within such a measurable distance as the Führer seemed to assume, the Führer put the summer of 1938 as the date which seemed to him possible for this. In reply to considerations offered by Field Marshal von Blomberg and General von Fritsch regarding the attitude of Britain and France, the Führer repeated his previous statements that he was convinced of Britain's nonparticipation, and therefore he did not believe in the probability of belligerent action by France against Germany. Should the

Mediterranean conflict under discussion lead to a general mobilization in Europe, then we must immediately begin action against the Czechs. On the other hand, should the powers not engaged in the war declare themselves disinterested, then Germany would have to adopt a similar attitude to this for the time being.

Colonel General Göring thought that, in view of the Führer's statement, we should consider liquidating our military undertakings in Spain. The Führer agrees to this with the limitation that he thinks he should reserve a decision for a proper moment.

The second part of the conference was concerned with concrete questions of armament.

HOSSBACH

CERTIFIED CORRECT:
Colonel (General Staff)

Source: *Documents on German Foreign Policy, 1918–1945*, Series D, vol. I (London, HMSO, 1949), pp. 29–30

Document 8.6 is a record of a meeting Hitler held towards the end of 1937 with his top military staff and his Foreign Minister in which he outlined the aims of German policy and the possible courses it might follow. These are not official minutes in a formal sense, rather an account that Friedrich Hossbach, Hitler's military adjutant, made from memory some five days later. The Hossbach Memorandum was used as a key prosecution document at the Nuremberg Trials when it was cited as a timetable for German aggression. Although there is no serious reason to doubt its accuracy, it is, in fact, a copy of a copy – the original having disappeared.

Hitler began by asserting that the subject of the meeting was too important for a full cabinet discussion. The preservation of the German racial community depended on 'living space', and this could only be achieved by the use of force ('and this was never without attendant risk'). Germany, however, would only be fully prepared for war in the mid 1940s but could not afford to wait that long. If an opportunity presented itself before that date, it must be taken. In order to improve Germany's 'politico-military situation', the first objective was the defeat of Czechoslovakia and Austria. Hossbach noted that the 'Führer believed that almost certainly Britain, and probably France … had tacitly written off the Czechs and were reconciled to the fact that this question would be cleared up in due course by Germany'. Hitler was also confident that Mussolini would not object to an *anschluss* with Austria.

As we have seen, German foreign policy after 1937 bore a striking resemblance to the strategy minuted by General Hossbach. If the Hossbach Memorandum was a premeditated masterplan for European domination, then whatever foreign policy the democracies adopted would have led to eventual conflict. Appeasement can then be discounted as the root cause of war, as war would have been inevitable. Alternatively, it is possible to argue that Hitler was not planning war but setting out long-term aims and taking the opportunity outside a minuted cabinet meeting to think aloud and make warlike noises. By adopting a position of appeasement, Britain and France tempted Hitler to gamble further and to take bigger risks, convinced that they would remain passive.

My own feeling is that the Hossbach Memorandum records Hitler attempting to win the support of his General Staff and Foreign Minister for the acquisition of living space in Eastern Europe within a specified time limit, and by force if necessary. The sense of urgency that Hitler conveyed is in marked contrast to the anxiety expressed by Blomberg and Fritsch (and later by Neurath) about the consequences of precipitate German military action. Within weeks of the meeting, the army had set out a strategic plan for an offensive against Czechoslovakia, and a few months later a bloodless purge removed the remnants of the conservative 'old guard' who had failed to respond more positively to Hitler's plans. The meeting of 5 November represented a dramatic turning point that led to Hitler assuming control of the armed forces and in the process emasculating the army as an independent force. By mid-1938 Hitler had sufficiently weakened potential opposition from conservative elites and could now initiate an expansionist foreign policy in pursuit of German hegemony.

Following the invasion of Czechoslovakia in March 1939, Britain abandoned appeasement; and on 31 March, Chamberlain announced that Britain and France would guarantee Poland's independence. On 3 April the German General Staff was ordered to prepare for war against Poland. German grievances against Poland stemmed from the 1919 peace settlements and the loss of the Polish corridor, which now separated East Prussia from the rest of Germany, and the former German port of Danzig, which was made an 'open' city under the League of Nation's jurisdiction. Document 8.7 is a propaganda postcard intended to persuade British public opinion that the loss of Danzig in 1919 'would be like dividing Britain into two parts'. Germans were encouraged to send the postcard to acquaintances and friends in Britain. Distinguished individuals were also targeted by the Nazi government.

8.7 A Nazi postcard justifying German claims to Danzig, 1939 (see p. 197)

Soon after the announcement of the League of Nations guarantee, the British and French started negotiations with the Soviet Union to establish a common front against Germany. However, longstanding Anglo-French mistrust of the motives of the Soviet Union, together with Poland's refusal in August to allow Russian troops on its territory in the event of a war between the Soviet Union and Germany, finally sank the negotiations. The Germans, on the other hand, keen to prevent such a *rapprochement*, stepped in and persuaded Stalin to sign a non-aggression pact on 23 August, with secret clauses on the partition of Poland.

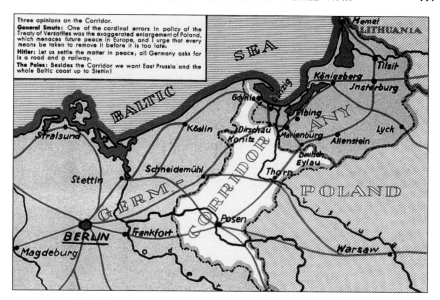

Three opinions on the Corridor.

General Smuts: One of the cardinal errors in policy of the Treaty of Versailles was the exaggerated enlargement of Poland, which menaces future peace in Europe, and I urge that every means be taken to remove it before it is too late.

Hitler: Let us settle the matter in peace; all Germany asks for is a road and a railway.

The Poles: Besides the Corridor we want East Prussia and the whole Baltic coast up to Stettin!

What would you say if Great Britain were to be treated in this way and a corridor and canal after the model of the Polish Corridor forced upon her territory in order to give Ireland a direct connection with the North Sea? Would Great Britain agree to such a frontier?

Source: University of Kent at Canterbury, Centre for the Study of Propaganda

The signing of the Nazi–Soviet Pact was perhaps one of the most controversial acts in the period leading up to the Second World War. Writing some years later in his memoirs, Nikita Khrushchev referred to the Soviet Union's motives in signing the pact.

8.8 Khrushchev on the signing of the Nazi–Soviet Non-Aggression Pact, 23 August 1939

Anyway, we met for dinner at Stalin's that Sunday in August 1939, and while the trophies of our hunt were being prepared for the table, Stalin told us that Ribbentrop had brought with him a draft of a friendship and non-aggression treaty which we had signed. Stalin seemed very pleased with himself. He said that when the English and French who were still in Moscow found out about the treaty the next day, they would immediately leave for home. The English and French representatives who came to Moscow to talk with Voroshilov didn't really want to join forces with us against Germany at all. Our discussions with them were fruitless. We knew that they weren't serious about an alliance with us and that their real goal was to incite Hitler against us. We were just as glad to see them leave.

That's how the Ribbentrop-Molotov Pact, as it was called in the West, came into being. We knew perfectly well that Hitler was trying to trick us with the treaty. I heard with my own ears how Stalin said, 'Of course it's all a game to see who can fool whom. I know what Hitler's up to. He thinks he's outsmarted me, but actually it's I who have tricked him!' Stalin told Voroshilov, Beria, myself, and some other members of the Politbureau that because of this treaty the war would pass us by for a while longer. We would be able to stay neutral and save our strength. Then we would see what happened.

Of course there were some people who thought that since Hitler wanted to negotiate with us, he must be too frightened of us to attack. This interpretation of the treaty was very flattering to us. Many people in the USSR eagerly believed it and congratulated themselves. But we, the leaders of the Government, knew better. We weren't fooling ourselves. We knew that eventually we would be drawn into the war, although I suppose Stalin hoped that the English and French might exhaust Hitler and foil his plan to crush the West first and then to turn east. This hope of Stalin's must have been part of the strategy behind our agreement to sign the treaty.

I believe that the Ribbentrop-Molotov Pact of 1939 was historically inevitable, given the circumstances of the time, and that in the final analysis it was profitable for the Soviet Union. It was like a gambit in chess: if we hadn't made that move, the war should have started earlier, much to our disadvantage. As it was, we were given a respite. I think the vast majority of the Party considered the signing of the treaty tactically wise on our part, even though nobody could say so publicly. We couldn't even discuss the treaty at Party meetings. For us to have explained our reasons for signing the treaty in straightforward newspaper language would have been offensive, and besides, nobody would have believed us. It was very hard for us – as Communists, as anti-fascists, as people unalterably opposed to the philosophical and political position of the fascists – to accept the idea of joining forces with Germany. It was difficult enough for us to accept this paradox ourselves. It would have been impossible to explain it to the man in the street. Therefore we couldn't admit outright that we had reached an agreement on peaceful coexistence with Hitler. Coexistence would have been possible with the Germans in general, but not with the Hitlerite fascists.

For their part, the Germans too were using the treaty as a manoeuvre to win time. Their idea was to divide and conquer the nations which had united against Germany in the First World War and which might unite against Germany again. Hitler wanted to deal with his adversaries one at a time. He was convinced that Germany had been defeated in the First World War because she had tried to fight on two fronts at once. The treaty he signed with us was his way of trying to limit the coming war to one front.

Source: *Khrushchev Remembers* (London, 1971), vol. 1, pp. 150–2

The first striking revelation of this meeting between Stalin and his advisers (which took place after a hunting session), was that that top Politburo members like Khrushchev did not know that the pact with Germany had been signed. From the discussion that took place, Stalin, at least, was convinced that Britain and France were not serious about an alliance ('didn't really want to join forces with us … at all'). Nevertheless, at the time, the signing of the pact was widely viewed as a cynical reversal of ideological allegiances. It appeared to undermine the Anti-Comintern Pact and be at odds with Hitler's talk of a crusade against Bolshevism. Khrushchev's record confirms that the Soviets were under no illusions about Hitler's intentions and anticipated that 'eventually we would be drawn into the war'. According to Khrushchev, both sides viewed the treaty as an exercise in short-term pragmatic politics. Germany sought to avoid a war on two fronts and Stalin, having purged his High Command (see Chapter 7), used the treaty 'as a manoeuvre to win time'. In a secret clause to the treaty, Germany and Russia agreed to establish spheres of influence in Eastern and Central Europe, with the immediate partition of Poland. Hitler fixed the date for his attack on Poland for 26 August.

Hitler believed that the announcement of the non-aggression pact would demonstrate to the British and the French the futility of their promises to Poland. Chamberlain, however, continued to back Poland, and on 25 August signed an Anglo-Polish mutual assistance treaty while still seeking to achieve a negotiated settlement. When Germany invaded Poland on 1 September, the British government issued an ultimatum to Germany which expired on 3 September. First Britain and then France declared war on the same day, and thus the Second World War began.

The cartoonist David Low satirised the balance of power in Europe in May 1940 and suggested a new 'concert of Europe' dominated by dictatorships.

8.9 'The Harmony Boys', a cartoon by David Low in the *Evening Standard*, 2 May 1940

Source: Centre for the Study of Cartoons and Caricature,
University of Kent, Canterbury

In May 1940, the 'harmony boys' did indeed pose a real threat to European democracy. Poland had succumbed to the Nazi *blitzkrieg* and Russian troops had invaded its eastern provinces. Norway and Denmark had been over-run in April, and towards the end of May British troops were evacuated from Dunkirk. This cartoon shows Hitler orchestrating the totalitarian challenge made up of Mussolini, Franco and Stalin, none of whom was yet in the war. Hitler is seen to be manipulating the others. In fact, by depicting Stalin as Hitler's puppet, Low misunderstood the Soviet Union's motives for signing the non-aggression pact. Within a month of the publication of this cartoon, Britain stood even more alone as a deeply divided France (see Chapter 2) capitulated on 22 June at Compiègne, where the armistice ending the First World War had been signed. One week earlier a reluctant Mussolini had been persuaded to declare war on Britain and France. The other dictator in the cartoon, Franco, managed to keep Spain, gravely weakened by the civil war, out of the conflict. (More accurately,

Hitler was not prepared to press Spain to enter the war on the basis of the terms demanded by Franco.)

On 22 June 1941, Germany launched 'Operation Barbarossa', the invasion of the Soviet Union. Although anticipating a similar victory in the east to that achieved by *blitzkrieg* in the west, Hitler had underestimated Russia's resources and resolve. This error of judgement was compounded by Germany's gratuitous declaration of war on the United States after the Japanese had bombed Pearl Harbor. What had started as a European conflict was now a world war. Fascism was everywhere in retreat, but its total destruction would require two extra-European powers – the USA and the USSR – to occupy the imperial capital of Berlin, thus radically transforming the balance of power in Europe.

CHRONOLOGY: THE APPROACH TO THE SECOND WORLD WAR

Spanish Civil War

1931	April	Spain becomes a Republic after King Alfonso XIII abdicates.
	December	Republican Constitution announced.
1933	November	Falange (*Falango Espanola*) established as a right-wing movement opposed to the Republic.
1936	February	Popular Front wins elections in Spain and Azaña is elected President.
	17 July	Rising of the army in Morocco under General Franco. The revolt spreads to the Spanish mainland, which signifies the beginning of the Spanish Civil War.
	18 July	Franco issues his manifesto referred to as 'Manifesto of Las Palmas'.
	September	Non-intervention Committee established in London.
	October	Franco is unconstitutionally appointed head of state by Nationalists.
	November	After Nationalist forces advance on Madrid, Franco government is recognised by Germany and Italy and Republican government flees to Valencia.
1937	April	Franco calls for the unification of all Nationalist groupings into one movement.
	26 April	The Basque city of Guernica is destroyed by German Condor Legion.
	19 June	The Basque captial of Bilbao is captured by the Nationalists.
	October	Republican government flees to Barcelona.
1939	26 January	Barcelona falls to Nationalist forces.
	28 March	Nationalist forces enter Madrid
	1 April	Franco proclaims an end to the Civil War.

The Munich Crisis and the origins of the Second World War

1938	20 February	In a Reichstag speech Hitler maintains that millions of Germans on the frontiers of the Reich require protection.
	6 March	Schuschnigg's proposal of a plebiscite on the future independence of Austria. Announced on 9 March, voting was to take place on the 13th.
	10 March	Hitler mobilises German forces for immediate invasion of Austria.
	11 March	Hitler's ultimatum demanding that the plebiscite not be held, accepted by Schuschnigg.

	12 March	German forces march into Austria.
	13 March	Austria is declared part of Greater German Reich.
	28 March	Nazi agitation encourages Henlein, leader of Sudeten Germans in Czechoslovakia to make unreasonable demands designed to break up the Czech state.
	9 May	Russia promises to assist Czechoslovakia if Poland and Romania allow passage of Russian troops. Both refuse.
	21 May	Partial mobilisation of Czech reservists.
	22 May	Germany warned by Britain not to start military action in Czechoslovakia.
	15 September	Chamberlain goes to Berchtesgaden for meeting with Hitler, who restates German determination to annex the Sudetenland on the principle of self-determination.
	18 September	Britain and France agree that Czechs should hand over territory in areas where over half of the population is German.
	20–1 September	The Czech government initially rejects the Anglo-French proposals, but accepts them on the 21st.
	22 September	Meeting between Hitler and Chamberlain at Bad Godesberg. Hitler insists on immediate occupation of the Sudetenland, stating that German forces would invade on 28 September. The Czech cabinet resigns.
	29 September	At the Munich conference Chamberlain, Daladier, Hitler and Mussolini agree that Sudetenland be transferred to Germany, while guaranteeing the remaining Czech frontiers.
	30 September	Hitler and Chamberlain sign 'peace in our time' communiqué.
1939	31 March	Britain and France promise aid to Poland in the event of a threat to Polish sovereignty.
	7 April	Italy invades Albania. Spain joins the anti-Comintern Pact.
	16–18 April	The Soviet Union proposes a defensive alliance with Britain and France, but Britain and France prevaricate.
	27 April	Britain introduces conscription.
	22 May	Hitler and Mussolini sign the 'Pact of Steel' – a ten-year political and military alliance.
	23 August	Signing of Nazi–Soviet Non-Aggression Pact. Secret clauses agree on the partition of Poland. Chamberlain warns Hitler that Britain will stand by Poland, but accepts the need for a settlement of the Danzig question. Hitler states that Germany's interest in Danzig and the Corridor must be satisfied. The Poles refuse to enter negotiations with the Germans. Hitler brings forward his preparations to invade Poland to the 26th (from 1 September).
	25 August	Anglo-Polish mutual assistance pact signed in London. Hitler makes a 'last offer' on Polish question and postpones his attack until 1 September.
	31 August	Hitler orders attack on Poland.
	1 September	German forces invade Poland and annex Danzig. Britain and France demand withdrawal of German troops.
	2 September	Britain sends ultimatum to Germany, which is refused.
	3 September	Britain and France declare war on Germany.
	17 September	Soviet Union invades eastern Poland.
	30 November	Soviet Union invades Finland.

BIBLIOGRAPHY

Sources and documents

Documents on the Spanish Civil War can be found in D.A. Puzzo, *Spanish Civil War* (1962) and C.F. Delzell, *Mediterranean Fascism 1919–1945* (1970). For contemporary accounts by those who fought in the conflict see G. Orwell, *Homage to Catalonia* (1938) and F. Borkenau, *The Spanish Cockpit* (1937). R. Fraser, *Blood of Spain* (1979) contains eyewitness accounts of the war. For an interesting exercise in the oral history of the conflict, see N. MacMaster, *Spanish Fighters* (1990).

On the origins of the Second World War, A. Adamthwaite, *The Lost Peace* (1980) provides an invaluable documentary source on the whole period. H. Jacobsen and A. Smith (ed.), *World War II* (1980) contains documents relating to the military and strategy. Hitler's speeches, some of which are on German foreign policy, are available in N.H. Baynes (ed.), *The Speeches of Adolf Hitler, April 1922–August 1939* (1942) and on Italy, *Ciano's Diaries, 1937–8* (1952) and *1939–43* (1947). For Britain, see Lord Avon, *Facing the Dictators* (1962) and *The Reckoning* (1965) and W.S. Churchill, *The Second World War, Vol. I, The Gathering Storm* (1949); for France, C. de Gaulle, *War Memoirs* (3 vols, 1955–9); and for Russia, see I. Maisky, *Who Helped Hitler?* (1964).

Secondary works

The origins of the Spanish Civil War are analysed in P. Preston, *The Coming of the Spanish Civil War* (1994 edn). General histories of the civil war in Spain include: S.M. Ellwood, *The Spanish Civil War* (1991); H. Thomas, *The Spanish Civil War* (1977 edn); G. Jackson, *The Spanish Republic and the Civil War 1931–39* (1965). G. Brenan, *The Spanish Labyrinth* (1943) remains a perceptive and indispensable source. Biographies of Franco include: G. Hills, *Franco, the Man and his Nation* (1967); J. Trythall, *Franco* (1970); B. Crozier, *Franco* (1967); and, more recently, P. Preston, *Franco* (1993) and S. Ellward, *Franco* (1993).

For the inter-war period in general, E.H. Carr, *The Twenty Years Crisis* (new edn, 1981) remains a stimulating analysis. R.A.C. Parker, *Europe, 1919–45* (1969) is a solid general introduction. More recently, M. Kitchen, *Europe Between the Wars* (1990) provides a compelling political overview.

On 1919 and its immediate aftermath, A.J. Mayer, *The Policy and Diplomacy of Peacemaking* (1968); I. J. Lederer (ed.), The Versailles Settlement (1974); G. Schulz, *Revolution and Peace Treaties* (1972); S. Marks, *The Illusion of Peace* (1976) all provide useful information. F.P. Walters, *A History of the League of Nations* (1960) remains the most comprehensive account of the League, but see also S.R. Gibbons and P. Morican, *League of Nations and UNO* (1970) and P. Raffo, *The League of Nations* (1974). F.H. Hinsley, *Power and the Pursuit of Peace* (1967) contains a lively discussion of the theory and practice of international relations during this period.

On the immediate causes of the Second World War, see A.J.P. Taylor, *The Origins of the Second World War* (1963), which is still exciting and very readable, though its arguments have been severely questioned. The major contributors to the 'origins' debate are contained in E.M. Robertson (ed.), *The Origins of the Second World War* (1971). More recently, the Taylor controversy was re-examined in G. Martel (ed.), *The Origins of the Second World War Reconsidered: The A.J.P. Taylor Debate After Twenty-Five Years* (1986). On the 1930s especially, see also C. Thorne, *The Approach of War* (1967); D.C. Watt, *Too Serious a Business* (1975); A. Adamthwaite, *The Making of the Second World War* (1977). A recent synthesis is provided in P. Bell, *The Origins of the Second World War in Europe* (1986) and an accessible collection of essays can be found in P. Finney (ed.), *The Origins of the Second World War* (1997).

On specific events and issues, N. Rostow, *Anglo-French Relations, 1934–6* (1984) analyses western policies at a key period, whilst K. Robbins, *Munich* (1968) and T. Taylor, *Munich* (1979) look at the most criticised episode in 1930s diplomacy. For a short but fascinating biography of Neville Chamberlain, see P. Neville, *Neville Chamberlain: A Study in Failure?* (1992). See also J. Charmley, *Chamberlain and the Lost Peace* (1989). S. Newman, *March, 1939* (1976) concentrates on the British guarantee to Poland, which was so vital in the outbreak of war. For a discussion of the Soviet Union's road to war see G. Roberts, *The Soviet Union and the Origins of the Second World War* (1995) and J. Erickson and D. Dilks (eds), *Barbarossa* (1994). On French policy see especially A. Adamthwaite, *France and the Coming of the Second World War* (1977). On Germany, see G.L. Weinberg, *The Foreign Policy of Hitler's Germany: Starting World War II* (1980) and more recently Weinberg's valuable collection of essays, *Germany, Hitler and World War II* (1995); see also W. Carr, *Arms, Autarky and Aggression* (1972) and K. Hildebrand, *The Foreign Policy of the Third Reich* (1973). On the Nazi war economy, R. Overy, *War and Economy in the Third Reich* (1994). On British appeasement in general see especially M. Gilbert, *The Roots of Appeasement* (1966); K. Middlemas, *Diplomacy of Illusion* (1972); W.R. Rock, *British Appeasement in the 1930s* (1976); R.A.C. Parker, *Chamberlain and Appeasement. British Policy and the Coming of the Second World War* (1993). See also the essays by N. Medlicott and M. Howard in D. Dilks (ed.), *Retreat from Power: Studies of Britain's Foreign Policy of the Twentieth Century: Vol. 1, 1906–1939* (1981).

Articles

On the Spanish Civil War, see P. Preston, 'Spanish Civil War; Right versus Left in the 1930s', *M.H.R.* (1991) and G. Jackson, 'The Spanish Popular Front 1934–37', *J.C.H.* (1970). See also special editions of *H.T.* (1986 and 1989).

Among the numerous articles on the various crises of the 1930s, see L. Hill, 'Three Crises 1938–39' ,*J.C.H.*(1968); R.A.C. Parker, 'Great Britain, France and the Ethiopian Crisis, 1935–6', *E.H.R.*, (1974); R. Eatwell, 'Munich, Public Opinion and the Popular Front' *J.C.H.*(1971); C.A. Macdonald, 'Britain, France and the April Crisis of 1939', *E.S.R.* (1972); D. Carlton, 'Eden, Blum, and the Origins of Non-Intervention', *J.C.H.* (1971) and M. Newman, 'The origins of Munich', *H.J.* (1978).

On Hitler's foreign policy, see P.A. Reynolds, 'Hitler's War' *H.* (1961);

M.Hauner, 'Did Hitler Want a World Dominion?', *J.C.H.* (1978) and H.W. Koch, 'Barbarossa' *H.J.* (1983). On the domestic factors influencing German foreign policy see, R. Overy, 'Mobilisation for Total War in Germany, 1939–41', *E.H.R.* (1988). For a stimulating overview see, D. Reynolds, 'Power, wealth and war in the modern world', *H.J.* (1989).

9

The origins of the Cold War

The Europea n alliance system that had been meticulously erected by Bismarck after 1871, and which formed the starting point for this book, lay in ruins in 1945. All hope of returning to the European *status quo* of 1914 had been shattered. Indeed, the fate of the historic states of Europe which had dominated the world in the late nineteenth century now depended on two great 'superpowers' that had come together late in the war to form an unlikely alliance against fascism. Looking back to 1945, it is not surprising that the Grand Alliance did not survive the end of hostilities. The decision to fight on until Germany surrendered unconditionally created a power vacuum in the centre of Europe that America and the Soviet Union filled enthusiastically. Differences that had been played down during the war became more and more evident as hostilities drew to a close. The first major test of the Grand Alliance was the meeting of the 'Big Three' at Yalta, in the Crimea, in February 1945.

The changing face of Europe

The Yalta Conference was attended by Joseph Stalin, US President Franklin D. Roosevelt and British Prime Minister Winston Churchill. The so-called 'Big Three' had met for the first time in November 1943 at the Tehran Conference, when a provisional agreement was reached over a territorial settlement in eastern Europe. Churchill then visited Stalin in Moscow in October 1944, and the two leaders concluded a secret agreement on 'spheres of influence'. Romania and Bulgaria were to be ceded to Russian influence, Greece to Britain, and Yugoslavia and Hungary equally between Russia and Britain. At Yalta the following February, the Big Three attempted to agree on the outlines for peace that would follow their anticipated military victory over Germany and Japan.

9.1 Yalta Conference protocol declaration on liberated Europe, 11 February 1945

The following declaration has been approved:

'The Premier of the Union of Soviet Socialist Republics, the Prime Minister of the United Kingdom and the President of the United States of America have consulted with each other in the common interests of the peoples of their countries and those of liberated Europe. They jointly declare their mutual agreement to concert during the temporary period of instability in liberated Europe the policies of their three governments in assisting the peoples liberated from the domination of Nazi Germany and the peoples of the former Axis satellite states of Europe to solve by democratic means their pressing political and economic problems.

'The establishment of order in Europe and the re-building of national economic life must be achieved by processes which will enable the liberated peoples to destroy the last vestiges of Nazism and Fascism and to create democratic institutions of their own choice. This is a principle of the Atlantic Charter – the right of all peoples to choose the form of government under which they will live – the restoration of sovereign rights and self-government to those peoples who have been forcibly deprived of them by the aggressor nations.

'To foster the conditions in which the liberated peoples may exercise these rights, the three governments will jointly assist the people in any European liberated state or former Axis satellite state in Europe where in their judgment conditions require (*a*) to establish conditions of internal peace; (*b*) to carry out emergency measures for the relief of distressed peoples; (*c*) to form interim governmental authorities broadly representative of all democratic elements in the population and pledged to the earliest possible establishment through free elections of governments responsive to the will of the people; and (*d*) to facilitate where necessary the holding of such elections.

'The three governments will consult the other United Nations and provisional authorities or other governments in Europe when matters of direct interest to them are under consideration.

'When, in the opinion of the three governments, conditions in any European liberated state or any former Axis satellite state in Europe make such action necessary, they will immediately consult together on the measures necessary to discharge the joint responsibilities set forth in this declaration.

'By this declaration we reaffirm our faith in the principles of the Atlantic Charter, our pledge in the Declaration by the United Nations, and our determination to build in co-operation with other peace-loving nations world order under law, dedicated to peace, security, freedom and general well-being of all mankind.

'In issuing this declaration, the Three Powers express the hope that the Provisional Government of the French Republic may be associated with them in the procedure suggested.'

YALTA CONFERENCE PROTOCOL (FRENCH ZONE AND REPARATIONS), 11 FEBRUARY 1945

IV. Zone of Occupation for the French and Control Commission for Germany

It was agreed that a zone in Germany, to be occupied by the French Forces, should be allocated to France. This zone would be formed out of the British and American zones, and its extent would be settled by the British and Americans in consultation with the French Provisional Government.

It was also agreed that the French Provisional Government should be invited to become a member of the Allied Control Commission for Germany.

V. Reparation

The following Protocol has been approved:

Protocol

Conversations between the Heads of the three Governments at the Crimea Conference on the question of reparation in kind from Germany

The Heads of the three Governments have agreed as follows:

1. Germany must pay in kind for the losses caused by her to the Allied nations in the course of the war. Reparations are to be received in the first instance by those countries which have borne the main burden of the war, have suffered the heaviest losses, and have organised victory over the enemy.

2. Reparation in kind is to be exacted from Germany in three following forms:

(a) Removals within two years from the surrender of Germany or the cessation of organised resistance from the national wealth of Germany located on the terri-tory of Germany herself as well as outside her territory (equipment, machine-tools, ships, rolling stock, German investments abroad, shares of indus-trial, transport and other enterprises in Germany, etc.), these removals to be carried out chiefly for the purpose of destroying the war potential of Germany.

(b) Annual deliveries of goods from current production for a period to be fixed.

(c) Use of German labour.

3. For the working out on the above principles of a detailed plan for exaction of reparation from Germany an Allied Reparation Commission will be set up in Moscow. It will consist of three representatives – one from the Union of Soviet Socialist Republics, one from the United Kingdom and one from the United States of America.

4. With regard to the fixing of the total sum of the reparation as well as the distribution of it among the countries which suffered from the German aggression the Soviet and American delegations agreed as follows:

> 'The Moscow Reparation Commission should take in its initial studies as a basis for discussion the suggestion of the Soviet Government that the total sum of the reparation in accordance with the points (a) and (b) of the paragraph 2 should be 20 billion dollars and that 50 per cent of it should go to the Union of Soviet Socialist Republics.'

The British delegation was of the opinion that pending consideration of the reparation question by the Moscow Reparation Commission no figures of reparation should be mentioned.

The above Soviet-American proposal has been passed to the Moscow Reparation Commission as one of the proposals to be considered by the Commission.

YALTA CONFERENCE (POLAND), 11 FEBRUARY 1945

The following Declaration on Poland was agreed by the Conference:

'A new situation has been created in Poland as a result of her complete liberation by the Red Army. This calls for the establishment of a Polish Provisional Government which can be more broadly based than was possible before the recent liberation of the Western part of Poland. The Provisional Government which is now functioning in Poland should therefore be reorganised on a broader democratic basis with the inclusion of democratic leaders from Poland itself and from Poles abroad. This new Government should then be called the Polish Provisional Government of National Unity.

'M. Molotov, Mr Harriman and Sir A. Clark Kerr are authorised as a commission to consult in the first instance in Moscow with members of the present Provisional Government and with other Polish democratic leaders from within Poland and from abroad, with a view to the reorganisation of the present Government along the above lines. This Polish Provisional Government of National Unity shall be pledged to the holding of free and unfettered elections as soon as possible on the basis of universal suffrage and secret ballot. In these elections all democratic and anti-Nazi parties shall have the right to take part and to put forward candidates.

'When a Polish Provisional Government of National Unity has been properly formed in conformity with the above, the Government of the USSR, which now maintains diplomatic relations with the present Provisional Government of Poland, and the Government of the United Kingdom and the Government of the USA will establish diplomatic relations with the new Polish Provisional Government of National Unity, and will exchange Ambassadors by whose reports the respective Governments will be kept informed about the situation in Poland.

'The three Heads of Government consider that the Eastern frontier of Poland should follow the Curzon Line with digressions from it in some regions of five to eight kilometres in favour of Poland. They recognise that Poland must receive substantial accessions of territory in the North and West. They feel that the opinion of the new Polish Provisional Government of National Unity should be sought in due course on the extent of these accessions and that the final delimitation of the Western frontier of Poland should thereafter await the Peace Conference.

Source: *British and Foreign State Papers* (London, HMSO); quoted in Charles I. Bevans (ed.) *Treaties and Other International Agreements of the U.S.A., 1776–1949* (Washington, DC, 1968 onwards)

A number of deals were struck at Yalta. First of all, the Protocol acknowledged the Atlantic Charter, which was a statement of principles set out by Churchill and Roosevelt in August 1941 on the future conduct of international affairs. In their 'Declaration on Liberated Europe', the three powers pledged themselves to allow European states to 'create democratic institutions of their own choice', thereby anticipating regimes 'broadly representative of all democratic elements' based on 'free elections of governments responsive to the will of the people'. A permanent body, the United Nations Organisation (UNO), was to be set up to deal with international problems. Germany was to be divided into zones of military occupation, and an Allied Control Commission (including France) was to administer Germany on the basis of 'disarmament, demilitarisation, and dismemberment'. The question of reparations was also accepted in principle. What the document doesn't tell you is that Stalin had agreed to join the war against Japan on condition that the Soviet Union received territory in Manchuria and the island of Sakhalin.

The Yalta Conference was particularly concerned with settling the Polish question. All sides recognised that its resolution would largely determine the fate of eastern Europe. As the Red Army swept through Poland in 1944, it set up a Communist government in Lublin, even though the Polish government-in-exile was based in London. After long negotiations, it was agreed at Yalta that a 'Provisional Government of National Unity' should be formed (made up of the Lublin group and representatives of the London Poles), pledged to the 'holding of free and unfettered elections as soon as possible on the basis of universal suffrage and secret ballot'. The cession of Poland's eastern territories to Russia and the acquisition of German provinces in the north and west was approved in principle, but would await a final decision at the peace conference.

Yalta was hailed as a diplomatic triumph for an alliance that confidently anticipated imminent military victory, yet restrained itself from squabbling over the spoils of war. However it is very revealing that the deal struck, although reasonable, barely concealed the lack of trust among the Allies. Given the state of hostility that existed between the USA and the Soviet Union since the Bolshevik Revolution, it seems extraordinary that so much was left to chance.

However, in February 1945 fundamental differences could be overlooked or postponed in the interests of defeating Germany and Japan.

These differences became considerably clearer several months later when the next conference was held, at Potsdam outside the ruins of Berlin (Document 9.2). Harry S. Truman had acceded to the US presidency following the death of Roosevelt in April and, during the conference, Clement Atlee was elected the new Prime Minister in Britain, replacing Churchill. Stalin remained an ominously powerful presence.

9.2 The Potsdam Agreement, 2 August 1945

PROTOCOL OF BERLIN (POTSDAM) CONFERENCE

I. ESTABLISHMENT OF A COUNCIL OF FOREIGN MINISTERS

A. The Conference reached the following Agreement for the establishment of a Council of Foreign Ministers to do the necessary preparatory work for the peace settlements:

(1)   There shall be established a Council composed of the Foreign Ministers of the United Kingdom, the Union of Soviet Socialist Republics, China, France and the United States.

(2)   (i)   The Council shall normally meet in London, which shall be the permanent seat of the joint Secretariat which the Council will form. Each of the Foreign Ministers will be accompanied by a high-ranking Deputy, duly authorised to carry on the work of the Council in the absence of his Foreign Minister, and by a small staff of technical advisers.

(ii)   The first meeting of the Council shall be held in London not later than the 1 September, 1945. Meetings may be held by common agreement in other capitals as may be agreed from time to time.

(3)   (i)   As its immediate important task, the Council shall be authorised to draw up, with a view to their submission to the United Nations, treaties of peace with Italy, Romania, Bulgaria, Hungary and Finland, and to propose settlements of territorial questions outstanding on the termination of the war in Europe. The Council shall be utilised for the preparation of a peace settlement for Germany to be accepted by the Government of Germany when a Government adequate for the purpose is established. ...

II. THE PRINCIPLES TO GOVERN THE TREATMENT OF GERMANY IN THE INITIAL CONTROL PERIOD

A. Political principles

1. In accordance with the Agreement on Control Machinery in Germany, supreme authority in Germany is exercised, on instructions from their respective Governments, by the Commanders-in-Chief of the armed forces of the United States of America, the United Kingdom, the Union of Soviet Socialist Republics and the French Republic, each in his own zone of occupation, and also jointly, in matters affecting Germany as a whole, in their capacity as members of the Control Council.

2. So far as is practicable, there shall be uniformity of treatment of the German population throughout Germany.

3. The purposes of the occupation of Germany by which the Control Council shall be guided are:

(i)   The complete disarmament and demilitarisation of Germany and the elimination or control of all German industry that could be used for military production.

(ii) To convince the German people that they have suffered a total military defeat and that they cannot escape responsibility for what they have brought upon themselves, since their own ruthless warfare and the fanatical Nazi resistance have destroyed the German economy and made chaos and suffering inevitable. …

(iv) To prepare for the eventual reconstruction of German political life on a democratic basis and for eventual peaceful cooperation in international life by Germany. …

9. The administration in Germany should be directed towards the decentralisation of the political structure and the development of local responsibility. To this end:

(i)   Local self-government shall be restored throughout Germany on democratic principles and in particular through elective councils as rapidly as is consistent with military security and the purposes of military occupation;

(ii) all democratic political parties with rights of assembly and of public discussion shall be allowed and encouraged throughout Germany;

(iii) representative and elective principles shall be introduced into regional, provincial, and State (Land) administration as rapidly as may be justified by the successful application of these principles in local self-government;

(iv) for the time being, no central German Government shall be established. Notwithstanding this, however, certain essential central German administrative departments, headed by State Secretaries, shall be established, particularly in the fields of finance, transport, communications, foreign trade, and industry. Such departments will act under the direction of the Control Council.

B. Economic principles

... 11. In order to eliminate Germany's war potential, the production of arms, ammunition, and implements of war as well as all types of aircraft and sea-going ships shall be prohibited and prevented. Production of metals, chemicals, machinery, and other items that are directly necessary to a war economy, shall be rigidly controlled and restricted to Germany's approved post-war peacetime needs to meet the objectives stated in paragraph 15. Productive capacity not needed for permitted production shall be removed in accordance with the reparations plan recommended by the Allied Commission on reparations and approved by the Governments concerned or, if not removed, shall be destroyed.

12. At the earliest practicable date, the German economy shall be decentralised for the purpose of eliminating the present excessive concentration of economic power as exemplified in particular by cartels, syndicates, trusts, and other monopolistic arrangements.

13. In organising the German economy, primary emphasis shall be given to the development of agriculture and peaceful domestic industries.

14. During the period of occupation Germany shall be treated as a single economic unit. To this end common policies shall be established in regard to:

(a)   mining and industrial production and its allocation;
(b)   agriculture, forestry, and fishing;
(c)   wages, prices, and rationing;
(d)   import and export programmes for Germany as a whole;
(e)   currency and banking, central taxation, and customs;
(f)   reparation and removal of industrial war potential;
(g)   transportation and communications.

In applying these policies account shall be taken, where appropriate, of varying local conditions.

15. Allied controls shall be imposed upon the German economy but only to the extent necessary:

(a)   to carry out programmes of industrial disarmament and demilitarisation, of reparations, and of approved exports and imports;
(b)   to assure the production and maintenance of goods and services required to meet the needs of the occupying forces and displaced persons in Germany and essential to maintain in Germany average living standards not exceeding the

average of the standards of living of European countries. (European countries means all European countries excluding the United Kingdom and the Union of Soviet Socialist Republics);

(c) to ensure in the manner determined by the Control Council the equitable distribution of essential commodities between the several zones so as to produce a balanced economy throughout Germany and reduce the need for imports; …

19. Payment of reparations should leave enough resources to enable the German people to subsist without external assistance. In working out the economic balance of Germany the necessary means must be provided to pay for imports approved by the Control Council in Germany. The proceeds of exports from current production and stocks shall be available in the first place for payment for such imports.

Source: *British and Foreign State Papers* (London, HMSO); quoted in Charles I.
Bevans (ed.), *Treaties and the International Agreements of the U.S.A., 1776–1949*
(Washington, DC, 1918 onwards)

The Potsdam Protocol sets out the broad lines of agreement. A Council of Foreign Ministers representing the 'Big Five' (Britain, the USSR, China, France and the USA) would draw up peace treaties for Germany and the Axis satellite states. It was agreed that the unity of Germany should be preserved, but Article 3 (ii) of the 'political principles' stated that one of the purposes of the four-power occupation was to 'convince the German people that they have suffered a total military defeat and that they cannot escape responsibility for what they have brought upon themselves'. The Allies were clearly concerned to avoid a recurrence of the 'stab-in-the-back' myth that developed after the terms of the Versailles Treaty had been made known, which claimed that Germany had never been defeated on the battlefield. To this end, German political life was to be reconstructed on 'a democratic basis' in order to prepare Germany 'for eventual peaceful cooperation in international life' (Article 3 (iv)). It was also agreed that the Soviet Union could take reparations from its own zone of occupation plus a further 25 per cent of all machinery and industrial plant that was unnecessary for the German peace economy from the western zones (III, 4 (a, b)).

Article 13 of the 'economic principles' stated: 'In organising the German economy, primary emphasis shall be given to the development of agriculture and peaceful domestic industries.' This illustrates the extent to which the Allies were prepared to be punitive in their economic treatment of Germany. One of the American proposals for post-war Germany was the so-called Morgenthau Plan, which envisaged the destruction of heavy industry and the pastoralisation of Germany into a primarily agricultural country. Although the proposal was attractive to those who feared a revitalised German economy, it ignored the prevailing realities of Germany's economic situation, which required exports to

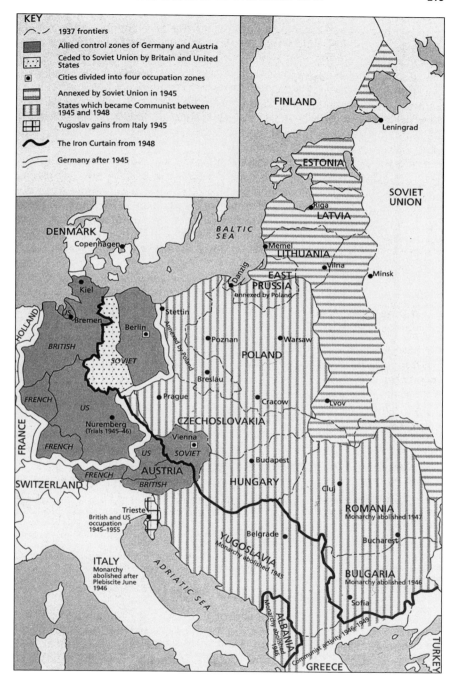

KEY

〜-〜 1937 frontiers

▨ Allied control zones of Germany and Austria

⬚ Ceded to Soviet Union by Britain and United States

◉ Cities divided into four occupation zones

▤ Annexed by Soviet Union in 1945

▥ States which became Communist between 1945 and 1948

▦ Yugoslav gains from Italy 1945

∿ The Iron Curtain from 1948

〜 Germany after 1945

Map 6 Europe after 1945

pay for the foodstuffs for a starving and displaced population. Moreover, the broad aims outlined at Potsdam failed to be specific enough to be applied uniformly across the four zones of occupation. This was because the Allies could not agree to implement a common policy across the whole country apart from the decision to keep Germany under military occupation. As the Grand Alliance began to disintegrate amidst growing antagonism, Germany became an intractable European problem that neither the United States nor the USSR was prepared to release into the camp of its adversary – a symbol of the cold diplomatic war of mistrust.

Pending a final treaty, the Potsdam Conference agreed to the transfer of part of East Prussia to the Soviet Union; and the western frontier of Poland, incorporating the areas of Germany's eastern territory, was accepted on a temporary basis as running along the Oder and western Neisse rivers. Germany was thus effectively moved well to the west of the frontier that had been accepted in principle at Yalta.

Overshadowing the discussions at Potsdam was the question of the Soviet Union's participation in the war against Japan. Truman had gone to Potsdam partly to ensure Soviet involvement, but he concealed from Stalin the existence of an atomic bomb that the United States had secretly tested. Thus although the Soviet Union declared war on Japan on 8 August and invaded Manchuria on 10 August, the USA dropped two atomic bombs on Japan, bringing the war in the Far East to a swift end without the need for Soviet intervention. The US administration believed that possessing the atomic bomb would strengthen its hand in negotiating with Stalin. In fact, it only increased the Soviets' resolve to develop their own atomic capability. While the dropping of the atomic bombs did end the Second World War, they also marked the beginning of the cold diplomatic war between the former allies.

The 'Truman Doctrine' and Marshall Aid

Potsdam marked a transitional period of the Cold War. Truman had left the conference alarmed at what he believed was the failure of the Soviets to uphold the principles of the Atlantic Charter and Yalta. Unlike Roosevelt, Truman was less committed to a Soviet sphere of influence and saw the spread of communism in eastern Europe as further evidence that Stalin was bent on expansionism. Winston Churchill was also worried by the potential growth of Soviet influence, and it was against this background that he made his famous 'iron curtain' speech at Fulton, Missouri in March 1946.

9.3 Winston Churchill's speech at Fulton, Missouri, USA, 5 March 1946

A shadow has fallen upon the scenes so lately lighted by the Allied victory. Nobody knows what Soviet Russia and its Communist international organisation intends to do in the immediate future, or what are the limits, if any, to their expansive and proselytising tendencies. I have a strong admiration and regard for the valiant Russian people and for my war-time comrade, Marshal Stalin. There is sympathy and goodwill in Britain – and, I doubt not, here also – towards the peoples of all the Russias, and a resolve to persevere through many differences and rebuffs in establishing lasting friendships. We understand the Russian need to be secure on her western frontiers from all renewal of German aggression. We welcome her to her rightful place among the leading nations of the world. Above all, we welcome constant, frequent, and growing contacts between the Russian people and our own people on both sides of the Atlantic. It is my duty, however, to place before you certain facts about the present position in Europe.

From Stettin, in the Baltic, to Trieste, in the Adriatic, an iron curtain has descended across the continent. Behind that line lie all the capitals of the ancient States of Central and Eastern Europe – Warsaw, Berlin, Prague, Vienna, Budapest, Belgrade, Bucharest, and Sofia. All these famous cities, and the populations around them, lie in the Soviet sphere, and all are subject in one form or another, not only to Soviet influence, but to a very high and increasing measure of control from Moscow. Athens alone, with its immortal glories, is free to decide its future at an election under British, American, and French observation. The Russian-dominated Polish Government has been encouraged to make enormous and wrongful inroads upon Germany, and mass expulsions of millions of Germans on a scale grievous and undreamed of are now taking place. The Communist parties, which were very small in all these Eastern States of Europe, have been raised to pre-eminence and power far beyond their numbers, and are seeking everywhere to obtain totalitarian control. Police governments are prevailing in nearly every case, and so far, except in Czechoslovakia, there is no true democracy. Turkey and Persia are both profoundly alarmed and disturbed at the claims which are made upon them and at the pressure being exerted by the Moscow Government. An attempt is being made by the Russians in Berlin to build up a quasi-Communist party in their zone of occupied Germany by showing special favours to groups of Left-wing German leaders.

At the end of the fighting last June, the American and British armies withdrew westwards, in accordance with an earlier agreement, to a depth at some points of 150 miles on a front of nearly 400 miles, to allow the Russians to occupy this vast expanse of territory which the Western democracies had conquered. If, now, the Soviet Government tries, by separate action, to build up a pro-Communist Germany in their areas, this will cause new serious difficulties in the British and American zones, and will give the defeated Germans the power of putting themselves up to auction between the Soviets and the Western democracies. Whatever conclusions may be drawn from these facts – and facts they are – this is certainly not the liberated Europe we fought to build up. Nor is it one which contains the essentials of permanent peace.

From what I have seen of our Russian friends and allies during the war, I am convinced that there is nothing they admire so much as strength, and there is nothing for which they have less respect than for military weakness. ... If the western democracies stand together in strict adherence to the principles of the United Nations Charter, their influence for furthering these principles will be immense and no one is likely to molest them. If, however, they become divided or falter in their duty, and if these all-important years are allowed to slip away, then indeed catastrophe may overwhelm us all.

Source: *Congressional Record*, Washington, DC, 79th Congress, 2nd Session, 1946

By the time Churchill had made this speech, pro-Communist coalition governments had been established in Poland, Hungary, Romania, Bulgaria and Albania (see Map 6). The Second World War left the Red Army occupying most of eastern Europe and dominating the region in a manner that years of Comintern propaganda had failed to achieve. Although Churchill was no longer British Prime Minister when he made his speech at Fulton, he nevertheless carried enormous prestige. Coining a phrase that has since become commonplace, Churchill described the new Soviet sphere of influence thus: 'From Stettin, in the Baltic to Trieste, in the Adriatic, an iron curtain has descended across the continent.' While acknowledging the 'Russian need to be secure on her western frontiers from all renewal of German aggression', he warned of the dangers of the potential growth of Russian influence and called for a Western alliance that would withstand the Communist threat. Recognising the collapse of the Grand Alliance, Churchill warned that this placed the Germans in a position of power to 'auction themselves' between the former allies.

Churchill's speech represented an invitation to form an anti-Soviet alliance and came less than a year after Potsdam. Stalin denounced the speech and accused Churchill of being a war-monger, citing British and United States duplicity and failure to share the secrets of the atomic bomb. While the former allies blamed each other for breaking faith over Potsdam, the map of the Cold War was being ever more firmly drawn across Europe.

Undeterred by Churchill's Fulton speech, the Soviet Union continued to establish obedient satellite states from Poland to Bulgaria. In Yugoslavia this met with resistance, as Belgrade had been liberated not by the Red Army but by the partisan forces led by Marshal Tito, who continued to resent Soviet interference. The USA was also concerned by the strength of Communist parties in western Europe, notably France and Italy, where they had played a significant role in resistance movements and had been included in post-war coalition governments. However, it was Soviet pressure on Greece, Turkey and Iran that aroused the greatest alarm. In February 1947 the British government announced that it could no longer afford to maintain military and economic aid to Greece and Turkey.

In the light of these events President Truman was encouraged to prevent further Soviet expansion by adopting a policy of 'containment'. This involved a much more interventionist role in the affairs of western Europe. In March 1947 Truman addressed both Houses of Congress and announced the 'Truman Doctrine'.

9.4 The Truman Doctrine. Address to US Congress, 12 March 1947

At the present moment in world history nearly every nation must choose between alternative ways of life. The choice is too often not a free one.

One way of life is based upon the will of the majority, and is distinguished by free institutions, representative government, free elections, guarantees of individual liberty, freedom of speech and religion, and freedom from political oppression.

The second way of life is based upon the will of a minority forcibly imposed upon the majority. It relies upon terror and oppression, a controlled press and radio, fixed elections, and the suppression of personal freedoms.

I believe that it must be the policy of the United States to support free peoples who are resisting attempted subjugation by armed minorities or by outside pressures.

I believe that we must assist free peoples to work out their own destinies in their own way. ...

The seeds of totalitarian regimes are nurtured by misery and want. They spread and grow in the evil soil of poverty and strife. They reach their full growth when the hope of a people for a better life has died.

We must keep that hope alive.

The free peoples of the world look to us for support in maintaining their freedoms.

If we falter in our leadership, we may endanger the peace of the world – and we shall surely endanger the welfare of our own Nation.

Great responsibilities have been placed upon us by the swift movement of events. I am confident that the Congress will face these responsibilities squarely.

Source: *Public Papers of the Presidents of the United States ... , Harry S. Truman, 1947; reprinted in W. LaFeber (ed.), The Origins of the Cold War 1941–47: A Historical Problem with Interpretations and Documents* (New York, 1971), pp. 154–6

Truman asked Congress for $300 million for Greece and $100 million for Turkey. In order to persuade Congress to release this money Truman linked the loan to the struggle against communism and a choice between alternative ways of life: 'One way of life is based upon the will of the majority, and is distinguished by free institutions, representative government, free elections ... '; the second way of life 'is based upon the will of a minority forcibly imposed on the majority. It relies on terror and oppression'. Truman had in mind the threat posed by the Soviet Union to freedom throughout Europe, and added: 'I believe that it must be the policy of the United States to support free peoples who are resisting attempted subjugation by armed minorities or by outside pressures'.

Although the Truman Doctrine sprang from events in Greece and Turkey, it was clearly intended to have a wider relevance, the implication being that the USA was committed to resisting Soviet expansion and Communist influence everywhere. Truman escalated the differences between the United States and the

Soviet Union into a choice between 'democracy' and 'totalitarianism'. Congress agreed to the release of funds, and in 1949 the bloody civil war in Greece ended in defeat for the Communists, while Turkey remained within the western sphere of influence.

The adoption of the Truman Doctrine opened the way for its economic corollary, the so-called 'Marshall Plan' – a massive programme of aid to restore the European economies. By the spring of 1947 the devastation caused by the Second World War still prevented economic recovery. In June 1947 the American Secretary of State, George Marshall, announced his Economic Recovery Programme in a speech at Harvard University.

9.5 The Marshall Plan. Speech of 5 June 1947 at Harvard University

It is logical that the United States should do whatever it is able to do to assist in the return of normal economic health in the world, without which there can be no political stability and no assured peace. Our policy is directed not against any country or doctrine but against hunger, poverty, desperation, and chaos. Its purpose should be the revival of a working economy in the world so as to permit the emergence of political and social conditions in which free institutions can exist. ...

It is already evident that, before the United States Government can proceed much further in its efforts to alleviate the situation and help start the European world on its way to recovery, there must be some agreement among the countries of Europe as to the requirements of the situation and the part those countries themselves will take in order to give proper effect to whatever action might be undertaken by this Government. It would be neither fitting nor efficacious for this Government to undertake to draw up unilaterally a program designed to place Europe on its feet economically. This is the business of the Europeans. The initiative, I think, must come from Europe. The role of this country should consist of friendly aid in the drafting of a European program and of later support of such a program so far as it may be practical for us to do so. The program should be a joint one, agreed to by a number, if not all, European nations.

Source: *Department of State Bulletin*, **XVI**, 15 June 1947, p. 1160

Marshall's plan offered economic and financial assistance wherever it was needed. 'Our policy', he declared, 'is directed not against any country or doctrine but against hunger, poverty, desperation, and chaos'. The initiative would come from Europe, and the Americans anticipated that 'a number, if not all European nations' would agree to the programme. Marshall referred to 'friendly aid' providing a 'cure not a palliative'. The Truman Doctrine and the Marshall Plan – which have been referred to as 'two halves of the same walnut' – served the United States' political and economic interests. Not only were they intended to contain communism and bring about economic recovery in Europe, but in return recipient countries would be expected to purchase US goods and provide investment opportunities for American capital.

By September 1947, sixteen nations from western Europe had drawn up a plan for using Marshall aid, and during the next four years they would receive over $13,000 million between them. Whatever the motives behind American policy, the Marshall Plan was a major factor in the successful reconstruction of western Europe. Although the Soviets' response to the Marshall Plan was initially positive, when the time came in July to send delegates to Paris to draw up a common recovery programme plan, they refused to attend, rejecting Marshall aid outright as 'dollar imperialism'. Moreover, the Soviet Union exerted pressure on Russia's eastern European neighbours, who had shown considerable enthusiasm for the aid programme, not to attend the Paris conference. The Soviet view of the Truman Doctrine and Marshall Aid was summed up by Andrei Vyshinsky, the Deputy Foreign Minister, in a speech to the United Nations in September 1947.

9.6 The Soviet view of the Truman Doctrine and the Marshall Plan: Andrei Vyshinsky, address to the United Nations, 18 September 1947

The so-called Truman Doctrine and the Marshall Plan are particularly glaring examples of the manner in which the principles of the United Nations are violated, of the way in which the Organization is ignored.

As the experience of the past few months has shown, the proclamation of this doctrine meant that the United States Government has moved toward a direct renunciation of the principles of international collaboration and concerted action by the great Powers and toward attempts to impose its will on other independent states, while at the same time obviously using the economic resources distributed as relief to individual needy nations as an instrument of political pressure. This is clearly proved by the measures taken by the United States Government with regard to Greece and Turkey which ignore and bypass the United Nations as well as by the measures proposed under the so-called Marshall Plan in Europe. This policy conflicts sharply with the principles expressed by the General Assembly in its resolution of 11 December 1946, which declares that relief supplies to other countries 'should ... at no time be used as a political weapon'.

As is now clear, the Marshall Plan constitutes in essence merely a variant of the Truman Doctrine adapted to the conditions of postwar Europe. In bringing forward this plan, the United States Government apparently counted on the cooperation of the Governments of the United Kingdom and France to confront the European countries in need of relief with the necessity of renouncing their inalienable right to dispose of their economic resources and to plan their national economy in their own way. The United States also counted on making all these countries directly dependent on the interests of American monopolies, which are striving to avert the approaching depression by an accelerated export of commodities and capital to Europe. ...

It is becoming more and more evident to everyone that the implementation of the Marshall Plan will mean placing European countries under the economic and political control of the United States and direct interference by the latter in the internal affairs of those countries.

Moreover, this Plan is an attempt to split Europe into two camps and, with the help of the United Kingdom and France, to complete the formation of a *bloc* of several European countries hostile to the interests of the democratic countries of Eastern Europe and most particularly to the interests of the Soviet Union.

An important feature of this Plan is the attempt to confront the countries of Eastern Europe with a *bloc* of Western European States including Western Germany. The intention is to make use of Western Germany and German heavy industry (the Ruhr) as one of the most important economic bases for American expansion in Europe, in disregard of the national interests of the countries which suffered from German aggression.

Source: United Nations General Assembly, Official Records, Plenary Meetings, 18 September 1947, pp. 86–8

Vyshinsky accused the United States of imposing its will on independent states by 'placing European countries under [its] economic and political control'. According to the Soviets, the ramifications of the Truman Doctrine and the Marshall Plan would be to 'split Europe into two camps … and complete the formation of a bloc … hostile … to the Soviet Union'. This is precisely the pattern that would emerge. The irony of the situation is that the Truman Doctrine, which set out to contain Russian expansionism, provoked Soviet fears of US imperialist intentions and led to the breakdown of trust and co-operation between the two superpowers.

The conventional Cold War view of Stalin's aggressive ambitions was expressed in a David Low cartoon of 1948. In this cartoon Stalin is crouched in a deep armchair while his Foreign Minister spins the globe of the world and asks: 'Who's next to be liberated from freedom, comrade?' On the table is a switchboard representing the nations of Europe. Stalin is about to casually reach over and 'turn off the lights' of freedom for the unlucky nation selected.

9.7 'Who's next to be liberated?', cartoon by David Low in the *Evening Standard*, 2 March 1948 (see p. 223)

Observing the proceedings from the picture on Stalin's desk is a rather powerless US Secretary of State, George Marshall. This was a typically pessimistic view of Soviet foreign policy in the late 1940s, held by former allies who, only a few years previously, had warmly depicted Stalin as 'Uncle Joe'.

The Soviet response to the Truman Doctrine and the Marshall Plan was to

**Source: Centre for the Study of Cartoons and Caricature, University of Kent,
Canterbury**

establish the Cominform (Communist Information Bureau) in September 1947.
This organisation was a revival of the pre-war Comintern (Communist
International) and provided the Soviets with the means to tighten their grip on
the eastern European satellite countries, which were expected to trade only with
Cominform members. In 1948 the western European recipients of Marshall Aid
established the Organization for European Economic Cooperation (OEEC) to
administer this aid, and this became one of the first instruments of western solidarity in the Cold War. The western Europeans also united together in military
alliances. In March 1948 Britain, France and the three Benelux countries signed
the Brussels Treaty (see Chapter 10) and, in April 1949, the North Atlantic
Treaty (NATO) brought together the signatories of the Brussels Treaty with
Cananda, Denmark, Iceland, Italy, Norway, Portugal and the United States, who
all pledged to regard an attack on one of them as an attack on them all. The
formation of NATO confirmed the dissolution of the Grand Alliance.
Predictably, Stalin responded by setting up the Council for Mutual Economic
Assistance (Comecon) in January 1949 to co-ordinate socialist economic planning in Eastern Europe, and in May 1955 the Soviet Union's answer to NATO,
the Warsaw Pact, was formed.

The Cold War resulted in a Europe divided into two hostile and irreconcilable ideological camps, sustained by different economic systems and protected by
military pacts, which in turn led to an escalating nuclear arms race. The gulf of
mistrust continued to separate east and west and to prevent *détente* taking place.
Occasionally the cold diplomatic war would ignite into open confrontation, as

during the Berlin Blockade (1948), the abortive uprisings in Poland and Hungary (1956), the building of the Berlin Wall (1961) and the 'Prague Spring' (1968). However, despite these crises, Europe managed to avoid direct military conflict, and in the 1970s *détente* and disarmament appeared to herald a new age of conciliation. When Mikhail Gorbachev came to power in 1985, he abandoned Marxist dogma and began to modernise the USSR using the new catchwords *glasnot* (openness) and *perestroika* (restructuring) (see Chapter 10). The collapse of the USSR in 1991 unquestionably marked the end of the Cold War but unleashed an equally unsettling new phase of European nationalism in eastern Europe.

CHRONOLOGY: THE ORIGINS OF THE COLD WAR

1943	28 November– 1 December	Meeting of Big Three (Churchill, Roosevelt and Stalin) at Tehran. They discuss arrangements for the allied landings in Europe and a renewed Soviet offensive against Germany. Also agree on a provisional territorial settlement in eastern Europe – including Polish frontiers.
1944	21 August– 9 October	Dumbarton Oaks Conference draws up broad framework of the United Nations.
1945	4–11 February	Meeting at Yalta between Churchill, Roosevelt and Stalin decides upon four occupation zones in Germany, the prosecution of war criminals, and prepares Allied Control Council to run Germany on the basis of 'complete disarmament, demilitarisation and dismemberment'. Declaration on Liberated Europe signed by the three powers to allow European states to 'create democratic conditions of their own choice'.
	17 July–1 August	Potsdam Meeting attended by Stalin, Truman and Churchill (after 25 July Attlee) finalises four-power agreement on administration of Germany, which is to be treated as a single economic unit, and the territorial settlements in eastern Europe. The Oder-Neisse line is to mark the new boundary between Germany and Poland.
	November	Tito elected President of Yugoslavia.
1946	5 March	Churchill's 'Iron Curtain' speech at Fulton, Missouri.
1947	12 March	President Truman, in a speech to Congress, outlines the Truman Doctrine 'to support free peoples who are resisting attempted subjugation by armed minorities or by outside pressures'.
	22 April	Truman Doctrine passed by Congress.
	5 June	George Marshall, American Secretary of State, calls for a European recovery programme supported by American aid.
	12–15 June	Non-communist nations of Europe set up Committee of European Economic Co-operation to draft European Recovery Programme.
	5 October	Molotov announces formation of Cominform or Communist Information Bureau (successor to Comintern).
1948	17 March	Belgium, France, Luxembourg, The Netherlands and Great Britain sign the Brussels Treaty Organisation for mutual military and economic assistance.

	April	Paris Treaty sets up Organization for European Economic Cooperation to facilitate Marshall Aid.
	24 June	Russians impose a complete blockade of Berlin.
	25 June	Allies begin Berlin airlift.
	June	Stalin and Tito quarrel. Yugoslavia expelled from Cominform.
1949	January	Council for Mutual Economic Assistance (CMEA) or Comecon, set up to co-ordinate economic development of the communist countries.
	4 April	Creation of North Atlantic Treaty Organisation (NATO) signed by members of Brussels Treaty Organisation, with Canada, Denmark, Iceland, Italy, Norway, Portugal and the United States. It pledges mutual military assistance.
	12 May	Berlin blockade lifted.
	May	Federal Republic of Germany (West Germany) comes into existence.
	October	German Democratic Republic (East Germany) comes into existence.
1952	27 May	Belgium, France, Italy, Luxembourg, The Netherlands, and West Germany sign mutual defence treaty for proposed creation of a European Defence Community.
1953	5 March	Death of Stalin.
	June	Risings in East Germany suppressed.
	September	Khrushchev appointed First Secretary of the Communist Party.
1955	9 May	West Germany admitted to NATO.
	14 May	Treaty of Friendship, Cooperation and Mutual Assistance (Warsaw Pact) formed.

BIBLIOGRAPHY

Sources and documents

A selection of documents can be found in M. McCauley, *The Origins of the Cold War* (1991 edn). A perceptive and brief commentary with documents is R. Morgan, *The Unsettled Peace: A Study of the Cold War in Europe* (1974). See also, W. Lafeber (ed.), *The Origins of the Cold War 1941–47* (1971); M. Carlyle (ed.), *Documents on International Affairs, 1947–8* (1952) and *1949–50* (1953); T.H. Etzold and J.L. Gaddis (eds), *Containment: Documents on American Foreign Policy and Strategy 1945–50* (1978). A valuable source book on Germany during this period is, M. Malzahn, *Germany 1945–49* (1991). There are numerous memoirs on the Cold War, including A. Eden, *The Eden Memoirs: The Reckoning* (1965); H.S. Truman, *Year of Decisions, 1945* (1955) and *Years of Trial and Hope, 1946–53* (1956); G. Kennan, *Memoirs 1950–63* (1972); D. Acheson, *Present at the Creation* (1970).

Secondary works

There are several general works on the period, mainly American. J.W. Spanier, *American Foreign Policy since the Second World War* (1980), is pro-American; S.E. Ambrose, *Rise to Globalism* (1983) and W. Lafeber, *America, Russia and the Cold War* (1982) are more critical of US policy. L.J. Halle, *The Cold War as History* (1967) remains a balanced assessment. More recent work includes, D. Yergin, *The Shattered Peace: The Origins of the Cold War and the National Security State* (1980) and an excellent political history by J. Young, *Cold War in Europe, 1945–89* (1991) and Young again, *Cold War and Detente 1941–91* (1993). The post-war peace settlements are analysed in J. Wheeler-Bennet and A. Nicholls, *The Semblance of Peace: The Political Settlement after the Second World War* (1972). On Britain see W.N. Medlicott, *British Foreign Policy since Versailles* (1940). Soviet policy is the subject of A.B. Ulam, *Expansion and Coexistence The History of Soviet Foreign Policy 1917–73* (1973) and T.W. Wolfe, *Soviet Power and Europe, 1945–70* (1970).

For more sympathetic accounts of American foreign policy, see G.F. Hudson, *The Hard and Bitter Peace* (1966) and H.L. Feis, *From Trust to Terror* (1970). G. and J. Kolko, *The Limits of Power* (1972) and D. Horrowitz, *The Free World Colossus: A Critique of American Foreign Policy in the Cold War* (1965), both adopt a highly critical approach. J.L. Gaddis, *The United States and the Origins of the Cold War* (1973) is excellent, and on the British see V. Rothwell, *Britain and the Cold War, 1941–7* (1983). Marshall Aid is analysed in J. Gimbel, *The Origins of the Marshall Plan* (1976) and H. Arkes, *Bureacracy, the Marshall Plan and the National Interest* (1972).

Articles

For the origins of the Cold War, see the special edition of *J.C.H.* (1968). See also D. Reynolds, 'The Origins of the Cold War: The European Dimension, 1944–1951', *H.J.* (1985). A thoughtful account of the 'two halves of the chestnut' is provided in G. Warner, 'The Truman Doctrine and the Marshall Plan', *International Affairs* (1974). Of vital importance to the framing of America's anti-communist policy was G.F. Kennan, 'The Sources of Soviet Conduct', *Foreign Affairs* (1947). A. Schlesinger, 'Origins of the Cold War', *Foreign Affairs* (1967) gives an intelligent, short discussion. Kennan's position in the immediate post-war period is critically analysed by D. Mayers, 'Soviet War Aims and the Grand Alliance: George Kennan's Views, 1944–46', *J.C.H.* (1986). An attempt to reappraise the historiographical debate is summarised in M. Leigh, 'Is there a Revisionist Thesis on the Origins of the Cold War?', *Political Science Quarterly* (1974). A thoughtful overview of these early crucial years is provided by R. Ovendale, 'Britain, the U.S.A. and the European Cold War, 1945–8', *H.* (1982).

10

European integration

The move towards closer western European co-operation has been the most striking development since the end of the Second World War. As we have seen in Chapter 9, the onset of the Cold War, and in particular the threat posed by Soviet-sponsored communism, persuaded the western democracies that European reconstruction based on democratic principles would require a common economic, political and military effort. The initial move towards European integration took place alongside the Berlin blockade, which, although lifted in May 1949, resulted in the formation of the Federal Republic of Germany (West Germany) and the German Democratic Republic (East Germany). The division of Germany only served to accelerate the desire to draw up a joint programme of needs, resources and requirements to consolidate western Europe.

Early post-war co-operation

The roots and antecedents of European integration can be traced back to the 1920s and 1930s, but the Second World War and the experience of occupation under Hitler's so-called 'new order' provided a new impetus for pan-European union. Many of the resistance groups fighting to overthrow fascist occupation were convinced that their own institutions had been found wanting. Liberation meant more than simply reinstating the old status quo; it was an opportunity to establish a genuine new order that would break down frontiers. In 1944, for example, the exiled governments of Belgium, The Netherlands and Luxembourg agreed to form a customs union, and this came into operation in 1948. The Organization for European Economic Co-operation (OEEC) was established in 1948 to administer Marshall Aid among its member countries, which had agreed to work co-operatively for economic recovery on a regional rather than on a strictly national basis. In March 1948 Britain and France joined the three Benelux countries and signed the Treaty of Brussels, the preamble to which appears as Document 10.1.

10.1 The Brussels Treaty (Preamble), 17 March 1948

The titular heads of the participating States:

Resolved to reaffirm their faith in fundamental human rights, in the dignity and worth of the human person and in the other ideals proclaimed in the Charter of the United Nations; To fortify and preserve the principles of democracy, personal freedom and political liberty, the constitutional traditions and the rule of law, which are their common heritage; To strengthen, with these aims in view, the economic, social and cultural ties by which they are already united; To co-operate loyally and to co-ordinate their efforts to create in Western Europe a firm basis for European economic recovery;

To afford assistance to each other, in accordance with the Charter of the United Nations, in maintaining international peace and security and in resisting any policy of aggression; To take such steps as may be held to be necessary in the event of a renewal by Germany of a policy of aggression; To associate progressively in the pursuance of these aims with other States inspired by the same ideals and animated by the like determination;

Desiring for these purposes to conclude a treaty for collaboration in economic, social and cultural matters and for collective self-defence;

Have appointed … their plenipotentiaries … who … have agreed as follows:

Source: Cmnd 7367 (London, HMSO, 1948)

The Treaty of Brussels was important because it was the forerunner of much bigger schemes. The preamble reaffirmed the United Nations Charter, and the determination to preserve the 'principles of democracy, personal freedom … political liberty … and the rule of law'. It was couched in idealist language and claimed the moral high ground in reaffirming human rights. Although German aggression was mentioned, the real threat was the Soviet Union, and the preamble can be seen as a response to the Soviet's action in eastern Europe and its failure to uphold the Yalta and Potsdam agreements. In order to strengthen these aims the signatories pledged collaboration 'for collective self-defence' and for providing 'a firm basis for European economic recovery'.

The desire for mutual defence would result in the formation of NATO in 1949, and in the same year the Council of Europe was established as a product of those articles of the Brussels Treaty that provided for social and cultural co-operation. Membership of the Council of Europe was identical with that of the OEEC, although its role was vague and its power negligible – essentially it agreed to respect the rule of law and fundamental human rights.

In May 1950 France proposed setting up a European Coal and Steel Community. The idea was the brainchild of the economist and politician Jean

Monnet, who had earlier produced the Monnet Plan for French economic reorganisation.

10.2 Jean Monnet, memorandum to Robert Schuman and George Bidault, 4 May 1950

Wherever we look in the present world situation we see nothing but deadlock – whether it be the increasing acceptance of a war that is thought to be inevitable, the problem of Germany, the continuation of French recovery, the organization of Europe, the very place of France in Europe and in the world.

From such a situation there is only one way of escape: concrete, resolute action on a limited but decisive point, bringing about on this point a fundamental change, and gradually modifying the very terms of all the problems.

It is in this spirit that the attached proposal has been drawn up. The reflections below summarize the observations that led to it.

I

Men's minds are becoming focused on an object at once simple and dangerous: the cold war.

All proposals and all actions are interpreted by public opinion as a contribution to the cold war.

The cold war, whose essential objective is to make the opponent give way, is the first phase of real war.

This prospect creates among leaders a rigidity of mind that is characteristic of the pursuit of a single object. The search for solutions to problems ceases. This rigidity of mind and of objective, on both sides, leads inevitably to a clash, which is in the ineluctable logic of this way of looking at things. From this clash will come war.

In effect, we are already at war.

The course of events must be changed. To do this, men's minds must be changed. Words are not enough. Only immediate action on an essential point can change the present static situation. This action must be radical, real, immediate, and dramatic; it must change things and make a reality of the hopes which people are on the point of abandoning. And thereby give the peoples of the 'free' countries faith in the more distant goals that will be put to them, and the active determination to pursue them.

II

The German situation is rapidly becoming a cancer that will be dangerous to peace in the near future, and to France immediately, if its development is not directed towards hope for the Germans and collaboration with the free peoples.

This situation cannot be dealt with by the unification of Germany, for that would require an agreement between the USA and the USSR, which for the moment is impossible to conceive. ...

We must not try to solve the German problem, which cannot be solved in the present situation. We must change the context by transforming it.

We must undertake a dynamic action which transforms the German situation and gives direction to the minds of the Germans – not seek a static solution based on things as they are.

III

The continuation of France's recovery will be halted if the question of German industrial production and its competitive capacity is not rapidly solved.

The basis of the superiority which French industrialists traditionally recognize in Germany is her ability to produce steel at a price that France cannot match. From this they conclude that the whole of French production is thereby handicapped.

Already Germany is asking to increase her production from 11 to 14 million tons. We shall refuse, but the Americans will insist. Finally, we shall state our reservations but we shall give in. At the same time, French production is levelling off or even falling.

Merely to state these facts makes it unnecessary to describe in great detail what the consequences will be: Germany expanding; German dumping on export markets; a call for the protection of French industries; the halting or camouflage of trade liberalization; the re-establishment of pre-war cartels; perhaps an orientation of German expansion towards the East, a prelude to political agreements; France fallen back into the rut of limited, protected production …

The USA do not want things to take this course. They will accept an alternative solution if it is dynamic and constructive, especially if it is proposed by France.

With the solution proposed there is no more question of domination by German industry, which could create fear in Europe, a source of constant troubles, and would finally prevent Europe being unified and lead once more to the ruin of Germany herself. This solution, on the contrary, creates for industry – German, French, and European – the conditions for joint expansion, in competition but without domination.

From the French point of view, such a solution gives French industry the same start as German industry; it eliminates the dumping on export markets which would otherwise be practised by the German steel industry; and it enables the French steel industry to participate in European expansion, without fear of dumping and without the temptation to form a cartel. Fear on the part of industrialists, which would lead to Malthusianism, to the halting of 'liberalization', and finally back to the well-worn ruts of the past, will be eliminated. The biggest obstacle to the continuation of French industrial progress will have been removed.

IV

Until now, we have been engaged in an effort to organize the West economically, militarily, and politically: OEEC, the Brussels Pact, Strasbourg.

Two years' experience, the discussions in OEEC on payments agreements, the liberalization of trade, etc., the armament programme submitted to the last Brussels meeting, the discussions in Strasbourg, the efforts – still without concrete results – to achieve a Franco-Italian customs union, all show that we are making no real progress towards the goal we have set ourselves, which is the organization of Europe, its economic development, and its collective security.

Britain, however anxious she may be to collaborate with Europe, will agree to nothing that might result in a loosening of her ties with the Dominions or a commitment to Europe going beyond those undertaken by America herself.

Germany, an essential element in Europe, cannot be drawn into the European organization in the present state of things, for the reasons given above.

It is certain that to continue the action undertaken along the lines we have adopted will lead to an impasse, and moreover may let slip the moment when this organization of Europe would have been possible.

As it is, the peoples of Europe hear nothing but words. Soon, they will no longer believe in the idea which Governments persist in offering them, and which gets no further than empty speeches and futile meetings.

American public opinion will not support common action and American participation if Europe does not show itself dynamic.

For future peace, the creation of a dynamic Europe is indispensable. An association of the 'free' peoples, in which the USA will participate, does not exclude the building of Europe; on the contrary, because this association will be based on liberty, and therefore on diversity. Europe will, if it adapts to new conditions in the world, develop its creative abilities and thus, gradually, emerge as a stabilizing force.

We must therefore abandon the forms of the past and enter the path of transformation, both by creating common basic economic conditions and by setting up new authorities accepted by the sovereign nations.

Europe has never existed. It is not the addition of sovereign nations met together in councils that makes an entity of them. We must genuinely create Europe; it must become manifest to itself and to American public opinion; and it must have confidence in its own future.

This creation, at the moment when association with an America of such power is in question, is indispensable in order to make clear that the countries of Europe are not taking the easy way out, that they are not giving way to fear, that they believe in themselves, and that they are setting up without delay the first machinery for building a Europe within the new community of free and peaceful peoples, to which it will bring stability and the continuation of its creative thinking.

V

At the present moment, Europe can be brought to birth only by France. Only France can speak and act. But if France does not speak and act now, what will happen?

A group will form around the United States, but in order to wage the cold war with greater force. The obvious reason is that the countries of Europe are afraid and are seeking help. Britain will draw closer and closer to the United States; Germany will develop rapidly, and we shall not be able to prevent her being armed. France will be trapped again in her former Malthusianism, and this will lead inevitably to her being effaced.

VI

Since the Liberation, the French, far from being cast down by suffering, have shown vitality and faith in the future: increased production, modernization, the transformation of agriculture, the development of the French Union, etc.

During these years the French have forgotten Germany and German competition. They believed in peace. Suddenly they have rediscovered Germany and war.

The growth of German production, and the organization of the cold war, would revive past fears and set off Malthusian reflexes. The French would relapse into their old timidity, at the very moment when boldness would enable them to eliminate these two dangers and cause the French spirit to make the progress for which it is ready.

At this juncture, France is singled out by destiny. If she takes the initiative that will eliminate fear, revive faith in the future, and make possible the creation of a force for peace, she will have liberated Europe. And in a liberated Europe, the spirit of men born on the soil of France, living in freedom and in steadily improving material and social conditions, will continue to make the contribution that is essentially theirs.

Source: Quoted in Richard Vaughan (ed.), *Post-war Integration in Europe* (New York, 1976), pp. 51–6, trans. Richard Mayne

---

Jean Monnet had been the first Deputy Secretary-General of the League of Nations and one of the most energetic proponents of a united Europe. As Minister of Commerce in the first post-war French government, Monnet had instigated an ambitious plan for reconstructing the French economy. In this memorandum to Robert Schuman (France's Foreign Minister) and George Bidault (who had represented France at OEEC meetings), Monnet sketches a western Europe paralysed by the 'deadlock' of the Cold War. According to Monnet, France and Europe must break free of the rigidity caused by the ideological straitjacket. Central to future planning was the German question and the importance of absorbing Germany's productive capacity and economic resources into an acceptable European framework. In other words, Monnet feared the revival of the Ruhr's economic predominance in the same way that Clemenceau had after the First World War. The main point of Monnet's argument, however, appears to be that the historic rivalry between France and Germany must end, and be replaced by a new relationship based on co-operation. France is 'singled out by destiny' and must take the initiative ('Only France can speak and act'). Schuman, as French Foreign Minister, is urged to 'abandon forms of the past and enter the path of transformation, both by creating common basic economic conditions and by setting up new authorities accepted by the sovereign nation'.

Beginnings of the European Economic Community

Schuman took up this challenge and, on 9 May 1950, he proposed that the 'entire Franco-German production of coal and steel be placed under a joint High Authority, within an organisation open to the participation of other European nations'. This provided the impetus for the establishment of a European Coal and Steel Community (ECSC). A treaty (Document 10.3) translating this idea into reality was signed in Paris on 18 April of the following year.

10.3 Treaty establishing the European Coal and Steel Community (ECSC), 18 April 1951

The President of the Federal Republic of Germany, His Royal Highness the Prince Royal of Belgium, the President of the French Republic, the President of the Italian Republic, Her Royal Highness the Grand Duchess of Luxembourg, Her Majesty the Queen of the Netherlands.

Considering that world peace can be safeguarded only by creative efforts commensurate with the dangers that threaten it,

Convinced that the contribution which an organized and vital Europe can make to civilization is indispensable to the maintenance of peaceful relations,

Recognizing that Europe can be built only through practical achievements which will first of all create real solidarity, and through the establishment of common bases for economic development,

Anxious to help, by expanding their basic production, to raise the standard of living and further the works of peace,

Resolved to substitute for age-old rivalries the merging of their essential interests; to create, by establishing an economic community, the basis for a broader and deeper community among peoples long divided by bloody conflicts; and to lay the foundations for institutions which will give direction to a destiny henceforward shared,

Have decided to create a European Coal and Steel Community. ...

Article 1: By the present Treaty the High Contracting Parties institute among themselves a EUROPEAN AND COAL AND STEEL COMMUNITY, based on a common market, common objectives, and common institutions.

Article 2: The mission of the European Coal and Steel Community is to contribute to economic expansion, development and employment and the improvement of the standard of living in the participating countries through the institution, in harmony with the general economy of the member States, of a common market as defined in Article 4. ...

Article 4: The following are recognised to be incompatible with the common market for coal and steel, and are, therefore abolished and prohibited within the Community ...

a) import and export duties, or charges ... on the movement of coal and steel;
b) measures or practices discriminating against producers, among buyers or among consumers, specifically as concerns prices, delivery terms and transportation rates, as well as measures or practices which hamper the buyer in the free choice of his supplier;
c) subsidies or State assistance, or special charges imposed by the State, in any form whatsoever;
d) restrictive practices tending towards the division of markets or the exploitation of the consumer.

Article 8: The High Authority shall be responsible for assuring the fulfilment of the purposes stated in the present Treaty under the terms thereof. ...

Source: Cmnd 4863 (London, HMSO, 1951)

The Schuman Plan reflected the desire to make more concrete progress in the direction of European federation than was proving possible in the Council of Ministers. Five countries accepted the French proposal – Belgium, the Federal Republic of Germany, Italy, Luxembourg and The Netherlands. The one notable exception was the United Kingdom, which remained unwilling to accept the basic condition of executive control by an independent 'high authority'. Ratification by the individual parliaments took a further year, and the ECSC was formally established on 25 July 1952. The United Kingdom became associated with it through a standing Council of Association, set up at the end of 1954.

The ECSC treaty recorded the desire of the six contracting countries to 'substitute for age-old rivalries the merging of their essential interests; to create ... an economic community ... and lay the foundations for institutions that will give direction to a henceforward shared destiny'. The 'mission' of the ECSC is set out in Article 2, and Article 4 is of particular interest because it defined, in a negative way, principles that were deemed incompatible with the common market, and therefore to be abolished. All duties on coal and steel between the six were removed, and a high authority was to be the executive institution charged with administering and organising the joint programme of economic expansion. In view of the powers conferred, the governments also set up a Common Assembly to exercise democratic control, in accordance with the accepted practice in the member states. The Common Assembly held its first sitting in Strasbourg on 10 September 1952. There were at that time seventy-eight 'representatives of the peoples of the Member States'.

In September 1952, the Common Assembly formed a broader-based *ad hoc* Assembly and framed a draft constitution which served as the foundation for a European political community. Although a large majority of the Assembly agreed to this in 1953, it fizzled out when the proposed European Defence Community (EDC) failed to materialise in 1954 because the French National Assembly refused to ratify it. The *ad hoc* Assembly was located in Paris and, for a while, the two assemblies existed side by side.

From 1955 onwards, Europe resumed its fragmentary approach towards integration. Detailed discussion continued over German rearmament and the failure to establish a European defence community. The success of the ECSC in increasing coal and steel production persuaded its members that free trade should be extended to all industries in order to establish comprehensive economic integration. At the Messina Conference (Sicily) in June 1955 the Six decided that the success of the ECSC warranted further steps towards European integration. Under the Treaties of Rome, signed on 25 March 1957, the European Economic Community (EEC) and the European Atomic Energy Community (Eurotom) were established.

10.4 The Treaty of Rome, 25 March 1957

His Majesty the King of the Belgians, the President of the Federal Republic of Germany, the President of the French Republic, the President of the Italian Republic, Her Royal Highness the Grand Duchess of Luxembourg, Her Majesty the Queen of the Netherlands,

Determined to lay the foundations of an ever closer union among the peoples of Europe,

Resolved to ensure the economic and social progress of their countries by common action to eliminate the barriers which divide Europe,

Affirming as the essential objective of their efforts the constant improvement of the living and working conditions of their peoples,

Recognizing that the removal of existing obstacles calls for concerted action in order to guarantee steady expansion, balanced trade and fair competition,

Anxious to strengthen the unity of their economies and to ensure their harmonious development by reducing the differences existing between the various regions and the backwardness of the less favoured regions,

Desiring to contribute, by means of a common commercial policy, to the progressive abolition of restrictions on international trade,

Intending to confirm the solidarity which binds Europe and the overseas countries and desiring to ensure the development of their prosperity, in accordance with the principles of the Charter of the United Nations,

Resolved by thus pooling their resources to preserve and strengthen peace and liberty, and calling upon the other peoples of Europe who share their ideal to join in their efforts,

Have decided to create a European Economic Community. ...

PART ONE – PRINCIPLES

Article 1

By the present Treaty, the High Contracting Parties establish among themselves a European Economic Community.

Article 2

It shall be the aim of the Community, by establishing a Common Market and progressively approximating the economic policies of Member States, to promote throughout the Community a harmonious development of economic activities, a continuous and balanced expansion, an increased stability, an accelerated raising of the standard of living and closer relations between its Member States.

Article 3

For the purposes set out in the preceding Article, the activities of the Community shall include, under the conditions and with the timing provided for in this Treaty:

(a) the elimination, as between Member States, of customs duties and of quantitative restrictions in regard to the importation and exportation of goods, as well as of all other measures with equivalent effect;

(b) the establishment of a common customs tariff and a common commercial policy towards third countries;

(c) the abolition, as between Member States, of the obstacles to the free movement of persons, services and capital;

(d) the inauguration of a common agricultural policy;

(e) the inauguration of a common transport policy;

(f) the establishment of a system ensuring that competition shall not be distorted in the Common Market;

(g) the application of procedures which shall make it possible to coordinate the economic policies of Member States and to remedy disequilibria in their balances of payments;

(h) the approximation of their respective municipal law to the extent necessary for the functioning of the Common Market;

(i) the creation of a European Social Fund in order to improve the possibilities of employment for workers and to contribute to the raising of their standard of living;

(j) the establishment of a European Investment Bank intended to facilitate the economic expansion of the Community through the creation of new resources; and

(k) the association of overseas countries and territories with the Community with a view to increasing trade and to pursuing jointly their effort towards economic and social development.

Article 4

1. The achievement of the tasks entrusted to the Community shall be ensured by:

an Assembly,
a Council,
a Commission, and
a Court of Justice.

Each of these institutions shall act within the limits of the powers conferred upon it by this Treaty.

2. The Council and the Commission shall be assisted by an Economic and Social Committee acting in a consultative capacity.

Article 5

Member States shall take all general or particular measures which are appropriate for ensuring the carrying out of the obligations arising out of this Treaty or resulting from the acts of the institutions of the Community. They shall facilitate the achievement of the Community's aims.

They shall abstain from any measures likely to jeopardise the attainment of the objectives of this Treaty. ...

Article 8

1. The Common Market shall be progressively established in the course of a transitional period of twelve years.

The transitional period shall be divided into three stages of four years each; the length of each stage may be modified in accordance with the provisions set out below. ...

Source: Cmnd 4864 (London, HMSO, 1957)

Following the example of the ECSC, the Treaty of Rome provided for executive, parliamentary, judicial and intergovernmental organisations. Five main bodies were to govern the activities of the EEC: the Commission, responsible for formulating policy; the Council of Ministers, approving proposals; an Assembly or Parliament (since 1979 directly elected by voters in all member states), with advisory powers only; a Secretariat and a Court of Justice. Articles 1–8 set out the principles on which the Community was to be based. The Treaty of Rome broadened the scope of Community activity with a view to putting an end to the economic divisions of Europe. The treaty provided for the progressive abolition, over a twelve-year period, of all custom duties and quotas. The Six also agreed to work towards a customs union, with the free movement of goods, capital and labour. Special regulations, however, were provided for the controversial common agricultural policy. The preamble records the determination to 'lay the foundations of an ever closer union among the peoples of Europe … to ensure the economic and social progress of their countries by common action'. The title 'European Economic Community', rather than simply 'the Common Market', emphasised the intention to extend harmonisation beyond free trade in a common market. Obviously something much wider than economic co-operation was envisaged by federalists, who wanted a political union.

The ideological division of Europe between East and West was compounded by the growing division between the Six ('Little Europe') and the rest. In November 1959 the remaining states within the OEEC, which preferred looser economic and political integration, formed the European Free Trade Association (EFTA); this comprised Britain, Sweden, Norway, Denmark, Switzerland, Austria and Portugal. However, it soon became clear that EFTA could not match the growth of the EEC, and the two blocs attempted to reconcile their differences. In October 1961 Britain had a change of mind and opened negotiations for entry into the EEC.

The outstanding success of the EEC in achieving unparalleled economic growth provided a focus for those who demanded political federation. However, moves towards greater political unity were successfully forestalled by General de Gaulle after his return to power in France in 1958. In a famous press conference in 1962, de Gaulle outlined his objections to political integration.

10.5 Charles de Gaulle, press conference statement on European integration, 15 May 1962

I would like incidentally, since the opportunity has arisen, to point out to you, gentlemen of the press – and you are perhaps going to be very surprised by this – that I have never personally, in any of my statements, spoken of a 'Europe of nations', although it is always being claimed that I have done so. It is not, of course, that I am repudiating my own; quite on the contrary, I am more attached to France than ever, and I do not believe that Europe can have any living reality if it does not include France and her Frenchmen, Germany and its Germans, Italy and its Italians, and so forth. Dante, Goethe, Chateaubriand belong to all Europe to the very extent that they were respectively and eminently Italian, German and French. They would not have served Europe very well if they had been stateless or if they had thought and written in some kind of integrated Esperanto or Volapük.

But it is true that the nation is a human and sentimental element, whereas Europe can be built on the basis of active, authoritative and responsible elements. What elements? The states, of course; for, in this respect; it is only the states that are valid, legitimate and capable of achievement. I have already said, and I repeat, that at the present time there cannot be any other Europe than a Europe of states, apart, of course, from myths, stories and parades. What is happening with regard to the Economic Community proves this every day, for it is the states, and only the states, that created this Economic Community, that furnished it with funds, that provided it with staff members; and it is the states that give it reality and efficiency, all the more so as it is impossible to take any far-reaching economic measure without committing a political action. ...

In fact, the economic development of Europe cannot be assured without its political union and, in this regard, I want to point out the arbitrary nature of a certain idea that was voiced during the recent discussions in Paris and that claimed to keep economic matters out of the meetings of the heads of state or government, whereas, for each of them, in their respective countries, economy is the constant and primary issue.

I should like to speak more particularly about the objection to integration. The objection is presented to us with the words, 'Let us merge the six states into a supranational entity; this way, things will be quite simple and practical.' But such an entity cannot be found without there being in Europe today a federator with sufficient power, authority and skill. That is why one falls back on a type of hybrid, in which the six states would undertake to comply with what will be decided upon by a certain majority. At the same time, although there are already six national parliaments, plus the European Parliament, plus the Consultative Assembly of the Council of Europe – which did, it is true, predate the conception of the Six and which, I am told, is dying on the shore where it was abandoned – we must, it seems, elect yet another parliament, a so-called European one – which would lay down the law for the six states.

There are ideas that may, perhaps, beguile certain minds, but I certainly do not see how they could be carried out in practice, even if there were six signatures on the dotted line. Is there a France, a Germany, an Italy, a Holland, a Belgium, a Luxembourg, that would be ready – in a matter that is important for them from the national or the international point of view – to do something that they would consider bad because this would be dictated to them by others? Would the French people, the German people, the Italian people, the Dutch people, the Belgian people, or the Luxembourg people dream of submitting to laws voted by foreign deputies if these laws were to run contrary to their own deep-seated will? This is not so; there is no way, at the present time, for a foreign majority to be able to constrain recalcitrant nations. It is true that, in this 'integrated' Europe, as they say, there would perhaps be no policy at all. This would simplify things a great deal. Indeed, once there would be no France and no Europe, once there would be no policy – since no one policy could be imposed on each of the six states – one would refrain from making any policies at all. But then, perhaps, this world would follow the lead of some outsider who did have a policy. There would perhaps be a federator, but the federator would not be European. And it would not be an integrated Europe, it would be something quite different, much broader and much more extensive with, I repeat, a federator. Perhaps it is this which, sometimes and to a certain degree, is at the basis of some remarks of such or such an advocate of European integration. In that case, it would be best to say so.

You see, when one's mind dwells on matters of great import, it is pleasant to dream of the marvellous lamp that Aladdin had only to rub in order to soar above the real. But there is no magic formula that will make it possible to build something as difficult as a united Europe. Thus, let us place reality at the basis of the edifice and, when we shall have completed the work, this will be the time for us to lull ourselves to sleep with the tales of 'The Thousand and One Nights'.

Source: *French Embassy Information Bulletin*, May 1962; quoted in R. Vaughan (ed.), *Post-War Integration in Europe* (New York, 1976), pp. 158–61

De Gaulle made this statement when he was at the height of his popularity in France. He had taken no part in the formation of the EEC but he appreciated the opportunities that *restricted* membership offered to France – provided special provision continued to be made for French agriculture. Although de Gaulle regarded the EEC as a means of freeing western Europe from dependence on the USA, he opposed the independent authority and supra-nationalism of its institutions. In this statement he set out his objections to integration. By placing on record his conception of the 'Europe of nations' he distanced himself from the federalist cause. De Gaulle was concerned that Europe should remain an association of sovereign national states whose authority would not be replaced by supra-national organisations such as the European Parliament ('there cannot be any other Europe than the Europe of states').

In the 1960s de Gaulle continued to oppose further moves towards political union and most famously vetoed British entry in 1963 and again in 1967. After de Gaulle's resignation in 1969, the climate improved and his successor, Georges Pompidou, was more favourably disposed to enlarging Community membership. Accordingly, a communiqué was issued by the Heads of the Six in December 1969.

10.6 Statement by the EEC Heads of State, 2 December 1969

1 On the initiative of the Government of the French Republic and at the invitation of the Netherlands Government, the heads of State or Government and the Ministers for Foreign Affairs of the Member States of the European Communities

met at the Hague on December 1 and 2, 1969. The Commission of the European Communities was invited to participate in the work of the conference on the second day.

2 Now that the Common Market is about to enter upon its final stage, they considered that it was the duty of those who bear the highest political responsibility in each of the Member States to draw up a balance-sheet of the work already accomplished, to show their determination to continue it and to define the broad lines for the future.

3 Looking back on the road that has been traversed, and finding that never before have independent States pushed their cooperation further, they were unanimous in their opinion that by reason of the progress made, the Community has now arrived at a turning point in its history. Over and above the technical and legal sides of the problems involved, the expiry of the transitional period at the end of the year has, therefore, acquired major political significance. Entry upon the final stage of the Common Market not only means confirming the irreversible nature of the work accomplished by the Communities, but also means paving the way for a united Europe capable of assuming its responsibilities in the world of tomorrow and of making a contribution commensurate with its traditions and its mission.

4 The Heads of State or Government therefore wish to reaffirm their belief in the political objectives which give the Community its meaning and purport, their determination to carry their undertaking through to the end, and their confidence in the final success of their efforts. Indeed, they have a common conviction that a Europe composed of States which, in spite of their different national characteristics, are united in their essential interests, assured of its internal cohesion, true to its friendly relations with outside countries, conscious of the role it has to play in promoting the relaxation of international tension and the rapprochement among all peoples, and first and foremost among those of the entire Europe continent, is indispensable if a mainspring of development, progress and culture, world equilibrium and peace is to be preserved.

The European Communities remain the original nucleus from which European unity has been developed and intensified. The entry of other countries of this continent to the Communities — in accordance with the provisions of the Treaties of Rome — would undoubtedly help the Communities to grow in dimensions more in conformity with the present state of world economy and technology.

The creation of a special relationship with other European states which have expressed a desire to that effect would also contribute to this end. A development such as this would enable Europe to remain faithful to its traditions of being open to the world and increase its efforts on behalf of developing countries.

5 As regards the completion of the Communities, the Heads of State or Government reaffirmed the will of their Governments to pass from the transitional period to the final stage of the European Community. ...

Source: *European Community*, December 1969, p. 24; quoted in R. Vaughan (ed.), *Post-War Integration in Europe* (New York, 1976), pp. 180–1

After de Gaulle's resignation in April 1969, his successor, President Pompidou, though a Gaullist, was more sympathetic to the wishes of the five other members of the Community to expand. The intention to 'draw up a balance sheet of the work already accomplished' sprang from a French initiative. The communiqué referred to a 'turning point in its [EEC's] history'. There was also a legal obligation under the Treaty of Rome to reappraise the aims of the EEC after the twelve-year period of transition. Significantly, the fourth point recorded the wish of the Heads of State to 'reaffirm their belief in the *political* objectives which give the Community its meaning' (my italics). The decision that followed this meeting, to enlarge the Community and give it its own resources, provided the basis for Britain, under the leadership of Edward Heath, to negotiate entry into the EEC. Document 10.7 is a British cartoon by Arthur Horner exploring traditional British attitudes to Europe during the period of admission.

10.7 'Shotgun Wedding', cartoon by Arthur Horner, *New Statesman*, 14 May 1971

SHOTGUN WEDDING

Source: Centre for the Study of Cartoons and Caricature, University of Kent, Canterbury

Horner viewed British admission into the Community as a 'shotgun wedding'. In order to depict Britain's ambivalent attitude to Europe, Horner employed stereotypes from the nineteenth century. Prime Minister Heath, who negotiated with obstinate determination to achieve British admission, is portrayed as a rotund John Bull, forcing a reluctant Britannia into the Community. Behind Heath stands an accommodating 'groom' in the form of President Pompidou (depicted in a stereotypical Gallic stance, with a cigarette dangling from his mouth). The cartoon reminds us, albeit indirectly, that, after 1945, moves towards European integration were accompanied by a painful process of decolonisation and eventual loss of empires on the part of all the major western European states. In the case of Britain, a willingness to sever its former imperial links proved more painful than most. Nevertheless, in 1973 Britain, (together with Eire and Denmark) became full members and in June 1975 a referendum approved membership by a proportion of two to one.

Developments since the collapse of communism

The history of European integration is a history of ambitious schemes and frustrated expectations. The controversial Maastricht Treaty illustrates the fragility of the 'European idea' and the different interpretations that continue to hinder greater integration. For some years after the Treaty of Rome, the EEC was viewed as an exclusive, parochial grouping of the 'Little Six'. Over the years, however, its membership has increased and it has shown itself capable of expansion and growth. Greece gained membership in 1981, and Spain and Portugal in 1986. In January 1993, the 19 nations of the European Community and the European Free Trade Association (EFTA) formed the world's biggest integrated market, the European Economic Area (EEA). The EEA was seen by a number of EFTA countries as a first step towards full EC membership. In 1994 the Community (or European Union as it is now referred to) expanded to include Norway, Sweden, Finland and Austria, although in 1995 Norway subsequently opted out of membership after a referendum. At the time of writing (1999) Poland, Hungary, the Czech Republic, Estonia, and the Republic of Slovenia have had their EU membership accepted and are negotiating terms. Lithuania, Latvia, the Slovak Republic, Romania and Turkey have applied for entry and are awaiting negotiation. The widening of the scope and powers of its institutions has resulted in a bewildering array of economic and social legislation that impinges on the everyday lives of Europeans – and is not all entirely welcome! Although enlargement of the Union has imposed additional strains, the most controversial issue remains progress towards political union.

Since the late 1980s, three great interconnected changes have played a significant part in reshaping the EU. These developments pose crucial dilemmas for its future. The collapse of communism in eastern Europe allowed the reunification of Germany, which, in turn, precipitated the Maastricht Treaty. The impetus therefore, towards greater political and economic union came from events taking place in eastern Europe. Mikhail Gorbachev, who had been elected General

Secretary of the Communist Party of the Soviet Union in March 1985, was determined to try a new model of reviving socialism in the USSR. Gorbachev was convinced that Soviet society was suffocating from a lack of freedom, deprived of social energy and resistant to reform. Dissatisfaction with recurring economic crises led to calls for 'acceleration' (*uskoreine*) and more 'openness' (*glasnost*), before Gorbachev arrived at a broader concept that change or 'restructuring' (*perestroika*) was needed not just for the USSR but also in international affairs. In 1987 Gorbachev fundamentally revised the Soviet approach to Europe and talked about a 'common European home'.

10.8 Mikhail Gorbachev, 'Perestroika' and a 'Common European Home' (1987)

Europe is indeed a common home where geography and history have closely interwoven the destinies of dozens of countries and nations. Of course, each of them has its own problem, and each wants to live its own life, to follow its own traditions. Therefore, developing the metaphor, one may say: the home is common, that is true, but each family has its own apartment, and there are different entrances too. ...

The concept of a 'common European home' suggests above all a degree of integrity, even if its states belong to different social systems and opposing military-political alliances. ...

One can mention a number of objective circumstances which create the need for a pan-European policy:

1   Densely populated and highly urbanized, Europe bristles with weapons, both nuclear and conventional. It would not be enough to call it a 'powder keg' for today ...

2   Even a conventional war, to say nothing of a nuclear one, would be disastrous for Europe today ...

3   Europe is one of the most industrialised regions of the world. Its industry and transport have developed to the point where their danger to the environment is close to being critical. This problem has crossed far beyond national borders, and is now being shared by all of Europe.

4   Integrative processes are developing intensively in both parts of Europe. ... The requirements of economic development in both parts of Europe, as well as scientific and technological progress, prompt the search for some kind of mutually advantageous cooperation. What I mean is not some kind of 'European autarky', but better use of the aggregate potential of Europe for the benefit of its peoples, and in relations with the rest of the world.

5   The two parts of Europe have a lot of their own problems of an East–West dimension, but they also have a common interest in solving the extremely acute North–South problem ...

Our idea of a 'common European home' certainly does not involve shutting its doors to anybody. True, we would not like to see anyone kick in the doors of the European home and take the head of the table at somebody else's apartment. But then, that is the concern of the owner of the apartment. In the past, the Socialist countries responded positively to the participation of the United States and Canada in the Helsinki Process.

Source: Mikhail Gorbachev, *Perestroika* (London, 1987) pp. 195–6

Gorbachev's analysis of *perestroika* can be discovered in his book of the same name. While most of the book focused on the problems of the democratisation of social life and radical economic reforms in the Soviet Union, Gorbachev also reassessed the future of Europe in the context of the Cold War. By the time the book was published, Gorbachev enjoyed unprecedented popularity at home and abroad. In his book he referred to the Helsinki Process and *détente*, which was the product of the Conference on Security and Cooperation in Europe (CSCE) that reached agreement with the Final Act in 1975. The Conference had included the USSR and the United States, although at the time the Soviet Union did not fully accept the legitimacy of the American presence in Europe. In *Perestroika*, Gorbachev appears to recognise the reality of the United States' role in Europe and the need for both eastern and western Europe to assume wider, global responsibilities ('we have a common interest in solving the extremely acute North–South problem ... '). The 'common European home' and the new emphasis on a shared culture and history, suggested a more integrated, pan-European order with both Superpowers playing a part ('the home is common, but each family has its own apartment, and there are different entrances ... '). Gorbachev anticipates that it is within the institutional framework of the CSCE that this new home (or 'house') can be constructed.

In the summer of 1989 at a Warsaw Pact meeting, Gorbachev's 'new thinking' encouraged the communist regimes of eastern Europe to determine their own future by means of economic and political reforms. Poland took the lead and Solidarity became a political party and its leader Lech Walesa was elected president of Poland. (In 1995, Walesa would, in turn, be ousted and replaced by the ex-communist Aleksander Kwasniewski.) Hungary followed by dismantling its barriers to the west, which allowed thousands of East Germans on vacation to flee to the west. In East Germany, Erich Honecker and his regime were toppled and on 9 November 1989, the Berlin Wall was dismantled. The following month, in what Vaclav Havel referred to as the 'velvet revolution', communism was overthrown in Czechoslovakia. Only in Romania, where the ousted dictator Nicolai Ceauşescu and his wife were executed, did revolutionary change result in bloodshed.

10.9 The fall of the Berlin Wall, 9 November 1989

Source: Reuters

The photograph from the news agency, Reuters, captures the dismantling of the Berlin Wall that, since its erection in 1961, had symbolised the physical manifestation of the division of Europe into East and West. The breathtaking speed with which the communist regimes in eastern Europe toppled was totally unexpected and the sense of bewilderment is captured on the faces of the unarmed

East German border guards who, after the Wall had been breached, had to stand and witness thousands of joyous East Berliners swarm across, as a divided city reunited in a euphoric embrace.

When East Germans began to vote with their feet, the leaders of the Federal Republic of Germany seized the historic opportunity for unification. Recognising that the German question was one with far wider implications for the Warsaw Pact, NATO and the European Community, German Chancellor Helmut Kohl and Foreign Minister Hans-Dietrich Genscher sought to reassure both sides of the political divide. Their visit to Moscow in February 1990 secured Soviet endorsement of unification. For many Russians the occupation of East Germany symbolised the Great Patriotic Victory in the Second World War and recognition of the Soviet Union's superpower status. If the unification of Germany was to herald the end of the Cold War division of Europe, the Soviets in particular would need to be placated. In May 1990, Hans-Dietrich Genscher offered a reassuring insight into Russia's future role within Europe.

10.10 Hans-Dietrich Genscher, 'The USSR and Europe', May 1990

We do not want to push the Soviet Union to the edge of Europe. She should rather continue to be incorporated in Europe as a whole, and that includes the political dimension of Europe. ... We do not want anyone to feel themselves the loser because of German unification. ... The CSCE provides a guarantee for the Soviet Union that it can play a full role in Europe. The Soviet Union has opened its doors and in such a situation we must go through the door, not let someone slam it shut from this side.

Source: *The European*, 11–13 May 1990, p. 9

Genscher's statement recognised the pivotal role played by the USSR in the events that were unfolding ('The Soviet Union has opened its doors and in such a situation we must go through the door') and the desire that the Soviet Union 'should continue to be incorporated in Europe and that includes the political dimension of Europe'. Under Gorbachev's leadership the Soviet Union agreed that a unified Germany would be a member of NATO and would enter the EC. Currency union of East and West Germany took effect on 1 July 1990 and in October the unification of the two Germanies was completed, thus setting the seal upon the end of the Cold War division of Europe. Genscher also referred to the CSCE providing 'a guarantee for the Soviet Union that it can play a full role in Europe'. The Conference on Security and Cooperation in Europe culminated in November in the Paris Charter that boldly proclaimed: 'the era of confrontation and division of Europe has ended ... we declare that henceforth our relations will be founded on respect and cooperation'.

Gorbachev's decision to gamble on internal political and economic reforms and to insist that eastern European leaders could not expect support from the Soviet army to suppress dissenters at home had created the conditions for the overthrow of communism in eastern Europe. With the general decline of Soviet power, Gorbachev's 'European home' (referred to in Document 10.8) can be viewed as part of a policy intended to minimise the Soviet loss of influence in eastern Europe and to prevent it from being excluded from Europe as a whole. However Gorbachev's *perestroika* unleashed forces he could no longer control. An abortive *coup* to unseat him in August 1991 was only thwarted by the brave intervention of his implacable opponent, Boris Yeltsin. In setting ambitious but unrealistic targets, Gorbachev actually destabilised the existing Soviet economy. Gorbachev's six years at the helm resulted in radical disintegration from within: first the mighty power of the communist party was emasculated and by the end of 1991 the USSR was formally dissolved.

The end of the Cold War provided the political impetus to move forward with economic integration and the federalist dream to unify Europe. At the European Council Meeting in Maastricht in December 1991 the heads of government of the twelve EC member states reached agreement on political and economic monetary union and paved the way for the signing of the Treaty on European Union (TEU) in February 1992.

10.11 The Maastricht Treaty, 10 December 1991

TITLE I

COMMON PROVISIONS

Article A

By this Treaty, the High Contracting Parties establish among themselves a European Union, hereinafter called 'the Union'.

The Treaty marks a new stage in the process of creating an ever closer union among the peoples of Europe, in which decisions are taken as closely as possible to the citizen.

TITLE II

Article 2

The Community shall have as its task, by establishing a common market and an economic and monetary union and by implementing the common policies or activities referred to in Articles 3 and 3a, to promote throughout the Community a harmonious and balanced development of economic activities, sustainable and non-inflationary growth respecting the environment, a high degree of convergence of economic performance, a high level of employment and of social protection, the raising of the standard of living and quality of life, and economic and social cohesion and solidarity among Member States.

Article 3.b

The Community shall act within the limit of the powers conferred upon it by the Treaty and of the objectives assigned to it therein. In areas which do not fall within its exclusive competence, the Community shall take action, in accordance with the principle of subsidiarity, only if and in so far as the objectives of the proposed action cannot be sufficiently achieved by the member States and can therefore, by reason of the scale or effects of the proposed action, be better achieved by the Community. Any action by the Community shall not go beyond what is necessary to achieve the objectives of this Treaty.

Article 8

1 Citizenship of the Union is hereby established. Every person holding the nationality of a Member State shall be a citizen of the Union.

Article 102

Member States shall conduct their economic policies with a view to contributing to the achievement of the objectives of the Community, as defined in Article 2 ...

Article 103

Member States shall regard their economic policies as a matter of common concern and shall co-ordinate them with the Council. ...

Article 104

1 Overdraft facilities or any other type of credit facility with the European Central Bank [ECB] or the central banks of the Member States ... in favour of Community institutions or bodies ... shall be prohibited ...

Article 105

1 The primary objective of the European System of Central Banks [ESCB] shall be to maintain price stability. Without prejudice to the objective of price stability, the ESCB shall support the general economic policies in the Community with a view to contributing to the achievement of the objectives of the Community as laid down in Article 2.

Article 105a

1 The ECB shall have exclusive right to authorize the issue of bank notes within the Community. ... The bank notes issued by the ECB and the national central banks shall be the only such notes to have the status of legal tender within the Community.

TITLE V

Article J.1

1 The union and its Member States shall define and implement a common foreign and security policy. ...

2 The objectives ... shall be:

- to safeguard the common values, fundamental interests and independence of the Union;
- to strengthen the security of the Union and its Member States in all ways;
- to preserve peace and strengthen international security in accordance with the principles of the United Nations Charter as well as the principles of the Helsinki Act and the objectives of the Paris Charter;
- to promote international co-operation;
- to develop and consolidate democracy and the rule of law, and respect for human rights and fundamental freedoms.

TITLE VI

Article K

Co-operation in the fields of justice and home affairs shall be governed by the following provisions.

Article K.1

... Member States shall regard the following areas as matters of common interest:

1 asylum policy;
2 rules governing the crossing by persons of the external borders of the Member States and the exercise of control thereon;
3 immigration policy and policy regarding nationals of third countries;

    c] combatting unauthorized immigration ... ;

4   combatting drug addiction … ;
5   combatting fraud … ;
6   judicial co-operation in civil matters;
7   judicial co-operation in criminal matters;
8   customs co-operation;
9   police co-operation … ;

Article K.3

1 In the areas referred to in Article K.1, Member States shall inform and consult one another within the Council with a view to co-ordinating their action …

Source: HMSO, *The Treaty on European Union* **(Maastricht) 1992**

The Maastricht Treaty goes further than any previous EC agreement. In 61,351 words it expands the scope of existing responsibilities in the EU and brings new policy areas under the jurisdiction of its institutions. The first section, 'Common Provisions', sets the overall tone by referring to the Treaty as a 'new stage in the process of creating an ever closer union among the peoples of Europe' (Article A). The Maastricht Treaty established new 'pillars' of European government. That meant that EU powers in areas of justice, home affairs (Title VI, Articles K to K.9) and foreign policy (Title V, Articles J.4 to J.7) were to be exercised outside the Commission, with member states meeting in the Council of Ministers. Heads of government, meeting at summits as the European Council, were given powers to set broad policy guidelines, within which the Commission was expected to operate when it proposed legislation. In addition, the Treaty introduced the concept of European citizenship (Title II, Articles 8 to 8e).

The most significant provision of the Maastricht Treaty was the agreement to move towards stage three of economic and monetary union and the introduction of a single European currency (euro) and exchange-rate policy under the authority of a single central bank by 1 January 1999 (Title II, Articles 102 to 109). Maastricht set out convergence criteria (low debts, deficit and interest) that member states had to meet in order to qualify to join the euro in January 1999. States had to exhibit a high degree of price stability (that is, an inflation rate over the previous year could not exceed by more than 1.5 per cent that achieved by an average of the three best performing member states); to have had at least two years' membership of the narrow band of the Exchange Rate Mechanism (ERM) without a devaluation of the national currency; not to run an excessive government budget deficit (not exceeding 3 per cent of GDP or accumulated government debt that has not exceeded 60 per cent of GDP); and to provide evidence of convergence durability (that is, long-term interest rates have not exceeded by more than 2 per cent the average of the three best performing states for the previous year). The Maastrict Treaty provided a caveat that allowed exceptions for those countries which 'have reached a level that comes close to the

3 per cent annual deficit level'. The same applied for the government debt threshold of 60 per cent, which must be 'sufficiently diminishing and approaching the reference value at a satisfactory pace'.

Maastricht left several matters unresolved and was not, in fact, ratified until November 1993. The controversial concept of 'subsidiarity' is dealt with in Title II, Article 3b, which states that the EU shall only take action at a Community level if 'the objectives of the proposed action cannot be sufficiently achieved by member States'. It was agreed, however, that enlargement negotiations should continue. Faced with the prospect of further enlargement, as a result of the collapse of communism, it was becoming clear that the EU had to assume a central political role in the new Europe of the post-Cold War era.

The Maastricht agreement marked a significant stage in European integration, although it was made possible only after the United Kingdom and Denmark had been granted 'opt-outs' on economic and monetary union and Britain had been excluded from implementing the 'social chapter' ('Protocols'). Such 'opt-outs' reflected Britain's continuing ambivalence to further European integration. In December 1990 Britain ceased to be an island when the Channel Tunnel was completed; nevertheless, British governments have consistently remained suspicious of federalism. In 1998, however, 'New Labour' signed the social chapter, which committed the UK to introduce a minimum wage and to the principle of equal pay for male and female workers for equal work. Britain has supported enlargement (at the expense of political integration) and has suggested several levels of overlapping and different weighted membership, with the industrialised nations of the West retaining control. In January 1999 when the euro was introduced, Britain was conspicuous by its decision not to join the launch.

10.12 The launch of the euro, 1 January 1999

Source: *The Independent*

With the introduction of the euro in January 1999, the eleven EU states that joined relinquished an important element of national and fiscal sovereignty; namely, the autonomy to manipulate the quantity and the price of money. Moreover, under the Stability Pact, which is part of the EMU, those member states have also relinquished a degree of fiscal sovereignty to the European Central Bank (ECB) in Frankfurt, which has exclusive rights to authorise the issue of bank notes (Title II, Article 105a). No longer will individual states be allowed to resort to capricious deficit spending, or even national debt to solve short-term economic problems. The photograph shown in Document 10.12, taken outside a Paris bank at the time of the launch, unveils the conversion rate of franc to euro. A major dilemma connected to the introduction of the euro is what will happen if some states fail to maintain the convergence criteria set out under the Single European Act. The introduction of the euro also has significant political ramifications. Federalists claim that having established a common European currency the next step is to move towards a 'common government'. For many Europeans the euro is a make-or-break affair; either the EU will have to federate into a United States of Europe – or it will disintegrate. Maastricht and the euro have raised the spectre of whether or not it is possible to have monetary union without political union.

Although the EU has been engaged in a continuous process of enlargement, this very process has imposed additional strains, forcing a searching reappraisal of its institutions and policies. For the countries of central and eastern Europe who have submitted applications, membership of the Union is not likely to occur until after 2000. To double its membership would cripple the institutions of the EU. In 1999, the five largest states, Germany, France, Italy, Britain and Spain contain 80 per cent of the population of the EU, but command only just over half the votes in the Council of Ministers. If the ten (or more) ex-communist applicants were members, the share of these states would fall further, while the proportion of poor countries in the EU entitled to substantial subsidies would rise from four out of 15 to fourteen out of 25. A further problem, of an unwieldy European Parliament – with over 800 deputies and over 40 commissioners – will also have to be overcome. The challenge of enlargement will be resolved either through the full implementation or the conclusion of association agreements, and unquestionably the Union will have to adapt its institutions and policies accordingly.

Europe has the means to become the premier economic power of the twenty-first century. To achieve this Europe will require vision for the next fifty years. Turkey and Russia will ultimately have to be integrated into the EU; Turkey's entry will reassure Muslims that they have a future within Europe and that it is no longer an exclusively Christian community. Continuing pressure to enlarge the EU raises fundamental questions of exactly what sort of organisation the Community is – or should become. During the Cold War the EC was rarely called upon to play an independent political role. The collapse of the Soviet bloc left a military and political vacuum and offered the EU an unprecedented opportunity to reassert Europe's sovereignty over its own affairs. Its lack of a concerted foreign policy to resolve conflicts was first revealed in Bosnia and more recently in Kosovo.

Although, for federalists, the road to European unity has proved disappointingly slow, assessed in its historical context, the movement towards European integration that has taken place since the 1950s is unparalleled in European history. In the mid-1980s, the European Community rediscovered its dynamism and has undertaken significant new initiatives and bold steps towards closer European union. Unquestionably, the achievements of European integration have dispelled the apocalyptic view that European civilisation had reached its appointed end amidst the ruins of 1945. Western Europe has shown a remarkable capacity to survive the challenges of fascism and communism and retain its democratic ideas and institutions. The evolution of the EU will depend largely on how it copes with economic and monetary union and enlargement to the east. The challenge it faces in the twenty-first century is to embrace its poorer neighbours while staying prosperous and competitive.

CHRONOLOGY: EUROPEAN INTEGRATION

1948	16 April	Organization for European Economic Co-operation (OEEC) established to receive Marshall Aid from the United States, comprising Austria, the Benelux countries, Denmark, France, West Germany, Greece, Iceland, Ireland, Italy, Norway, Portugal, Spain, Sweden, Switzerland, Turkey and the United Kingdom.
1949		Council of Europe established in Strasbourg to facilitate 'political co-operation'.
1950		Memorandum sent by Jean Monnet to Robert Schuman and George Bidault.
1951		Paris Treaty established the European Coal and Steel Community (ECSC) between the Benelux countries, France, Italy and West Germany. 'The Six' set up a 'common market' in coal and steel. A European Commission is set up as the supreme authority. With a Council of Ministers, Court of Justice and an appointed Parliament, it is the prototype for the European Community.
1953		European Court of Human Rights set up in Strasbourg.
1955		Messina Conference of ECSC members to discuss a wider customs union.
1957		The Rome Treaties (25 March) between 'the Six' set up the European Economic Community (EEC) and Euratom.
1959		European Free Trade Association (EFTA) set up as a counterweight to the EEC, comprising Austria, Denmark, Norway, Portugal, Sweden, Switzerland and the United Kingdom.
1961		Britain, Ireland and Denmark apply for membership of the EEC.
1962		Norway applies for membership. Common Agricultural Policy (CAP) agreed between EEC members to come into operation in 1964: a system of high guaranteed prices for European farmers paid for out of a common agricultural fund with protective tariffs against imports.
1963		De Gaulle announces veto on British application for membership. Irish, Danish and Norwegian applications suspended.

1967		Britain, Ireland, Denmark and Norway re-apply to the EEC, but are still opposed by de Gaulle.
1970		Plans to enlarge the EEC and give it its own resources are agreed.
1973		Britain, Denmark and Ireland join the EEC but Norway declines to join after a referendum.
1975		Britain confirms membership of the EEC by referendum. Greece applies for membership as do Spain and Portugal.
1979		European Monetary System introduced with a common European Currency Unit (ECU) linking the exchange rates of individual countries. First direct elections held to the European Parliament.
1981		Greece becomes a member of the EEC, phased over five years.
1985		European Council adopts the Single European Act (SEA) – agreement on an internal single market by the end of 1992.
1985		Spain and Portugal sign accession treaty to join the EEC from 1 January 1986.
1989	9 November	The collapse of the Berlin Wall.
1991		Maastricht Summit accepts Treaty on European Union.
1992		Treaty on European Union (TEU) signed at Maastricht.
1994		Applications from Norway, Sweden, Finland and Austria to join are provisionally accepted.
1995		Norway says No in referendum to the delight of its fishermen and farmers and the dismay of Oslo.
1999	January	The introduction of the single currency (euro).

BIBLIOGRAPHY

Sources and documents

Two excellent collections of documents can be found in T. Salmon and Sir William Nicoll (eds), *Building European Union* (1997) and D. Weigall and P. Stirk (eds), *The Origins and Development of the European Community* (1992). Documents relating to European integration are included in W. Lipgens (ed.), *Documents on the History of European Integration* (1985); R. Vaughan (ed.), *Post-war Integration in Europe* (1976); A.H. Robertson *European Institutions; Cooperation, Integration, Unification* (1973). On Britain and the Community, see U. Kitzinger (ed.), *The Second Try: Labour and the E.E.C.* (1968).

Three contemporary accounts of the European unity movement by statesmen involved include: J. Monnet, *The Memoirs*, (1978); P.H. Spaak, *The Continuing Battle: Memories of a European 1936–66* (1971); K. Adenauer, *Memoirs, 1945–53* (1976). For an important account by one of the earliest pan-Europeans see R.N. Coudenhove-Kalergi, *Pan-Europe* (1926).

Secondary works

Wider analyses of European political development since 1945 that include sections on the moves towards European unity include: R. Morgan, *West European Politics since 1945* (1972); R. Mayne, *The Recovery of Europe* (1970); W. Laqueur, *Europe since Hitler* (1970); D. Urwin, *Western Europe since 1945* (1989 edn); P. Lane,

Europe Since 1945 (1985). For a general discussion of the European unity movement, see A. Daltrop, *Politics and the European Community* (1982); C. Mowat, *Creating the European Community* (1973).

For a detailed account of the early years of the movement towards European integration, see W. Lipgens, *A History of European Integration, 1945–7* (1982). J.W. Young, *Britain, France and the Unity of Europe, 1945–51* (1984) provides a concise analysis of the rivalry between Britain and France. On the ill-fated EDC, see E. Fursdon, *The European Defence Community* (1981). On the Common Market, see R. Pryce, *The Politics of the European Community* (1973). For British attitudes towards closer European integration, see S. Greenwood, *Britain and Europe Since 1945* (1992); S. George, *Britain and European Integration Since 1945* (1991); M. Camps, *Britain and the European Community, 1955–63* (1964); U. Kitzinger, *Diplomacy and Persuasion* (1974).

American relations with the European unity movement are covered in a number of works, including G. Lundestad, *'Empire' by Integration: The United States and European Integration, 1945–1997* (1998); K. Featherstone and R. Ginsberg, *The United States and the European Union in the 1990s: Partners in Transition* (1996); F. Heller and J. Gillingham (eds.), *The United States and the Integration of Europe: Legacies of the Postwar Era* (1996); D. Ellwood, *Rebuilding Europe: Western Europe, America and Postwar Reconstruction* (1993); R. Manderson-Jones, *Special Relationship* (1972); M. Beloff, *The United States and the Unity of Europe* (1963).

For more recent developments within the European Community, see B. Nelson, D. Roberts and W. Veit (eds), *The European Community in the 1990s* (1992); J. Pinder, *European Community. The Building of a Union* (1991); D. Urwin and W. Paterson, *Politics in Western Europe Today* (1990); W. Feld, *The European Community in World Affairs* (1976); J. Fitzmaurice, *The European Parliament* (1978); V. Herman and J. Lodge, *The European Parliament and the European Community* (1978).

Postscript

The book started with Germany's emergence under Bismarck as the strongest power in Europe and has traced the evolution of the European state system through to the final decades of the twentieth century. Having defeated German hegemony and survived Soviet Russian claims to superpower status that threatened to divide Europe irrevocably, we are now witnessing moves towards a refraction of sovereignty and a policy of co-operation within the European Union.

Arguably the most revolutionary movement in European history has been the progress made in integrating states of western Europe with the ultimate objective of a united European state. The history of Europe since 1871 has been dominated by the German Question – by the need, and the general failure, to absorb the economic capacity and resources of Germany into an acceptable European political framework. An attempt to solve this problem has been, in my view, the greatest single achievement of the European movement. Placed in the wider context of European history, the desire for and the successes of European integration (governed by the need for economic reconstruction after 1945) should not be underestimated – particularly the 'special relationship' between France and Germany that has evolved out of historic rivalry.

In recent years Europe's sharpest and clearest dividing line, the Iron Curtain, has suddenly disappeared and Germany is reunified. The speed of these events has created a new urgency to clarify what we mean by 'Europe' and European integration. 'Eastern Europe' no longer exists as a separate socio-economic or geographical region. There is now only 'Europe'. In political terms Europe has been identified with the European Community, yet until now, the EC has been a western European phenomenon.

With the collapse of Stalinist communism in eastern Europe, the tensions that were a recurrent feature of Europe prior to 1914 have erupted again. The case of former Yugoslavia and the ensuing civil war polarised around questions of ethnic identity and the desire for 'ethnic cleansing' have a disturbing, but familiar, resonance. Recent electoral successes in Russia for neo-fascist and aggressively nationalist forces provide an equally chilling reminder of the past. The great task facing the European movement is to rise to the challenge of successfully integrating eastern Europe into the economic prosperity and subsequent political stability of a 'European Community' – within a time span that will not frustrate raised expectations. It is a similar problem to the one faced by the great industrial nations of the West at the beginning of the twentieth century. As the twenty-first century approaches, Europe is living in anticipation of vast but still imponderable changes. One can only hope that in the 2000s Europe will demonstrate a greater willingness to embrace these challenges.

Index